I0214504

# Duryea
## The Movies

Duryea: The Movies

© 2013 Joseph Fusco

All rights reserved.

No part of this book may be reproduced in any form or by any means,
electronic, mechanical, digital, photocopying, or recording, except
for in the inclusion of a review, without permission in wriring
from the publisher.

For information, address:

BearManor Media
P. O. Box 71426
Albany, GA 31708

bearmanormedia.com


Edited by Michael Schemaille and Sarah DeSimone

Book design and layout by Brian Pearce | Red Jacket Press


Published in the USA by BearManor Media


ISBN—1-59393-890-X
978-1-59393-890-1

# Duryea
## The Movies

JOSEPH FUSCO

# Table of Contents

*A sleek portrait of Dan Duryea, an actor who created characters that combined suave gentility with cunning depravity.* 1954, UNIVERSAL PICTURES COMPANY, *Inc.*

# 1

# Introduction

Dan Duryea was a rare actor who had the knack of creating an impressive array of characters from a limited range of emotions. He used this array in different combinations and frequencies to create heroes and villains out of the same patterns. It was a matter of degree of righteous behavior tempered with malicious cowardice. Sometimes the touches were subtle, while at other times they were stark contrasts. That meant there were times when tags like 'hero' and 'villain' meant nothing.

Similar expressions and reactions could mean one thing or its opposite according to Duryea's acting technique. It was more complicated than the villain doing a sniveling boot-licking routine or a hero with his in-your-face sarcasm. A snarl could be a whine for a spineless deadbeat or a warning from a hard-nosed crime boss. A stare could mean abject surrender or an ultimatum that meant certain death. A temper tantrum could be the futile flare-up of a helpless loser or a triumphant outburst of someone mighty. Timid, two-faced cowardice and gorilla-like chest beating could be the cry of the concrete jungle or the whimpering surrender of a spoiled nobody.

Duryea's unique style was highlighted in classic dramas, crime *noirs*, pulp Westerns, soap opera romances, and low-budget independents from the 40s to the late 60s. He also had a television resume that covered all of the dramatic, comedy and Western genres of the 50s and 60s, including his own exotic adventure show in the 50s and a recurring role in a 60s prime-time soap opera. Not a bad set of credits for someone who once described himself as "a bread and butter actor!"

Dan Duryea was born on January 23, 1907 in White Plains, New York. He became interested in theater production while attending White Plains High School. English was his major at Cornell University but he still participated in theatre, even succeeding Franchot Tone as the president of Cornell's Dramatic Society. He graduated in 1928 and began work at The N.W. Ayer advertising agency in New York.

In 1931, he met Helen Bryan of Scarsdale, New York, and they married. The newlyweds moved to Philadelphia, where Duryea was to open an office for the advertising agency. Instead of finding success, he suffered a mild heart attack that ultimately forced him to seek a career change. Doctors' orders inspired him to seek out an enjoyable career, so Duryea headed for the summer stock straw hat circuit to seek work that would lead him to the New York stage after a road company of "Stepping Sisters" ran out of steam.

*Dan Duryea (right, pictured with Maurice Hunt, Peter Van Buren and Wendell Phillips) played a divinity student in the short-lived play,* Many Mansions. 1937, BEN PINOCHOT.

In 1935, Dan Duryea landed a bit part as a G-Man in Sidney Kingsley's *Dead End*, the startling Broadway play about New York slum life that created the legend of The Dead End Kids. After eighty-five weeks, he moved on to the role of Gimpty, the architect, before Samuel Goldwyn bought the rights to the play and brought it to his Hollywood sound stages. The principal cast members, The Dead End Kids, traveled west

*An upbeat photo of Dan Duryea and four starlets (left to right, Louise Jones, Alva Lacy, Shirley Mathison and Dee Van Enger) at Ocean Park, Coney Island of the West.* 1947, UNIVERSAL PICTURES COMPANY, INC.

but the rest of the cast was replaced by Hollywood actors and actresses. William Wyler directed the movie.

Duryea continued to act in the theater and played the part of a divinity student in *Many Mansions*. The next year, Duryea played his first Western bad man in *Missouri Legend*, appearing as Bob Ford, the coward who shot Jesse James. The play starred Dean Jagger, Dorothy Gish, Mildred Natwick, Russell Collins, and Jose Ferrer. The play was short lived, but it was enough to impress Herman Shumlin, the theater impresario. Shumlin cast Duryea as Leo Hubbard, the young weakling nephew in Lillian Hellman's *The Little Foxes*, starring Tallulah Bankhead.

It was a role that he would repeat in William Wyler's 1941 film version of the play, starring Bette Davis and produced by Sam Goldwyn. *The Little Foxes* started a film career in 1941 that continued until 1967 with *The Bamboo Saucer*, a Cold War science-fiction adventure.

Dan Duryea's last role was Eddie Jacks on the successful night-time soap opera, *Peyton Place*. He appeared during the show's 1967-1968,

*In Fritz Lang's* Scarlet Street, *Dan Duryea played his first impressionable villain, Johnny Prince (Dan Duryea), an amoral cad who abuses his lover, Kitty March (Joan Bennett).* 1945, UNIVERSAL PICTURES COMPANY, INC.

season, playing a sly home wrecker who returns to his wife seventeen years after he went out for a pack of smokes and didn't come home. Duryea died on June 7, 1968, six months after his wife had passed away.

The irony of Duryea's career is that the man who created a roster of scoundrels, connivers, murderers, and thieves was actually a mild man who enjoyed a fulfilling home life and a marriage that lasted thirty-six years and produced two sons. He shied away from the Hollywood social scene, choosing instead to enjoy his hobbies of building boats and racing yachts on Lake Arrowhead.

*Dan Duryea created a memorable western bad man with Waco Johnny Dean in the classic* Winchester '73. 1950, UNIVERSAL PICTURES COMPANY, INC.

*Dan Duryea stars as Dragon # 1 in* Five Golden Dragons, *a ridiculous spy thriller made by Hong Kong's Shaw Brothers.* 1965, WARNER-PATHE DISTRIBUTORS LTD.

*Dan Duryea's last role was Eddie Jacks, a conniving faithless husband who walked out on his wife only to return to her sixteen years later on TV's popular night time soap opera,* Peyton Place. 1967, TWENTIETH CENTURY FOX TELEVISION.

# 2

# The Little Foxes

*The Little Foxes* is an MGM screen adaptation of Lillian Hellman's 1939 Broadway play. It was produced by Samuel Goldwyn, directed by William Wyler, and filmed by Gregg Toland. The drama focuses on the members of a dissipated Southern family trying to make a successful transition to the twentieth-century machine age. They are a second generation of carpetbaggers and all they have left are dreams of past glory. Desperation and crass measures are some of the things they stoop to in order to make a lucrative investment in a cotton mill.

Regina (Bette Davis) is a strong-willed opportunist who has the business acumen and power of veto that allows her to outmaneuver her brothers, Oscar and Ben (Charles Dingle and Carl Benton Reid). They are desperate and kept in line by her resolute manipulation. She becomes the creative force behind the plan to adapt to the industrial age because only she has the vision to see the benefits of a partnership with Mr. Marshall (Russell Hicks), an industrialist and opera patron.

All the deal needs is the financial support of Regina's ailing estranged husband, Horace Giddens (Herbert Marshall). To Regina and her brothers, Horace is the period at the end of the sentence, as his approval is needed to make the deal final. His daughter, Alexandra (Teresa Wright), loves him dearly and is used to lure him back to the estate so he can be persuaded to kick in his share.

Horace Giddens is an ailing patriarch, a man living alone and away from the madness that was once his family. He genuinely loves his daughter but cannot deal with his wife's ravenous appetite or the pushy hustles of his brothers-in-law. Giddens seems detached from this and often resorts to taking his medicine when his nerves flare up. He is dead-set against approving his wife's participation in her brothers' deal to buy into the cotton mill.

Regina controls her invalid husband even though he is the only person who understands her. His ailment makes him vulnerable to her will and that is the reason that she dominates him. She uses his aversion to the merger as a bargaining tool with her brothers. The weaklings can't deal with the suspense and will resort to larceny to make the partnership work. This includes temporarily appropriating some of the bonds that Giddens keeps in a safety deposit bank at the bank where nephew Leo Hubbard (Dan Duryea) works.

Regina's nephew is a rude, lazy, good-for-nothing until he tells his father about the valuable bonds in a safety deposit box. That is when he becomes a player by being a pawn. Leo is supercilious, a lazy man with grand ambitions who stands in his father's shadow and picks the old man's pockets when he can get away with it. Leo is weak, a pile of leaves swept around by the wind blown by his father and uncle. Easily manipulated by his father's ambition to be the main player in the family, Leo Hubbard is a vacillating parasite, but then so are most of the players in this drama.

Bette Davis is remarkable as the cunning yet vulnerable matriarch of the Giddens clan. She may be conniving and manipulative, but she is running on empty and is in desperate need of a refill. Failure to gain a controlling share in the prospective cotton mill will mean becoming a cipher in the new century.

*Regina Giddens (Bette Davis) is the rapacious matriarch of a southern family trying to adapt to the 20th Century in* The Little Foxes. 1941, LOEW'S INC.

She is full of as much fear as she is hopeful, because her youth (and the dreams that went along with it) has slipped away.

Her pancake makeup and haggard reflection show her that she is trapped in a Limbo that will turn her into something worse than her dissipated sister-in-law or spineless brothers. Limbo will become Hell if she does not secure the finances she needs from her estranged husband.

Herbert Marshall excels at portraying a vulnerable man with a steel will. He has a conscience and realizes that the enterprise would ruin the town due to the investors' aim to pay substandard wages and secure land rights that do not belong to them.

His goodness and strong moral character are preserved in his daughter, Alexandra, played by Teresa Wright. Wright earned her place in 40s films by playing young, optimistic adolescents on the verge of womanhood. Her post-Gibson Girl-type characters were flowers blooming at the onset of spring, possessing an uplifting charm that was often a balm to the sickness that pervaded the lives of her supporting players.

Patricia Collinge gives the most remarkable performance of the film as Birdie, Leo's mother and Alexandra's aunt. She is preserved by alco-

*Regina (Bette Davis) is catered to by her weak nephew Leo (Dan Duryea) and her scheming brothers (Carl Benton Reid and Charles Dingle, left to right).* 1941, LOEW'S INC.

hol and fond memories of a proud past. Watching her performance is like seeing an ornate vase dropped to the floor and shattering in slow motion. Birdie's family were once true southern aristocrats, their honor well-preserved through adherence to a strict social code. The Civil War changed their fortunes and they fell prey to the rapacious merchant code of the Hubbard family. Charles Dingle plays the crude and uncouth Oscar Hubbard, the man who married Birdie in order to snap up what was left of the family dynasty. Alexandra is warned by her aunt that she will suffer the same fate if she does not break away from the family.

Her escape route is provided by an aspiring newspaperman played by Richard Carlson. This optimistic, chorus-like character was not in the original play but rather added for the movie. Alexandra runs off with him at the end of the movie, leaving Regina to wallow in her ill-gained success.

Dan Duryea recreates his stage role of Leo Hubbard, a dunce who is lazy and greedy, willing to reap the benefits of unrealized dreams or live on someone else's fortune. Supercilious and rapacious, he is a spoiled brat

*Leo Hubbard (Dan Duryea) listens to his father (Charles Dingle) explain the importance of social marriages while his bemused wife, Birdie (Patricia Collinge), listens ruefully.* 1941, LOEW'S INC.

turned loquacious bore. A schemer made of putty, Leo is the grifter who sells out himself every time he makes a score.

Leo wants to be rich and successful but does not have the drive to work for it. He has his father's dark heart, which makes him reckless because he does not think before he acts. His impulsiveness inspires small dreams and that's what his life is — a small dream. He needs to be rich in order to survive. Without money, he would be a casualty of life. That is also true of his father, aunt, and his Uncle Ben, who is portrayed as a frivolous bore by Carl Benton Reid.

There is a little touch of Leo Hubbard in the majority of Duryea's big screen roles. This applies to many of the heroes, too. It was Duryea's shadings and accents that produced the moral fiber of his characters and the degree of anguish they caused others in order to achieve an end that was either sanctified or damned. That is the only way his characters can be identified.

Seven years after *The Little Foxes*, Dan Duryea expanded the scope of the Leo Hubbard role when he played the character's father in *Another Part of the Forest*, made at Universal-International.

*Regina (Bette Davis) attempts to talk her husband Horace (Herbert Marshall) into financing a cotton mill enterprise.* 1941, LOEW'S INC.

*Another Part of the Forest* is Lillian Hellman's prequel to *The Little Foxes*. It provides a history of the Hubbard family twenty years before their attempt at resurrection in *The Little Foxes*. It is Universal-International's attempt at making a serious picture, but runs into trouble because very little about it can compare favorably with the film it is setting itself up to. The script, for the most part, is good. The performances range from excellent to perfunctory. What dooms it in comparison is the lack of style provided by the original's direction and cinematography.

William Wyler's mature direction was masterful in the way he moved the players like chess pieces that spoke over each other. He subtly brought out the nuances of the characters' inner anguish, including the dark sides of the socially redeeming characters. Gregg Toland's deep-focus camera work gave the film a rich-textured, sullen atmosphere. His scene compositions resembled turn-of-the-century photographs come to life. Wyler and Toland plus an expert cast created a three-dimensional world on a flat screen.

In *The Little Foxes*, the remnants of a family of ruined Southern aristocrats try to recapture lightning in the bottle again, a power surge they enjoyed during the years shown in *Another Part of the Forest*. In the prequel,

*The Hubbard clan (left to right): Marcus (Frederic March), Regina (Ann Blyth), Lavinia (Florence Eldridge), Oscar (Dan Duryea) and Ben (Edmond O'Brien).* 1948, UNIVERSAL PICTURES COMPANY, INC.

Ann Blyth is supposed to turn into Bette Davis and Dan Duryea gets to play his character's father.

The Hubbards are from the merchant class and they are resented by some of the townsfolk. There is whispering and backbiting about the success of their business. The elder Hubbard's moral character is an ink blot to some, and how this perception affects his family sets the tone for this post-Civil War drama.

The family's history is clarified and it is an ignominious one, at that. Klan tales, war profiteering, and atrocities are the ingredients of the merchant family that escaped its class through dark secrets of treachery. The family skeleton is responsible for the shift in the balance of power within the Hubbard family. To risk exposure, Pop relinquishes his fiefdom to Ben, his avaricious elder son.

Frederic March is excellent as the elder Hubbard and he does what he can with a few startling character faults and an unraveling and fall from power that happens too fast. It is hard to imagine that he would not try to wheel and deal with his eldest son to keep him from informing the town elders about who was responsible for the atrocities committed in the town during the war.

*The Hubbard brothers (Edmond O'Brien and Dan Duryea) and sister Regina (Anne Blyth) conspire against their fading father.* 1948, UNIVERSAL PICTURES COMPANY, INC.

Edmond O'Brien is the strong son who steps out from his father's shadow when he hears his mother misspeak about the old man's skeleton in the closet. His threats, demands, and rise to the seat of family power are too swift and could have provided grist for a family power play worth expanding on.

This sudden change of events shifts the balance of power from the father to the eldest son. The most startling thing about the new power scheme is the way Regina is reborn as a selfish manipulator in order to cozy up to the new head of the household.

Ann Blyth is beautiful and somewhat defiant as Regina Hubbard, but cannot give credibility to a character that will develop into Bette Davis. One can imagine Bette Davis eating Ann Blyth as if she were an after-dinner mint. The only thing that links the two performances is the cold and deliberate look Blyth displays when she realizes that the family power has passed from her father to her elder brother.

The only way to accept Ann Blyth is to believe that Regina was once as innocent as Alexandra, her daughter. Her fortune's loss and her brother's gain taught her a new meaning to survival. From that point

*Laurette Sincee (Dona Drake) is a spirited Can-Can dancer who puts some pep in Oscar Hubbard's (Dan Duryea) step.* 1948, UNIVERSAL PICTURES COMPANY, INC.

onward, it is possible to accept Blyth's sweet character eventually turning into Bette Davis' bitter crone.

Regina's first step toward one day becoming the family's matriarch occurs in the last scene of the movie, which is stolen by Florence Eldridge. She plays the matriarch of the Hubbard clan and she is part Rock of Gibraltar and part pillar of salt. She scores the film's focal point with her declaration, one that ends the movie and puts a cap on the family that was to evolve into *The Little Foxes*.

Duryea gives a fleshed out performance of the lanky, bilious coward that he played in *The Little Foxes*. Father and son are hardly distinguishable, so weak and mealy-mouthed. Duryea plays the father much the same as he played the son. His part in the prequel is larger so we can get a fuller portrait of the devilish, ne'er-do-well wastrel of a hated Southern family. The elder Hubbard, too, is a dim-wit, a flippant popinjay in love with a Can-Can girl and one who dresses in Klan regalia when driving Yankees out of town under the cover of night.

Having Duryea play the father of his character from *The Little Foxes* is interesting casting, but one of the things that work against the film. Duryea expands on Leo Hubbard, but it is unlikely that his father, so cold and manipulative in *The Little Foxes*, could have been anything like his son.

This also applies to Edmond O'Brien's performance as the young Ben. He is a chip off the old man's block in this film, but is portrayed as a sad and weak bachelor in *The Little Foxes*. It's as if the brothers exchanged personalities when they matured.

The genesis of Aunt Birdie depicts a twit with a loon's perspective of life. She is nothing like that in the Wyler film. As played by Betsy Blair, she is a genteel Southern doyenne weakened through attrition, her husband's family takeover of her family legacy due to a deal she asked for when things were rough.

This is played out in *Another Part of the Forest* and it becomes clear that she will lose everything her family has. The impact in this movie is nothing compared to the sane effect achieved by an unsettling performance of her older self by Patricia Collinge in *The Little Foxes*.

Dona Drake has a small part as Laurette Sincee, a Can-Can girl being romanced by Oscar Hubbard. She gives a vivacious performance as simpleton bimbo who does a mean Can-Can. Oscar wants to marry her but his father will not hear any of it. She irritates him to the point of his being stupefied by her.

*In* The Valley of Decision, *Dan Duryea played William Scott, Jr., the son of a steel magnate, one of the many MGM classics that were part of his early career.*
1945, LOEW'S INC.

# 3

# The Gilded Age

Greer Garson was the reigning queen of MGM during the war years. She combined a breathtaking aristocratic beauty with a strong-willed, working-class bravado. She plays the lightning rod for two scions of the Gilded Age in *Mrs. Parkington* and *Valley of Decision*. The movies are MGM spectacles that brilliantly chronicle the rise to power of families whose fortunes were made during the Gilded Age, an era of sumptuous wealth for the newly-formed American aristocracy.

Tay Garnett's films deal with a time when the robber barons were born, men who controlled the elements that created the new Industrial Revolution. The Gilded Age started with the post-Civil War years and reached its peak around the turn of the century. The Great War changed the world economy and the Gilded Age began to tarnish, eventually collapsing with the Great Depression of 1929.

*Mrs. Parkington* is the history of Susie Sparrow's marriage to the Major, a wealthy industrialist whose fortune was built on the mines. Major Augustus "Gus" Parkington's story is that of a time when the American frontier was being shaped into an empire by a handful of ambitious, if avaricious, men. It was an era when opportunists became industrialists and created an age of ostentatious wealth, and with it, a class system to rival Europe's.

The Major's investments in shipping, railroads, and the new automobile have made him rich beyond most men's dreams. He uses this wealth as a way to commemorate his wife's beauty. Susie "Sparrow" is his muse and motivation, the only person who is his equal in cunning and compassion.

Mrs. Parkington is a woman with a clear sense of morality. She was a helper in her mother's rooming house when she met the gregarious Major. Marriage followed shortly after her mother was caught in a cave-in and killed while delivering lunch to miners. Their marriage is the beginning of a journey that will span several decades, well into the early twentieth century.

Greer Garson projected a strange charm: wise, sensual, and cunning. She had a strong sex appeal made more alluring by her strength and wisdom. Mrs. Parkington is a noble woman of humble means who inherits the kingdom when she marries a dashing entrepreneur who creates an empire based on natural resources, the railroad, and the emerging automobile. In the film she starts as an octogenarian who takes a trip down memory lane when a family crisis makes her think about the man who started it all.

Walter Pidgeon is sublime as The Major. He is tall and debonair, gregarious and boorish, charming and obnoxious, spiteful and tenacious. The Major's upbeat ego offends many of the old world moneybags and they show their disapproval by shunning him. This proves to be their fault because he takes their snobbery and uses it to destroy them, one by one, on Wall Street. His wife is the only person who can stand up to him and make him come back for more.

Agnes Moorehead is delightful as Baroness Aspasia Conti, a French coquette who is more like the Major's mistress. She begrudgingly accepts his marriage to the servant girl and acquiesces to his wish that she educate Sparrow in the ways of the world.

Moorehead is worldly and charming, a bundle of elegant energy and French sensuality.

Cecil Kellaway plays the Prince of Wales with a lighthearted humor. He is also observant and respectful of customs when he steps in to favor Sparrow in a delicate situation regarding the Major and the Duchess after a fox hunt on the English estate.

*A poster for MGM's* Mrs. Parkington, *a sprawling drama about a turn-of-the century robber baron that stars Greer Garson and Walter Pidgeon.* 1944, LOEW'S INC.

Edward Arnold plays the son who has a financial scandal on his hands. It threatens the inheritances of his brothers and sisters. He is a flatterer who is on the verge of being exposed as an embezzler.

Gladys George plays a dissolute relative, one whose nerves are shattered by booze and neurosis. She is acerbic, quite a contrast to her role as the mother in *Valley of Decision.*

Duryea again plays a spoiled heir whose dependence on the family fortune has rendered him useless in the ways of independence and ambition.

Roger Stillwell is the complete opposite of his grandfather, the Major, who started out as a gambler with a silver mine and wound up a Wall Street scion before his death in an automobile race.

Roger Stillwell is lazy, lanky, and lachrymose. Unlike his grandfather, there is no need for him to leave his mark on the world because he will inherit part of his grandmother's fortune. This safety net is why Roger

*Susie Sparrow (Greer Garson) and The Major (Walter Pidgeon) are dismayed at another telegram expressing regret at not being able to attend his prestigious ball.* 1944, LOEW'S INC.

is a rude and selfish do-nothing. His impertinence fits in well with the second and third generation Parkingtons because most of them are decadent, hollow people.

Roger lacks the manners, bearing, and temperament of a wealthy man, electing instead to act like an ignorant boor. He refuses to shake the hand of his new brother-in-law (Rod Cameron), a cattle rancher. Instead, he whistles *Home on the Range* as he saunters across the room, marking his distance from the new family member.

He also callously rejects his father when the elder tells the family that he is about to be exposed as an embezzler. The rest of the family, with the exception of Mrs. Parkington and his daughter, could not care less about his predicament. They are worried about the family name being fed to the press.

Later, when Mrs. Parkington announces that she will use her fortune —
their inheritances — to bail him out, the family protests, threatening legal
action. Roger, showing no respect, accuses her of experiencing a second
childhood. The thought of losing his safety net appalls him and it seems
as if he will do anything to prevent his grandmother from carrying out
her promise.

*An elderly Mrs. Parkington (Greer Garson) welcomes her daughter's cattleman
beau (Rod Cameron) while the rest of the family condescends to acknowledge his
presence.* 1944, LOEW'S INC.

*The Valley of Decision* depicts the time when steel mills took over
America and a Scottish immigrant who created a steel empire deals with
the changes it has brought in production methods as well as Irish workers'
grievances. Greer Garson again stars as a noble woman of humble means
who inherits the kingdom, but not without heartache and misery.

She plays Mary Rafferty, the daughter of an embittered steel worker
who was injured in an accident at the steel mill. She exacerbates her
father's anger when she accepts a job as a maid in the house of the mill
owner. It does not help matters that she falls in love with Paul (Gregory
Peck), the eldest son. The tension provides for a Romeo-and-Juliet type
of romance. In this version, happenstance reunites the lovers and they

do it right the second time around after having been separated by family politics and feelings of guilt.

The movie is an incisive portrait of the formation of the steel mills. Rugged individualism pervades a movie filled with sons of thunder and lightning, spinners with steel backbones and fiery spleens. One wonders if a genetic code is responsible for the working and ruling classes. The

*Patrick Rafferty (Lionel Barrymore) strongly disapproves of the relationship between his daughter Mary (Greer Garson) and Paul (Gregory Peck), the son of his arch rival.* 1945, LOEW'S INC.

thing they have in common is the smokestacks that belch billowing, voluminous smoke. The difference is that the son of Scottish immigrants lives in the house on the hill and the progeny of the Irish immigrants live in the shanties of the valley.

William Scott, Sr. (Donald Crisp) is a fair-minded man who did not become corrupted by his enormous success. He is a sober-minded individual who is aware of his social status and the responsibilities that come with it. Scott is the immigrant son who made a fortune, but is still considered new money by the industrialists he competes with. Independent and proud, he is unwilling to lose his bearings by becoming part of a steel syndicate headed by Andrew Carnegie.

His noble character is reflected in the way he treats his workers, especially the irascible Pat Rafferty (Lionel Barrymore), who was crippled in an accident at the factory. Mr. Scott has compensated Rafferty with a weekly stipend, but the victim's pride has made him bitter and vengeful.

Lionel Barrymore is to be given a lot of credit for creating a full-bodied figure with the tempestuous nature of a raging tornado. He leads the strikers in a confrontation on the bridge and shoots the elder Scott to death, only to be shot dead by one of the strike breakers.

*Paul Scott is betrothed to Louis Kane (Jessica Tandy), although he is in love with Mary Rafferty.* 1945, LOEW'S INC.

The two men represent the two factions that forged steel out of their own blood. Both adversaries are children of the immigrants who dug into the mountains to create the mines. Now, one prides on himself on hard work and visionary ideas while the other relies on cunning and ambition to compensate for his inability to earn a decent wage to support his family.

The essence of dissolution, the bitter old man in the wheelchair is the impediment to the future. Pat Rafferty leads his working-class ruffians against the effete founder of the steel mills. It appears to be class warfare, but what it is comes closer to being mob rule. Through an unforeseen miscalculation, the sides collide with deadly consequences during a strike. The patriarchs are killed, but their offspring eventually marry. It is a new dawn in the age of industrialism.

The underlying industrial theme is a sub-plot to the personal stories and relationships that are interwoven into the social studies lesson. The setup is similar to the family rivalries in Romeo and Juliet.

Greer Garson is mesmerizing as the lady in ascension. She does it through humility, beauty, and a quick and sharp tongue. She appeals to the benignly arrogant Sir Paul, who admires the servant girl, but things go wrong between them because of caste restrictions.

Gregory Peck plays Paul, the son of the steel magnate. He is steadfast and strong, inheriting his father's vision for the future of the steel mills. It does not hurt that he is aided by a rustic genius, played by Preston Foster. Foster is the odd man out, an engineering genius who develops a blueprint for a new type of mill.

Marshall Thompson is the popinjay son with the drinking problem. He causes the cataclysm that that kills the heads of the families in the confrontation at the bridge. He was entrusted with the task of informing his brother, Willie, to call off the strike breakers because an agreement had been reached between the workers and the elder Scott. While waiting for his brother to arrive, he passes the time with a few that drinks that eventually make him too drunk to carry out the task.

His sister, Constance, is played by Marsha Hunt. She, too, is a spoiled brat but is taught about responsibility by Mary Rafferty, especially after she marries into royalty and goes to live abroad. Mary accompanies her out of fealty to the Scott family, who hope that Paul will marry his well-to-do fiancée, played with icy frippery by Jessica Tandy.

Dan Duryea is Willie, the middle son, the one who tires of the workers' demands. Duryea plays a decisive and brash younger brother of a fledgling Scottish steel magnate played by Gregory Peck. His break with the family in the way of useful politics ends with a mini-revolution that kills its captains. Willie butts heads with Paul and winds up losing it all when his kid brother has one too many send-me-offs at the bar.

Willie does not believe in progress and would readily sell the mines if it means that he would net two million dollars. He also does not believe in family honor, and he shows little gratitude to his immigrant

*William Scott, Sr. (Donald Crisp) breaks up a row between his sons, Willie (Dan Duryea) and Paul (Gregory Peck).* 1945, LOEW'S INC.

grandfather or the toll that had to be paid to make the mines the meat of the family's matter.

Willie Scott is the exception to the rule of the decadent aristocratic offspring. He is the son of a steel magnate, but does not rest on his father's laurels. He is more active and outspoken than the other roles played in the industrial jungles. That does not mean that he will not sell the family mines and factories if the price is right.

# 4

# Working Class Heroes

The Roaring 20s gave way to a global depression and then World War II. Hollywood chronicled these turbulent eras with dramas that stirred the soul and shook the emotions. *Pride of the Yankees* and *None But The Lonely Heart* are stories of the Depression and World War II told from both sides of the ocean and from two different points of view.

The new land of opportunity creates a modern folk legend and the shadow of the old giant obscures a working class hero. One is a scrappy American folk tale and the other a British survival story. Duryea plays a reporter adverse to the legend in *Pride of the Yankees* and a safe fish-and-chips man in *None but the Lonely Heart,* respectively.

*Pride of the Yankees* is the sentimental and emotional story of Lou Gehrig (Gary Cooper), the Yankee legend known as The Iron Man for his long consecutive streak of games played. Gehrig is the shy and unassuming child of German immigrants. His mother's dream is for Lou to become an architect, so he works his way through Columbia University. He excels at baseball, attracting the eyes of a scout for The New York Yankees.

Gehrig makes it to the big leagues but he is afraid that his mother will be disappointed when she finds out that he is a ballplayer instead of an architect. He is right; despite his fame and success, she is upset that he hasn't fulfilled her dreams for him. It is not until he becomes an American legend that she can accept the life that he has carved out for himself.

Gehrig's success in the game turns him into a superstar of the time. He gets to battle Babe Ruth for the supremacy of the sports pages. They are two larger-than-life figures that represent the two extremes of human nature. Ruth is convivial and Bacchus-like in his rapacious appetites, while Gehrig is the picture of quiet reserve, possessing a refined grace under pressure. Their rivalry creates a basis for a fairy tale that has its sadness within the charm.

*Pride of the Yankees* has all of the clichés, inanities, and apocryphal messianic episodes that make Hollywood biographic films fun to watch. What makes this film remarkable is the success of the actors in affecting the pathos, empathy, and soft heartedness of the audience by cutting through the sappy dialogue.

Gary Cooper, Teresa Wright, and Walter Brennan deliver the corniest lines to the dippiest musical accompaniment, but they still elicit the same type of catharsis you would get from a classical Greek tragedy. Gary Cooper delivers corn-pone dialog and Teresa Wright is too pure

*Title lobby card for* Pride of the Yankees, *starring Gary Cooper and Teresa Wright.* 1942, LOEW'S INC.

to be true, but they go beyond the cornball conventions to give powerful performances. Their courtship, marriage, fame, and tragic travail are all portrayed convincingly.

*Pride of the Yankees* is a storybook, feel-good film that celebrates legends such as Lou Gehrig and the New York Yankees. Babe Ruth is on hand to lend authenticity to this weepy sudser. Despite the way the film tugs at the heart strings it shows the greatness of the man, especially in the finale when Gehrig gives his famous farewell speech at Yankee Stadium.

Dan Duryea is a disparaging press box reporter who rebuffs Brennan's positive copy about Gehrig. Duryea's reactions and feelings about Gehrig change as the film progress as he is seen mostly from the press booth, mixing it up with Brennan.

*Babe Ruth shows Gary Cooper how to hold a bat like his character, Lou Gehrig.*
1942, LOEW'S INC.

*Lou Gehrig (Gary Cooper) and Babe Ruth (himself) humiliate a couple of press box critics, including one played by Dan Duryea (right).* 1942, LOEW'S INC.

*Pride of the Yankees* could very well be seen as a profile of courage in the immigrant chronicles. Crisis and old-world resolve are also the theme of *None but the Lonely Heart*. The difference is this profile in courage in played out in the shadows of a small obscure town in England. It's still a place haunted by the Reaper when it's time to pay a visit.

Ernie Mott (Cary Grant) is a loner and a vagabond who is fond of describing himself as someone with a heart that is "blacker than the Ace of Spades." His boon companion is a scraggly dog and they roam the countryside without a care in the world. He occasionally touches base in his hometown, where his mother runs a secondhand shop. It is where he recharges his batteries before he hits the road again.

It does not take long for the viewer to realize that Mott is a selfish Cockney blackheart instead of the free spirit that he pretends to be. A crisis of conscience upsets his world when he finds out that his mother is dying of cancer. Mott's struggle lies in curbing his wanderlust and fitting into the routine of running the shop while caring for his ill mother, Ma Mott (Ethel Barrymore). The challenge is staying in one place long enough to confront the biggest enigma of his life: himself.

He assumes the responsibility of running his mother's thrift shop. He is a Handy-Andy and the jack-of-all trades. The colors of his life turn into a shades of gray when he copes with the burden of his mother's crisis. The only sure thing in his life is his perfect pitch.

Economic pressures force the mother and son to operate outside the law. Ma Mott becomes a fence and Ernie Mott a petty thief as he gives in to pressure from Jim Mordinoy (George Coulouris), the local gangster. Mott is dating Ada (June Duprez), the gangster's ex-wife and this makes for a strange triangle.

The shady areas and ambiguous spots are balanced by the three women in Ernie Mott's life. Ethel Barrymore is a towering figure, Jane Wyatt is pure optimism, and June Duprez is callous remorse. They inhabit the world that Ernie Mott has settled in, and they expect a lot from him. They are selfish in the way they use him to nurture their feeble lives. He becomes middle-class yet accepts their sorrow. His foray into crime ends disastrously for him, but what makes things tragic is his mother's arrest for fencing stolen goods. This shock sends tremors through Mott's cocksure attitude and he begins to feel unsure as he faces the terror of making split decisions about long-term affairs.

Cary Grant is laconic as the attitudinal wayfarer. He receives a lesson in humility that brings out a dark side to Grant's acting ability. He rekindles his relationships with towering arrogance, only to give into the supporting players.

As Mott's mother, Ethel Barrymore has a quiet strength and mettle reserve that is stronger than anything Grant can come up with, which is why they work so well together. Barrymore is a quiet, but deep reservoir of joy and sorrow.

*Ernie Mott (Cary Grant) is a selfish vagabond with perfect pitch and a black heart.* 1944, RKO PICTURES.

Jane Duprez is sharp and defiant while being vulnerable and frightened. She hates the gangster life and promises to cut off Grant if he hooks up with her ex-husband. Duprez is desperate but not reckless.

George Coulouris is chilling as the gangster who gets what he wants and acts however he likes. He is brazen, brutal, and defiant. He sets himself up by being so tough, but it only takes one misstep to bring himself down. Coulouris is a successful small time crook who crosses wires and short circuits.

Jane Wyatt is Aggie Hunter, the cellist with the heart of gold. She is the lit hearth and spring fever aiming to please. Her true-heart, homespun charm is what attracts Mott after all is said and done. It's the wholesome middle-class life that attracts the jack-of-all trades who has tired of his wanderlust.

Barry Fitzgerald pulls out his leprechaun disguise in his role as Henry Twite, the family friend who is a font of old-world wisdom that sets Ernie Mott straight.

Dan Duryea plays Lew Tate, a snide fry cook at a fish and chips shop. He is a pampered mama's boy and shows it when he backs up his mother's criticism of the refrigerator that she received as a gift from Ernie. Duryea has two short scenes, one at the shop and the other in the apartment of Ernie's mother.

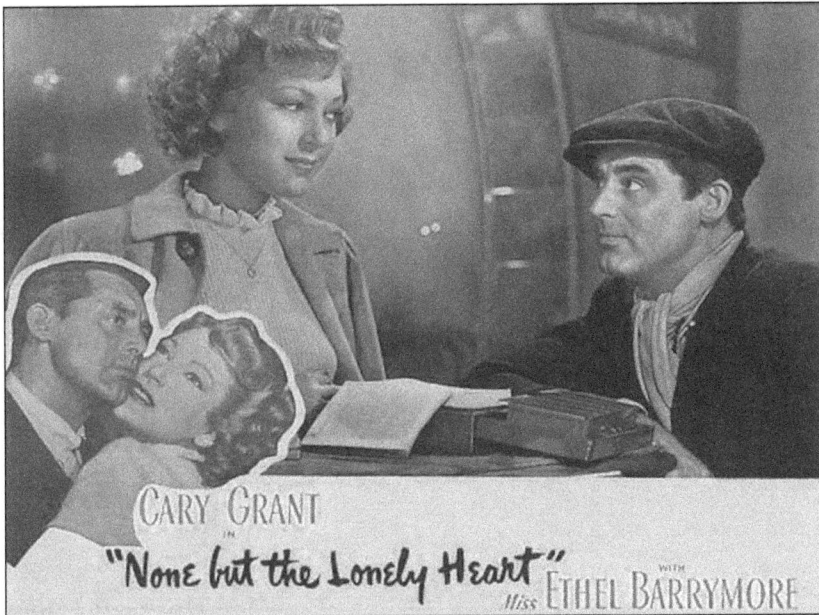

*Ernie Mott (Cary Grant) tries to charm Ada Brantline (June Duprez), a woman who has a dimmer view of human nature than he has.* 1944, RKO PICTURES.

*Ernie Mott (Cary Grant) provides the music for a neighborhood dance. Dan Duryea is part of the dancing couple, second from the left.* 1944, RKO PICTURES.

# 5

# WWII: Duty, Honor, and Espionage

Dan Duryea had supporting roles in three films that showed the ways in which World War II was fought: in the field, on the home front, and in the underground movement. In *Sahara*, Duryea plays a member of an American tank crew barely making their way through a desert trek without the added burden of having to haul a stranded British outfit and two marooned Axis soldiers.

*The Man from Frisco* depicts a shipbuilder with new ideas and a means of production to increase the manufacture of battleships needed for the war effort. Duryea is part of the old scheme, someone who supports the former boss who now seems antiquated because of the revolutionary production methods created by the man from Frisco.

Fritz Lang directed *The Ministry of Fear,* a contrived but enjoyable five-and-dime espionage thriller about underground Nazi sympathizers trying to get their hands on microfilm that has been mistakenly given to an American recently released from a sanitarium. Duryea plays a member of a subversive séance presided over by the hypnotic Hillary Brooke.

*Sahara* is an intriguing movie, a minor gem set in the desert during the Allied campaign against Rommel. Sgt. Joe Gunn (Humphrey Bogart), Waco Hoyt (Bruce Bennett), and Jimmy Doyle (Dan Duryea) pilot the tired tank Lulubelle, whose saga is about to become part of war history. Before it does, it will give a boost to the morale of a group of marooned Brits, an Italian P.O.W., and a downed German flyer.

Lulubelle and her pilots are the central characters in the drama, the only reason for the others to hope that they'll survive being stranded in the desert. The ragtag outfit consists of Bogie and his two men, a group of Brit soldiers they pick up at a derelict oasis, an Indian officer, a contrite Italian soldier, and a defiant, grounded German flyer. They brave the desert elements and their common enemy is thirst. Their water is running low and rationing is driving them mad.

Sgt. Gunn is the boss and he makes the life and death decisions that eat at his insides and irritate the others. The trouble is that beneath his tough guy exterior is someone who prizes life. That is why the German and Italian soldiers are allowed to accompany the stranded British troops and the Indian officer. He would have left them if not for the beckoning of his subordinates, international troops included.

It is this motley arrangement that adds more strain to the mission of survival. One Axis prisoner is overt in his loyalty, but the Italian seems to be appreciative, although he is not fully trusted by the others.

The survival equation is changed when they pick up the remnants of a British squadron. It becomes weakened when two more survivors turn out to be fascist soldiers. That is why questions of conscience pop up, including natural survival instincts and nationalism. Everyone gets to vent their spleens and they represent their sides of the story well.

Their salvation is an abandoned oasis where the well still drips a little water from the rocks. The Indian officer spends hours filling

*A Belgian movie poster for* Sahara, *an exciting WWII drama set in the African desert.* 1943, COLUMBIA PICTURES.

canteens and cups and sending them to the surface. That is how they survive. There are the sub-stories, such as that of the Italian P.O.W., who begs for his life in the name of his family. His is despised by the arrogant German soldier, who is defiant and cunning to the end. The Brits are righteous guys who agree to let Bogie call the shots.

They brave the desert looking for a water hole that will revive them. What they find is a devastated outpost that will serve as their fortress against an advancing and parched German division. Bogie and his boys will fight a fierce battle, but not without paying a price. The survivors leave behind the silent heroes, whose helmets hang on the butts of rifles dug into their memorial graves.

The director and cinematographer have created an impressive desert vision for the eyes and added a compelling atmosphere to the movie. The

*Sgt. Gunn (Humphrey Bogart) is a regular Joe from Brooklyn who finds himself in an extraordinary desert survival drama.* 1943, COLUMBIA PICTURES.

*Jimmy Doyle is the mid-western machine gunner for Lulubelle, a used-up tank on its last mission.* 1943, COLUMBIA PICTURES.

Sarge is one of those characters that become flesh and blood because of Bogie's acting.

Bogie plays a man with no past or origin. It's more than blood and guts that makes Sgt. Gunn a leader. He calls the shots because he has what it takes to coax Lulubelle to fight the desert's elements.

Bennett is the strong and silent type, someone who drives the tank and makes bets with Duryea about short term standoffs. He is doing it as it comes along; dealing with time as if it were something as endless as the sand.

Duryea is a happy-go-lucky optimist, someone who keeps things going with his farm boy energy. He is the machine gunner and can handle the rough stuff, but is able to smile and joke with Bogie and Bennett.

J. Carrol Naish and Kurt Krueger give passionate performances as the captured P.O.W.s. Louis Mercier is poetic and philosophical as Frenchie. Richard Nugent keeps a stiff upper lip as a British officer. Rex Ingram imbues his character, an Indian officer, with the solemn pride and determination that inspires the rest of the cast.

*Man from Frisco* is the story of an innovative builder who turns his mercurial genius toward building government ships for use in the European war effort. His revolutionary methods of production can increase output, earning him a trial period at the shipyards of the nation's most prominent shipbuilder. The clash between old and new, tried and true, versus bold and innovative creates a lot of friction in a movie that is Frank Capra-esque Americana mixed with industrial film footage of the shipyards.

Matt Braddock (Michael O'Shea) is an arrogant genius with a mission. Nothing will stand in his way, not even knowing that his new methods will forever change the small town by erasing the residents' lives and replacing them with a mad, mechanical world of his making.

An old-world icon, an old-world political system, an old-world way of life is usurped by the government when they give the mad genius total control of the shipyards so he can produce his revolutionary, pre-fabricated ships for the European war effort.

The old-school network, whose figurehead is the iconic Joel Kennedy (Gene Lockhart), is ordered to accommodate Braddock, but they offer subtle resistance. The only support comes in the form of the old guardian's young son, Russ (Tommy Bond). He is optimistic and supportive of Braddock and his pre-fabricated ship-building plan. Russ offers a strange mid-point in labor relations when he works for Braddock and lives at home.

The odd cog in the network is Jim Benson (Dan Duryea), the would-be son-in-law of the icon, who is in love with Diana Kennedy (Anne Shirley). The balance of romance changes when the arrogant and aggressive Mr.

Braddock throws his weight around. He brings in over a thousand workers and risks arrest by the town elders until a broadcast of the bombing at Pearl Harbor makes the old guard realize that they are obsolete.

The megalomaniacal Braddock builds his shipyard and pre-fabricated ships, but not without treachery and tomfoolery by Jim Benson, who is the cuckolded, would-be son-in-law suddenly squeezed out of the picture.

*Dan Duryea, Gene Lockhart, Anne Shirley and Michael O'Shea (left to right) star in* Man from Frisco. 1943, REPUBLIC PICTURES CORP.

He supervises the shipbuilding, but becomes purposely negligent due to his jealousy. This has tragic results, and Braddock is blamed for Tommy's death until Benson owns up to it in the end.

The home wartime effort ends with Braddock and Diana united in a tacked-on ending. The industrial drama that showcased the destruction of an old-time American town ends with a few cornball jokes about raising kids.

*Man From Frisco* is a hometown war drama. This story of shipbuilding is full of history and rich tradition. The clash of production methods is a contest of wills. It is almost stupefying to see the way Kennedy's world is washed away by Braddock's rude stampede. He is trampled under Braddock's brash new enterprise, the construction of a world that is built on his own terms.

*Matt Braddock (Michael O'Shea) upsets the status quo of a sleepy town with his new production methods.* 1943, REPUBLIC PICTURES CORP.

*A radio broadcast about the bombing of Pearl Harbor tips the balance of power in Matt Braddock's (Michael O'Shea) favor.* 1943, REPUBLIC PICTURES CORP.

No one has asked him to move, but he makes himself fair game when he challenges Braddock in the opening moves. Benson was Kennedy's loyal assistant before he became Braddock's hesitant foreman. His integrity is blinded by jealousy; it costs the life of youthful vision. Benson is still manipulative, although this time it was because he saw his girl kissing the arrogant interloper.

This results in sabotage that temporarily darkens Braddock's name. A heroic comeback thanks to strong scripting has him building the ship that will be christened in the name of the youthful visionary who lost his life to petty jealousies.

Michael O'Shea is irritating, but he accomplishes the mission. Along the way he wipes out a sleepy little town, destroys the old political regime, and dethrones the preeminent shipbuilder who once ruled the town and was an icon. O'Shea plays it arrogantly and effectively, as if he expects success and obeisance as part of his reward for being a genius.

Gene Lockhart plays a ball-less icon, one whose stature is more like a statue in the park. He is obsolete but still deserves the reverence of past accomplishments. He also plays the role of the past being thrust aside by the necessity of innovation.

Ann Shirley is caught between her father and Braddock, not to mention her relationship with Duryea. Shirley is the all-American, true-hearted, heartland girl. Whomever she chooses becomes the steer that leads the stampedes that trample anything that gets in their way.

In the end, Michael O'Shea stampedes Lockhart and Duryea while claiming Tommy Bond as his inspiring angel. He is played with the sincere earnestness that was supposed to epitomize the future captains of industry bred in American suburbia.

*Ministry of Fear* is a pocket-book espionage thriller where the action flows in and out of conflicts and resolutions with little or no trouble. There is a beginning, a middle, and an end with a bewildered hero, good and evil blonde seductresses, treasonous villains, and colorful supporting characters. It is well-made in a paint-by-the-numbers fashion by Fritz Lang.

Ray Milland is Stephen Neale, a troubled man who has served time in a mental hospital for the mercy killing of his wife. He becomes embroiled in a Nazi plot involving smuggled microfilm when he inadvertently intercepts the microfilm in a cake. It happens at a county fair where a fortune teller sets things up so that Neale wins the cake by guessing its weight. He is the wrong rigged winner and it sets off an intense manhunt in which Nazis and British authorities pursue Neale, who is aided by Marjorie Reynolds playing Carla Hilfe, a reluctant Fraulein.

It is the cat-and-mouse chase scenes that add suspense to the plot. Outwitting two pursuers does not give Neale much room to operate. Fair-handed law officer Inspector Prentice (Percy Waram), and pat script-writing enable Neale to scour a bombed-out field for the microfilm in the cake. Of course, he finds it in a bird's nest! This clears him in the eyes of the law, but does not get him out of the sight of the Nazis' scopes.

*A poster for Fritz Lang's, Ministry of Fear, an espionage thriller. That's Dan Duryea's character lying face up, on the left.* 1945, PARAMOUNT PICTURES.

*Ministry of Fear* is a wartime film that has split sides with heroes and patriots intermingling with each other and arousing antipathy and sympathy with every ploy or maneuver. There are those who have a split vision of Neale, who is considered a crazy American by some and a dangerous, patriotic spy by others. He is still needed because he can be used against the Axis powers.

Ray Milland's earnest performance gives the character credulity. Marjorie Reynolds is the Austrian freedom fighter who aids him in his escape. Carl Esmond is her wimpy brother, a man who reluctantly aids Milland before turning him over to the authorities. Percy Waram plays a vacillating top cop who is suspicious but obliging in Neale's attempts to clear himself.

*A fake spiritualist (Hillary Brooke) uses natural charm to bedevil Stephen Neale (Ray Milland).* 1945, PARAMOUNT PICTURES.

The distinguished Alan Napier plays Dr. Forrester, who works for National Security but secretly heads a Nazi spy ring that uses a charitable organization as its front. Hillary Brooke is a phony psychic who adds to the confusion that creates another front for the traitors.

Erskine Sanford adds color as George Rennit, an eccentric investigator who does not stick around to collect his fee. Dan Duryea plays Cost, a small-potatoes tailor who fails to get the cake and winds up a fall guy and a frame-up at a séance. The séance was not meant for him, and it lays him out with a phantom punch.

*Ministry of Fear* is an entertaining movie even though it is performed on stilts. Fritz Lang has given some of the scenes a mysterious ambience, but otherwise it's full of phony theatrics, such as the suitcase bomb in the hotel room, the phony subway bomb-shelter setting, and the bombing of the fields. The microfilm in the cake is a cheap enough gimmick, but finding the microfilm after the Nazi bombing stretches credulity a bit. The fortune-telling angle adds a touch of parlor-game amusement, but the presence of Hillary Brooke makes it hypnotic and worthwhile.

# 6

# Loose Screwballs: High and Low

Romantic comedy is one of film genres where a tight script is necessary for a successful result. The same goes for expert direction and tight editing, coupled with disciplined but zany acting and whimsical musical phrases that accent, not detract from, a scene. This perfect combination produces a snappy picture; anything less than this produces a strained result.

The degree of a romantic satire's success depends on whether or not the audience thinks that it fulfills the strict requirements of such a comedy style. It is one of the few genres where every facet has to work if the final result is to appear natural and not strained. A strong script is a necessity, but cannot be used to coast by on.

*Ball of Fire* and *That Kind of Woman* are romantic farces with a Damon Runyon-like flavor. Both movies have clever scripts but they do not share adept players, appropriate musical accents, seasoned direction, and rhythmic editing. *Ball of Fire* and *That Other Woman* are at the opposite ends of the scale and serve as two studies of the comedy-drama where daffiness and logic have to blend to create laughs and pathos.

*Ball of Fire* is a rare combination of drawing-room farce, screwball comedy, gangster movie, and class satire. Dan Duryea has a small part as Duke Pastrami, a low level hood who speaks the jargon of the streets. He gets some screen time during the expository scene where he and another goon hold professors and a sanitation man hostage while an underground marriage is being performed across the river.

He has a larger part as Ralph Cobb, a cuckolded suitor, in *That Other Woman*, a coming-of-age comedy for a secretary in love with a womanizing playboy architect. Duryea is her proper Southern gentleman beau, a Yankee-hating man who gets caught up in a convoluted scheme started by his fiancé in order to net her boss. He becomes an ex and an odd man down and out for the count. The real insult is his Southern etiquette being ridiculed by a sweet child of the South.

In *Ball of Fire*, a nightclub chanteuse wanted for questioning by the police finds sanctuary in a brownstone where eight professors are writing an encyclopedia. She serves as an authority on slang for Professor Potts (Gary Cooper), an awkward English professor who falls in love with her. He does not realize that she is the moll of a gangster who wants to marry her so she can't testify against him in a murder trial. The professor com-

*Title lobby card for Howard Hawks'* Ball of Fire, *starring Gary Cooper and Barbara Stanwyck.* 1942, LOEW'S INC.

plicates things by wanting to marry her after she teaches him how to kiss.

The staid routine of the professors' lives is interrupted by the ball of fire. They begin to think of love in the antiquated styles of their youth, from wearing spats to singing golden oldies. The only person not impressed by the burlesque queen is the maid, who believes that women like her cause the crumbling of civilization. She aims to do something about it when she reads the headlines reporting that the entertainer is wanted for questioning.

Gangsters enter the picture when they want to use her wedding with the professor as a pretext for a wedding between her and a crime boss, the gist being that a wife can't testify against her husband. It is when academia meets the underworld that a clash of attitudes produces a series of comical mishaps. True love triumphs when the professor and the singer marry, proving that the illogical forms the backbone of screwball comedies.

Mix your verbs and strangle your malapropisms and you have a *Ball of Fire*, a war of the words, a comedy drama that demonstrates that words have power and that a nation's stability rests in respect and

*Sugarpuss (Barbara Stanwyck) casts a spell on the bookish professors (Left to Right: Henry Travers, Oscar Homolka, Gary Cooper, Aubrey Mather, Leonid Kinskey, S.Z. Sakall, Richard Haydyn and Tully Marshall).* 1942, LOEW'S INC.

proper usage of its language. The question who has the clout to codify proper usage and what does it matter if communication is the final cause of *Ball of Fire*, a pleasant gangster comedy with the flair of a Damon Runyon yarn.

Fortunately, *Ball of Fire* is top-notch. The first rate script by Billy Wilder and Charles Bracket is perfectly balanced between mirth and pathos. Language has always been an expression of status and class. Street talk and proper English are only tolerated in their own milieu.

Barbara Stanwyck plays Sugarpuss with a brash and feisty sensuality. She is perky and frisky, relishing the way she disrupts the staid lives of the cloistered professors. She handles them with the ease and skill of a club hostess hustling a customer into buying an endless round of drinks for the house. It's all based on her sexual allure, something most of the professors know nothing about.

Gary Cooper displays his ability to play a shy, awkward man whose honest heart and decent moral code set him apart from the ruffians

*Duke Pastrami (Dan Duryea) is one of the two gangsters who keep the professors and guests hostage so his boss can marry Sugarpuss without their interference.* 1942, LOEW'S INC.

Sugarpuss is used to associating with. He falls in love with her, not realizing that she is a flirtatious tease who is leading him on.

Plot mechanics bring them together by the end of the film and it is not the first time that a cynical woman is won over by an innocent Cooper character. His righteousness impresses Sugarpuss, but he wins her over the old fashioned way by beating up his rival and bringing down his crime syndicate.

Picaresque characters have always been an asset to screwball comedies. It is one of the film genres where they fit in as normal characters. The professors and the working class players are a colorful bunch, but the groups are linguistic oddities. The professors are experts in the usage of modern English, and the working class characters communicate with neighborhood colloquialisms. It's a polite confrontation between two class systems but the gentility turns bombastic in the film's final reel.

Dana Andrews is the crime boss and Dan Duryea has a small role as Duke Pastrami, one of the wise-cracking, small-time hoods working for the big guy. The professors are played by the top characters actors of the era. Among them are Henry Travers, Oscar Homolka, S.Z. Sakall, Tully

*Gary Cooper takes direction from Howard Hawks while Oscar Homolka, Barbara Stanwyck, Aubrey Mather and S.Z. Sakall wait to resume the action.*
1942, LOEW'S INC.

Marshall, Richard Haydyn, Leonid Kinskey, and Aubrey Mather. Allen Jenkins plays a sanitation man who tutors Professor Potts in jive-talk, doing so with a snappy verve.

Speaking of snappy verve, Ms. Stanwyck sings *Drum Boogie* with Gene Krupa and his orchestra. She has a skillful interlude with him where she sings *sotto voce* and he solos with matchsticks.

Howard Hawks is in top form in a role akin to that of a traffic cop in Times Square during rush hour. He repeated this formula with a remake, *A Song Is Born*, with Danny Kaye and Virginia Mayo, which tells the story of a stripper on the lam and a college professor who has to invent a new lexicon when they meet.

*That Other Woman* has a tight script, but it is reduced to college level hi-jinks with dull leads and uninspired direction. Everything is present for a formidable comedy but it does not happen. James Ellison, Virginia Gilmore and Dan Duryea are a romantic triangle. Mistaken identity, romantic double-crosses, and clever writing shuffles them around town in a fox hunt that ends with a toe-to-toe blowout between Ellison and Duryea.

*Dan Duryea plays Ralph Cobb in* That Other Woman, *a Southern gentleman who loses his manners in a comedy of errors.* 1943, TWENTIETH CENTURY FOX.

Henry Summers (James Ellison) is a narcissistic architect who is irresistible to women and too weak to stave off the temptation that goes along with his magnetism. It has given him a mercurial attitude towards his work, where reaching a deadline means cramming three weeks' worth of work into a maddening night.

Emily Borden (Virginia Gilmore) is his perfect secretary because she is a Gal Friday who excels at arranging schedules, juggling clients, and evading paramours. She is an attractive woman who has fallen in love with Summers, but feels helpless because she believes that she lacks sex appeal.

Grandma (Alma Kruger) is a southern matriarch who is proud of her Victory Garden because it is her patriotic duty. She is a conspirator who looks out for the interests of her granddaughter, whom she believes is wasting her time with her suitor, Ralph Cobb (Dan Duryea), even though he is a southern gentleman with a sense of hospitality and an inbred mistrust of Yankees.

The dowager regales her granddaughter with tales of how she snagged Grandpa, telling of ruses that included letters of flattery and

Poster for That Other Woman, a romantic comedy starring James Ellison and Virginia Gilmore. 1943, TWENTIETH CENTURY FOX.

seduction, something she suggests her granddaughter should attempt if she wants to land Mr. Summers as her husband. The family tradition boasts the anonymous love letter gambit as a surefire way of fortifying the blood line.

It is fitting that a deceptive mash letter should get things moving with Mr. Summers because he is vulnerable to perfume-scented love notes with ornate penmanship. Grandma's advice becomes Miss Borden's burden and she mails it more out of compunction than compulsion.

This leads to a chain of events that fosters love while encouraging discouragement. This is done is screwball style, with clever lines and synchronized slapstick bits to enliven a subplot about a lover's misunderstanding and the fun of life-and-death chases based on mistaken identities.

Henry Summers, the narcissist, is knocked down a couple of pegs when he realizes there is more to a woman than a line on the expense account. Emily Borden discovers the inherent power of a plain Jane who becomes a lady on a court balcony.

Chivalry wears out easier than it used to when Ralph Cobb is cuckolded and cut out of the deal completely. Grandma maintains matriarchal status and has successfully passed down the tradition of the poisoned pen letter as being more prudent than an invitation to a shotgun wedding.

James Ellison plays his part like a wind up doll going through the motions. He never runs out of energy, playing his part well enough to get his character's intentions through to the audience. Virginia Gilmore is another wind-up toy playing her part the way it was written, so she compliments her lead as they run circles round each other in a game of charades mixed with masquerades.

Dan Duryea is Ralph Cobb, a Southern gentleman who courts Borden in the way of a Southern gentleman, only to be knocked on his pride by his rival. He plays it honest and noble throughout the movie and winds up confounded by a game of errors.

Duryea plays it well as the suspicious suitor who follows his fiancé upstate while her boss thinks that he is being shadowed by a gangster. Duryea plays it both ways, as a jealous shadow and a Southern cuckold.

Janis Carter is the know-it-all snoop who starts the chain of events that end with the architect and his secretary falling in love. Minerva Urecal plays a suspicious landlady who eyeballs Ellison and Borden as they try to book a room in her hotel in a small upstate town.

*A secretary (Virginia Gilmore), her boss (Ralph Ellison) and the other woman (Janis Carter) form an unusual romantic triangle.* 1943, TWENTIETH CENTURY FOX.

*Ralph Cobb (Dan Duryea) and Henry Summers (James Ellison) are about to fight over Emily Borden (Virginia Gilmore).* 1943, TWENTIETH CENTURY FOX.

# 7

# The Great
# Crime Spree of '45

Dan Duryea is identified chiefly with portraying screen villains who menaced their victims before being brought down by ironic twists of fate. Conniving, vain, sniveling, and overconfident to a fault, these characters epitomized the sleazy con-artists with oily smoothness and soprano intonations who dominated a group of stooges until they were ruined by a bitter ironic conclusion to one of their own failed schemes.

These villains suffered the pangs of karmic payback so many times they had to develop night vision to suit the shadows of their crime drama hells. That was true of Johnny Prince in *Scarlet Street* in 1945 and twenty years later for Carl Lutcher, the hired killer in *Walk a Tightrope* in 1965. It was the same thing for anyone with similar intentions who came along in between.

In 1945, Dan Duryea added a new genre to his repertoire of classical films and comedies when he appeared in a series of crime dramas that broadened the direction of his career. He created a group of complex and tortured characters in several lurid crime dramas. Two were directed by Fritz Lang, while Edward L. Cahn helmed a low budget pulp, and another starred Eric Von Stroheim.

*Woman In The Window, Scarlet Street, Main Street After Dark*, and *The Great Flamarion* — four crime dramas in one year, a collection of eccentric characters in movies with outrageous scenarios that are somewhat hilarious and outdated, and at times ingenious.

In *Main Street After Dark*, quickie master Edward L. Cahn directs Duryea in a movie about a crime family of paddy rollers. Ma (Selena Royale) heads the gang that rousts gullible servicemen in the military town the family operates in. Duryea is smooth and slips easily into the darkness after hustling innocent soldiers. He gets in over his head and nabs a bellyful of "crime does not pay" by the final credits.

One could look at *Main Street After Dark* as an educational film padded with crime drama vignettes. The subject is the police crackdown on con artists in a military town. The focus is on a family and Lt. Lorgan (Edward Arnold), the detective who hounds them to keep them in line. Thanks to the detective, the drama veers off into educational segments on surviving the scams the servicemen will face in town.

Selena Royale plays Ma Dibson, the matriarch of a family of crooks that thrives on the easy marks in their military service town. Their dupes

*The Dibson family is a clan of hustlers consisting of (left to right) Lefty (Tom Trout), Jessy Bell (Audrey Totter), Posey (Dan Duryea), Ma (Selena Royale), and Rosalie (Dorothy Ruth Morris).* 1944, LOEW'S, INC.

are mainly servicemen, and the family plies a variety of methods to snare their prizes. It all comes apart for the crime family when the eldest son is released from the pen after serving his stretch.

He cannot wait to get back in the game and eyeballs a payroll drop as his one big score. It is bungled and turns into a murder rap when he murders his boss. Lt. Lorgan dogs the family in a way that makes it seems like harassment until the film's climax. It becomes apparent that he knew what he was doing and that the villainous kin will be split up to face separate raps.

Edward Arnold is aggravating as the detective hot on the beat. He comes off like a patronizing big brother, but he is always there to make a bust. He is always smiling, whether he is giving a pep talk, conducting an unofficial interrogation, or cracking down on someone with the iron cuffs.

Selena Royale is the matriarch that rules the gang with an iron fist. She knits sweaters while listening to a police band and calls the shots that net wallets, knick-knacks, and other odds and ends. She is strictly a small-town crime queen, but one that uses her street savvy to stay one step ahead of the law.

Lefty (Tom Trout) is a two-dimensional cartoon tough guy right

*Posey (Dan Duryea) pulls an ingenious but heartless scam on two unsuspecting servicemen.* 1944, LOEW'S, INC.

out of the funny pages. The main difference is that he does not have a five o'clock shadow until his final shot when it turns into a twenty-year stretch. The cartoon tough guy has a wife, and she is played by Audrey Totter.

Totter has a bitter deadpan expression and a sexy pout that brings life to the stereotypical character of Jessy Bell Gibson, a hard-bitten, dime-a-dance girl. She resists his attempts to get her back into a life of crime, but she gives in to the pressure.

Dan Duryea is Posey, the pampered younger son who is the apple of his mother's eye. He is a pickpocket who is fawned over by his mother, turning him into a lazy good-for-nothing. He is soft, and that is what works against him in the big holdup.

*Posey (Dan Duryea) tries to talk his brother Lefty (Tom Trout) out of pulling an ill-planned robbery.* 1944, LOEW'S, INC.

*The Dibson clan is finally busted by the relentless Lt. Lorgan (Edward Arnold).* 1944, LOEW'S, INC.

Hume Cronin plays an unsettling and morbid antiques shop owner. He is a front and he is there to finance the undercurrent of the hustler squad's world. Lloyd Corrigan is his usual friendly boisterous self. This time his charm is not enough to impress everyone as his payroll is the countdown to his death.

Duryea goes from ill-fated, pampered pickpocket to a drunken husband whose sidestep becomes a misstep in *The Great Flamarion*. He is the marked husband in a spouse-sidekick act that accompanies a sharpshooter played by Erich Von Stroheim.

*The Great Flamarion (Erich Von Stroheim) and sidekick Connie (Mary Beth Hughes) plan to murder her husband during a performance.* 1945, REPUBLIC PICTURES.

The Great Flamarion is a Prussian marksman who showcases his shooting prowess by shooting at the husband-and-wife team who play an adulterous couple to his enraged cuckold. Offstage, the wife eventually ingratiates herself to manipulate the great showman into shooting her husband in a drunken misstep while going through this act.

If the dated histrionics of yesteryear's romanticism aren't enough to keep you in stitches, the ham acting of a once-upon-a-time great film director doing the Mad Prussian routine will have you in hysterics.

*The Great Flamarion* seems old for its time and is reminiscent of early films of the sound era because it is overly melodramatic and has a tinny soundtrack. It has its odd attraction because of the talent associated with it. The director is Anthony Mann and the star is Erich Von Stroheim. The *Sturm und Drang* of betrayed love in the theatre world makes it an interesting companion piece to the *Blue Angel*, although it is a minor connection.

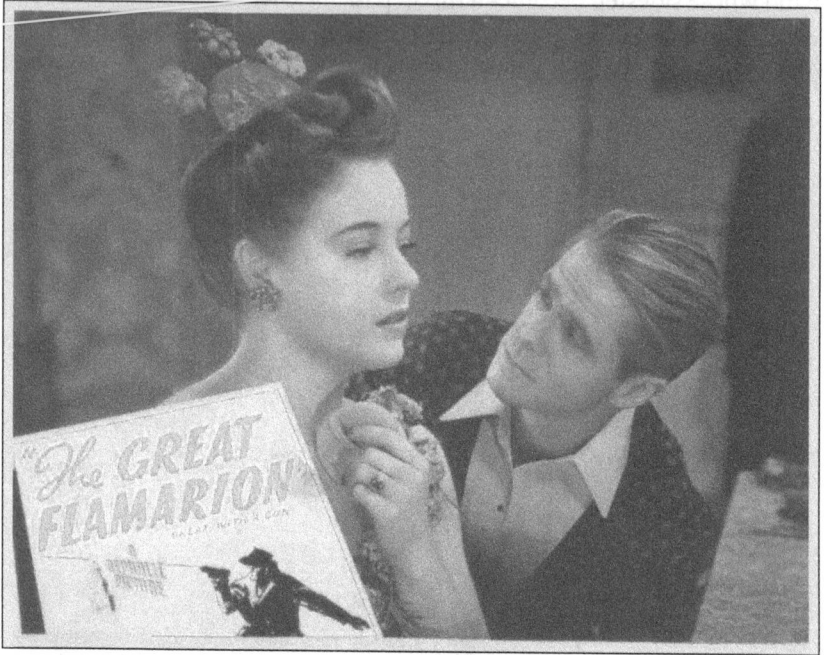

*Al Wallace (Dan Duryea) makes another empty promise to his wife Connie (Mary Beth Hughes) about giving up alcohol.* 1945, REPUBLIC PICTURES.

Flashbacks were the rage of many films in the 1940s, chiefly because of Orson Welles' masterful use of the technique in *Citizen Kane*. It eventually became a cheap gimmick among its many imitators, but it became a standard storytelling method. The usage of flashback in *The Great Flamarion* is basic.

The movie begins with a murder in a Mexican theater. A woman had been killed and her husband is the chief suspect. The real murderer is a wounded mystery man who falls from the rafters after everyone except the clown has left the wings. The dying man tells the clown his story, the legend of *The Great Flamarion*.

The legend is an expert marksman who showcases his shooting prowess in an absurd stage show. He plays the cuckolded lover who returns home to find his wife with another man. He shoots at them with his pistol, popping buttons, straps, and bottles. His aim is hair-raising and the audience is enthusiastic. *The Great Flamarion* enters and exits to thunderous applause every time he performs his act.

His assistants are played by Mary Beth Hughes and Dan Duryea. Al Wallace, the husband, is a drunkard and Connie, his wife, strives for a better

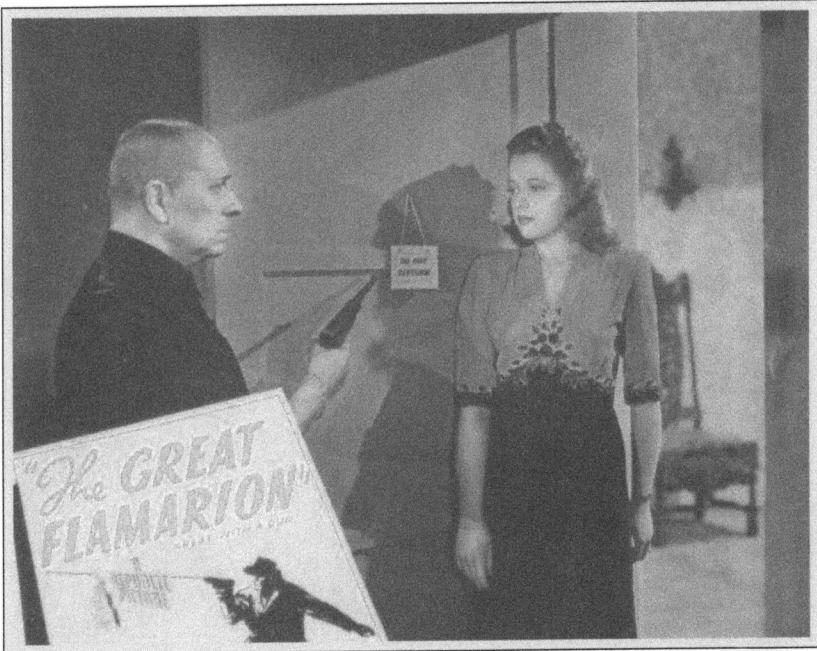

*The Great Flamarion (Erich Von Stroheim) reminds Connie (Mary Beth Hughes) of his prowess with a pistol.* 1945, REPUBLIC PICTURES.

life. She contrives a plot where the Great Flamarion would accidentally shoot her husband when he stumbles drunkenly onto the stage. The murder would be deemed an accident because of Wallace's drinking problem.

At first, Flamarion is a tough nut to crack. He is the stereotypical, highly-disciplined Prussian aristocrat. The act is the only thing that matters to him and his only concern is Wallace's drinking. His life consists of practicing to strengthen his eyes.

Flirtation and exhibitionism fail to excite Flamarion. He is immune to female wiles because of a failed relationship many years ago that turned him into the man of stone. His work is now his life and it occupies all of his time. It takes time to wear him down, but when Connie does, he is silly putty in her hands.

It does not take long to convince him to shoot her husband and make it look like an accident. The coroner rules the death accidental because of the high amount of alcohol in Wallace's blood. The successful plot is a pact to temporarily separate and meet at a later date where they can resume their love.

It is when Connie fails to show up at the designated spot, a hotel in Arizona, that Flamarion realizes that he was deceived. He becomes

*The Great Flamarion (Erich Von Stroheim) loses his self-control when Connie (Mary Beth Hughes) unsettles his Prussian code of arms.* 1945, REPUBLIC PICTURES.

obsessed with revenge and becomes destitute during his nationwide search for Connie, who has run off with the cyclist from their last act together.

The tip-off is that Connie is in Mexico and it is all settled at the theater when he strangles her backstage and she shoots him twice. He uses the wings to make his escape before he comes down to earth to tell the clown his story. The movie ends when Flamarion finishes his story and the flashback turns into the sympathetic clown nodding as the cops arrive to solve the crime.

*The Great Flamarion* is a shrill affair with overblown performances. Backstage rivalries make for great mystery and intrigue when handled with lurid melodramatics and ham acting. Histrionics and cliché dialogue comprise a noteworthy genre when a good cast and experienced crew squeeze the thrills and chills out of bits that have been reliable standbys since the silent era.

The movie benefits from the sinister character of Von Stroheim, a one-time cinematic giant whose career flourished in pre-Nazi Germany and Hollywood during the silent era. He later attained success in B-movies typecast as Mad Prussian types in post-war American melodramas. Erich Von Stroheim is hilarious as Flamarion, especially when he acts like a schoolboy in love.

Dan Duryea plays a dupe to the great Von Stroheim and attempts to keep himself from being the losing side of a lover's triangle. Duryea plays the spineless jelly-man, one who keeps his promises in a bottle. The goofball is Leo Hubbard under dire circumstances. Dissipated and cheapened by his spoiled sense of superiority, he now acts like a stooge in a marksman's side show.

In the end, Duryea's main nemesis is the bottle. It is no wonder that the ruined genius should push him out of the picture and lay claim to his wife. Mary Beth Hughes is a formidable vamp, although it is Flamarion's pent up desperation, not her seductive power, that makes her effective.

*Johnny Prince (Dan Duryea) is the rotten apple of Kitty March's (Joan Bennett) jaundiced eye in* Scarlet Street. 1945, UNIVERSAL PICTURES COMPANY, INC.

# 8

# A Fritz Lang Triangle

Fritz Lang directed Duryea as a misogynist cad in *The Woman in the Window* and *Scarlet Street.* In both films, Duryea's character harasses the lovely Joan Bennett and hustles the timid Edward G. Robinson into compromising his honor for the sexy vamp. The milquetoast is a timid cuckold who becomes a mother hen because of Bennett's domineering allure. Death and blackmail are Duryea's forte until he becomes a victim of his own schemes.

Alice Reed (Joan Bennett) is *The Woman in the Window*, a portrait of a seductive woman that inspires three middle-aged professional men to question their own virility. Professor Wanley (Edward G. Robinson) is a mild-mannered psychology professor who faces his mid-life changes with a sex-fantasy that turns into a bone-chilling nightmare. It starts with a captivating portrait on display in a gallery next to the men's club that he frequents.

One night, the painting inspires a conversation among the three friends at the social club. The DA (Raymond Massey) believes that a middle-aged man is like an unconditioned athlete who cannot rise to the task at hand. Many cases that cross his desk attest to the foibles of over-the-hill stallions that still pass themselves as colts. The doctor (Edmund Breon) reluctantly agrees, but Professor Wanley does not concede the point so easily.

The DA and the doctor leave their colleague to ponder his conceit, a perspective that leads to a chance encounter with the model. This leads to a round of cordials and a late night review of her portfolio. Murder, blackmail, and suicide follow, all because of an innocent flirtation with a painting.

*The Woman in the Window* is a gimmick-laden blackmail melodrama whose chief interest is the mesmerizing Joan Bennett. To look at her allows you to tolerate a pat plot development based on cardboard figures given life by the principal players. Edward G. Robinson and Dan Duryea breathe life into the stock characters of a milquetoast and sleek villain. They add a seedy vitality to Bennett's veneer of sophistication. A twist ending befits a morality tale where murder and suicide are suitors for the hand of a bored socialite-for-hire.

*The Woman in the Window* is another one of the crossword puzzles Fritz Lang directed during his WWII Hollywood exile. It is a compact and compelling movie, expertly acted and directed with Lang's concise flair. The viewer is swept along with the fluid plot development that

*Professor Richard Wanley (Edward G. Robinson) meets Alice (Joan Bennett), the woman of his dreams in* The Woman in the Window. 1944, RKO PICTURES.

flows like dream logic.

The repressed sexual fantasy unfolds naturally even though the plot seems illogical when examined. The forbidden impulse lies in falling in love with the sexy portrait. Self-censorship comes in the form of not wanting to take the cordials beyond a casual encounter. Fantasy and temptation are shown by giving in to her invitation of viewing her portfolio in the privacy of her apartment. Denial and chaos occur when he tries to deny his feelings and confronts her jealous keeper. Condemnation and punishment is manifested with a blackmail scheme and a sordid way to find absolution.

The first half of the movie plays like a police procedural, with the DA assuming the pompous, professorial tone of Sherlock Holmes. He reveals clues, deduces motives, and lays out assumptions that make

Professor Wanley feel uneasy. The movie's tone changes once Dan Duryea shows up as the blackmailer, an ex-cop turned private eye who has been shadowing the murder victim. The moment Duryea enters the movie, the DA disappears and it becomes Duryea's show. He becomes the character who calls all of the shots and decides which way the plot will develop.

*An impromptu lover's triangle turns into a nightmare for the ethics professor.*
1944, RKO PICTURES.

*Woman in the Window* has a special allure because such by-the-numbers movies are designed to make clichés enjoyable. Forget loose ends and a novelty ending, 'no questions asked' is the way to digest the movie's logic. So Alice Reed has nothing better to do than to look at the reactions on strangers' faces when they match her visage to the portrait in the window?

Of all the strangers she encounters, she invites the bulldog man up to her apartment. The seedy man in the straw hat can bluff his way into a blackmail scheme without resistance from Reed. The professor will dig a grave for himself when he buys poison for Alice Reed to use on the blackmailer. It all does not matter because a shaggy dog story is just a shaggy dog story.

Edward G. Robinson is likeable although it is unlikely that Bennett would take an interest in him, especially when she is the kept woman of a millionaire. The jealous outburst of the sugar daddy is extreme, but lays the groundwork for the scissors-in-the-back bit and the body-in-the-rug disposal. There is always a creepy peeper around to witness the disposal of the corpse. In this movie, it's Dan Duryea. He insinuates himself into

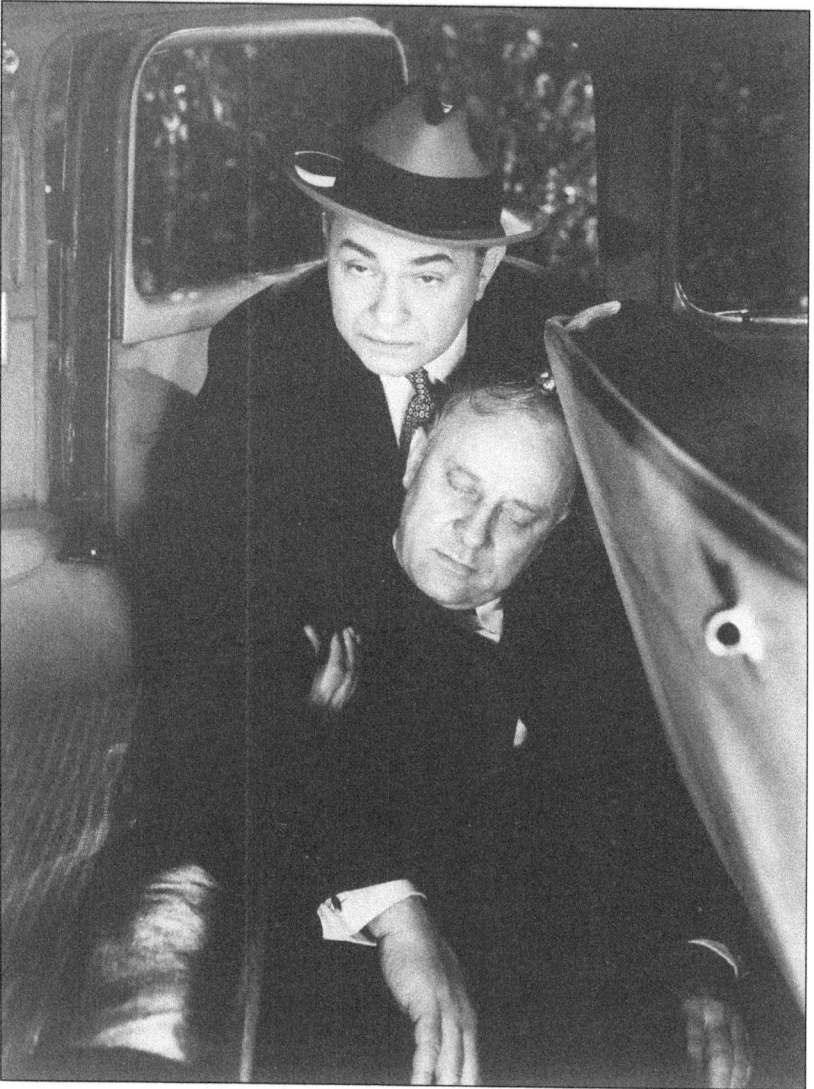

*Prof. Wanley (Edward G. Robinson) disposes of the weight of his guilt.* 1944, RKO PICTURES.

Bennett's life, complete with blackmail demands and a Plan B that serves as his magic carpet ride to a fade-out.

The ease with which he accomplishes his threats, demands, and set-ups is convenient but unrealistic. Bennett agrees to come with part of the money, and also uses poison in a cocktail toast. It does not work because Duryea is too smart for that.

*A shadow player (Dan Duryea) upsets the balance of power with a blackmail scheme.* 1944, RKO PICTURES.

However, he is not smart enough to avoid the shootout with cops that results in his death and accusations of being the original murderer. It is a smooth if implausible turn of events that clears Bennett. Too bad that the professor did not have nerves of steel and opted instead for a poisonous bromide. It's all a joke when the sandman collects the leftover laughs.

Joan Bennett is the main reason to disregard the absurdities of the plot. She is one of the last of the original dark-haired *femme fatale* before they became dominated by peroxide blondes. Her hypnotic eyes and neurotic manner legitimize the illogical dreamlike simplicity of the action.

Edward G. Robinson's inner satyr makes him a slave to Bennett. It's not just the painting; it's the polite come-on in the genteel form of a sidewalk pickup. It is abstract rudeness to him and it drives him crazy. He becomes a cuckold gone cuckoo in need of a Mickey Finn prescription.

Dan Duryea comes off like the shadow of Bennett and Robinson's skewed moral compasses. He is the built-in nemesis created by the loopholes of their plan. They killed Zeus, the great sugar daddy, and Duryea was the rude jester who appeared on the scene to exact payment for their folly.

Duryea witnesses the activities of the crime and deduces that the guilty parties are a model and her slave. He cashes in on it with sly inference and dream logic. Being justified in his attempt to collect a tariff on Bennett and Robinson's secret gives Duryea the liberty to break the law with impunity.

In *Scarlet Street*, Fritz Lang reunites his three principal players in a similar, ill-fated triangle. Dan Duryea and Joan Bennett play a sleazy couple that hustles Robinson for his paintings. Robinson is so lovestruck and timid that he considers it an honor that his paintings can bring wealth to his lover.

Three on a match leads to a streak of bad luck for Chris Cross (Edward G. Robinson). He is an honest and well-respected cashier for a prestigious banking firm. His life begins to fall apart on the night of his testimonial dinner after an act of heroism turns into a downward spiral. He rescues a woman from her abusive boyfriend only to become a hapless victim of their heartless manipulation.

A friendly drink and a conversation peppered with two-sided exaggerations leads to a strange affair between the timid painter and Kitty (Joan Bennett), the outgoing "actress." It turns into a tragic and violent scam because of the nefarious Johnny Prince (Dan Duryea), the sleazy boyfriend of the low-class femme fatale.

Prince is forever concocting get-rich quick schemes, usually at the expense of his girlfriend, who is madly in love with the abusive heel. His dream is to buy into a garage and force out the partners. The dream is given substance by Cross, the quiet cashier who also is a devoted Sunday painter.

His paintings become the focal point of the drama because they bring out the hidden personalities of the characters. They are something out of Rod Serling's *Night Gallery* because they have a quality that makes people feel differently about themselves.

Cross loves his paintings, but he is self-effacing when it comes to his talent. His wife thinks that they are garbage and they only make her more of a shrew. Prince thinks that they are the work of a hop-head, but becomes giddy with ambition when they command the attentions of an art critic and a gallery owner. Kitty is put off by them but finds self-worth when she takes credit for them. They will bring her fame in the art world, as will her grisly murder.

A series of clever plot twists worthy of a good pulp novel leads to a downbeat conclusion for all of the principals. Kitty is murdered by Cross. Prince is accused, convicted, and executed for the crime. Cross is driven

*Christopher Cross (Edward G. Robinson) is a star-crossed milquetoast in* Scarlet Street. 1945, UNIVERSAL PICTURES COMPANY, INC.

insane by guilt and becomes an unhappy wanderer. The final irony comes in the final scene when his portrait of Kitty commands $10,000 as the deluded bum passes the gallery where it has just been sold.

The plot to *Scarlet Street* is convoluted but the movie is captivating, mainly because of the three principal characters. Joan Bennett sizzles as usual. She is crude and vulgar this time around, possessing a rude sex

*Johnny Prince (Dan Duryea) appraises Criss Cross' bizarre Sunday paintings.*
1945, UNIVERSAL PICTURES COMPANY, INC.

appeal that overshadows her rough edges. She is crazy about Duryea, an abusive heel who sometimes hustles her to make money. In his straw hat and striped jacket, Dan Duryea looks more like a song-and-dance man from vaudeville than a pimp. He has a dancing partner, but she is no Irene Castle. Her love for Duryea is matched by her well-disguised contempt for Robinson.

Robinson again plays the kind-hearted milquetoast. He has celebrated twenty five years working as a cashier with a prestigious banking firm, has a nagging wife at home, and his friends are considerate of him. It all changes when he becomes involved with the woman he saved from a brutal attacker.

The rescue becomes a polite drink and a strange relationship is formed, a perverse marionette play with Duryea pulling the strings. It is not enough that Cross offers his paintings to Bennett; he has resorted to embezzling money from the firm that recently held a testimonial dinner in his honor. This is a convoluted way to dissolve his marriage.

Robinson is too dense to notice that Duryea is Bennett's paramour. The unsavory lover controls Bennett in every way and uses her to con the old man. It all unravels when Bennett can no longer conceal her contempt for the old man. She ridicules him and basically lets the whore inside chew the old man up and spit him out. It is the one time that Robinson cracks up and he does so with a creepy gusto.

*The mild-mannered cashier can't believe that he is also a cuckold.* 1945, UNIVERSAL PICTURES COMPANY, INC.

Duryea created his first really vicious sleaze ball character with the role of Johnny Prince. He was the template of the conniving heel, akin to Leo Hubbard's prototype of the vacillating weasel. Prince is a low-brow cad with a well-honed personality and a pimp's mentality.

*Scarlet Street* was Lang's remake of Renoir's *Le Chienne*. It has a strange charm to it and works well as a cheap and tawdry thriller. It is parts music-hall crudity, German Expressionism, minimalism and exploitation flick.

Lang's direction gives the movie a quaint touch, like a German silent movie with sound added to it. There are the usual Fritz Lang parlor tricks, visually and plot-wise. The first husband of Robinson's wife shows up after having been presumed drowned in the river. The circumstances of his survival stretch one's credulity although his demands for getaway money and how he gets it are comical. His temporary intrusion interrupts Bennett and Duryea's vicious hustle.

Another odd point is the brouhaha caused by Robinson's paintings. They have a primitive and naïve charm to them, but hardly possess the power to create a sensation. It is the art world's hysteria that gives the paintings a sense of worth, but they are really flimsy cartoons that make the fuss hilarious.

It is implausible that Duryea can pass off Bennett as the painter of the popular masterpieces that Robinson willingly gives her. An eccentric painter and a pompous art critic attest to her genius although one never sees a painter's studio in her home. The paintings are in the ludicrous style of a Sunday painter but they cause a rage in the art world.

Adding to the absurdity is Robinson's first wife believing that he

*Kitty March (Joan Bennett) and Johnny Prince (Dan Duryea) confront an ironic twist of fate.* 1945, UNIVERSAL PICTURES COMPANY, INC.

copied his style from the female impostor after she sees a painting in an art gallery window. One of the movie's charms and highlights is the rustic Greenwich Village neighborhood where Bennett has her love nest. Margaret Lindsay adds a sanitized sex appeal as Kitty's roommate. She has contempt for Prince, which Kitty mistakes as jealousy.

# 9

# Puttin' On The Ritz

Nightclubs once had a mythic aura about them because of their class, pizzazz, and glitter. The party and dining milieu was accentuated by floor shows and big bands that kept things hopping. Nightclubs during the 30s, early 40s, and the post-war years boasted an experience that soothed an audience out on the town to drown their miseries and kick up their heels.

They also provided a great atmosphere for any type of film, which was given that extra jolt by having a nightclub background to it. Nightclubs gave a film rhythm and intensity, adding a stylish, otherworldly element. That was as true for romantic comedies as it was for gangster movies. During the 40s, it was popular to blend genres and that was something Universal was good at doing.

Dan Duryea's association with a nightclub almost ends on a sour note in *Lady on a Train*. Deanna Durbin's dulcet tones save him from his darker self when truth becomes crime fiction on a honeymoon caboose. The same thing can be said about his perilous association with a nightclub in *White Tie and Tails*. Ella Raines is the steady influence this time around. She gets him into a jam and uses it to make him see the light about day jobs and the night life.

*Lady on a Train* is a whimsical murder-mystery, an attempt by Universal to alter Deanna Durbin's screen image without straying too far from her persona as a singing ingénue. She plays Nikki Collins, a lover of mystery novels who witnesses a Christmas Eve murder while riding a train into Grand Central.

The police don't believe her claims so she undertakes the task of investigating the murder, eventually persuading mystery writer Wayne Morgan (David Bruce) to reluctantly help her. She finds out through a newsreel that the victim was Mr. Waring, a wealthy shipping magnate who is reported to having died from an accident at his Long Island estate. This inspires Nikki to visit the estate for her inquest, where she unwittingly assumes the role of Margo Martin, a nightclub singer who is the disputed heir to the victim's estate.

This leads to a cat-and-mouse tale of mistaken identities as the schemers try to dissuade Nikki from continuing her investigation. This includes numerous murder attempts on her life, although her persecutors are not responsible for the original murder. The whole investigation becomes a trail of false leads and a string of red herrings.

*Lady on a Train* is typical of the films Universal turned out during the 1940s. It is a professionally-made movie, created by expert craftsmen who knew how to do their jobs well. It is entertaining because it follows a formula and evenly dispenses the thrills and humor.

Deanna Durbin is attractive and personable, showing a flair for sex appeal and comedy. She sings "Silent Night" over the phone to her father and performs "Night and Day" in a nightclub.

David Bruce was a bland star of the 40s and he plays the mystery writer who is drawn into a real mystery. His pencil mustache has more character than he does and he ambles his way through the film with an affable manner.

Dan Duryea again dons a trench coat and a fedora for *Lady on a Train* as a suspect who is sinister

*Poster for* Lady on a Train, *a comedy-drama starring Deanna Durbin.* 1945, UNIVERSAL PICTURES COMPANY, INC.

and suggestive of menace, although he is a diversion to the real murderer.

Ralph Bellamy plays his older brother and they are drawn into the scheme when they become infatuated with the nightclub singer who was the bait for their uncle, the murder victim. The brothers are the two swings of the pendulum, only one of them cuts for real.

George Couatouris is a nightclub owner who is responsible for the original extortion scheme that led to the murder of his lure, Margo Martin. She is a nightclub singer played by Maria Palmer and is used as bait to snare the aging millionaire. It becomes a case of mistaken identity when Nikki Collins temporarily assumes the singer's identity, implicating her in the shady goings-on, only one of them gets roses and the other winds up colder than chilled champagne.

*Nikki Collins (Deanna Durbin) mesmerizes two brothers (Dan Duryea and Ralph Bellamy) at an inquest.* 1945, UNIVERSAL PICTURES COMPANY, INC.

*Nikki Collins (Deanna Durbin) cradles Wayne Morgan (David Bruce), a mystery writer who faints during a real life murder investigation.* 1945, UNIVERSAL PICTURES COMPANY, INC.

Allen Jenkins is menacing as the nightclub owner's chauffeur and strong-arm thug. Edward Everett Horton is charming as a befuddled attorney for Collins' father. William Frawley has a comic bit as the cop who refuses to believe Collins' claims at the beginning of the movie. Lash LaRue, the Western legend, has a small part as a waiter at the club where Margo Martin sings.

*Charles Dumont (Dan Duryea) is the perfect gentleman's gentleman, much to the delight of the well-heeled Louise Bradford (Ella Raines).* 1947, UNIVERSAL PICTURES COMPANY, INC.

In *White Tie and Tails*, Dan Duryea is a gentleman's gentleman masquerading as the gentleman himself. He gets involved in an oddball adventure with a dark haired femme and a loony-tunes mobster.

White tie and tails is the disguise used by Charles Dumont, a major-domo, to enjoy the high life from the other side of the tracks. Dumont is the perfect butler, one who can coordinate clothes, mix

*Charles Dumont (Dan Duryea) puts on a front with the help of Emil (William Trenk), a cooperative maitre de.* 1947, UNIVERSAL PICTURES COMPANY, INC.

drinks, talk knowledgably about art, and bring order to the chaotic world of teenagers.

The butler is a brilliant man who enjoys the finer things in life and believes that the only way he'll ever enjoy them is by being butler to a wealthy family. This leads to a walk on the wild side.

He gets the chance to play the boss when the Latimer family he works for takes a holiday in Florida. Dumont dismisses the staff for a holiday of their own, only retaining the services of the chauffeur, George (Frank Jenks).

Dumont's first night on the town is the first of many missteps that will end with his ignominious dismissal, but happy days await him as befits the ending of a sophisticated comedy bordering on lunacy. His misadventure is actually a belated coming-of-age drama intended to work up the creativity and individualism that lie within him; all it took to bring it out was love.

On his first night out on the town, Dumont meets Louise Bradford (Ella Raines) at a nightclub and he is instantly smitten by her. There is an air of mystery to her that only makes his attraction stronger. George cautions him about taking the masquerade to the next level, but Dumont does not heed the advice.

Love and a heavy sense of chivalry implicate the butler in a crime of passion. He vouches for a gambling debt incurred by Louise's sister and winds up surrendering two paintings to Larry Lundie (William Bendix), the nightclub owner, as collateral. This theft becomes the basis of a series of wrong conclusions for the butler posing as the master. It all seems okay until the real master returns and notices something amiss about his prized paintings. The gangster mucks up things with his intrusion, the butler is fired and becomes reborn again. All's well that ends well when Dumont is dismissed for abusing the master's trust, but he gets to start a new life with Louise Bradford.

*Cover for a comic book rendition of* White Tie and Tails. 1947, UNIVERSAL PICTURES COMPANY, INC.

Dan Duryea is spry and sleek as Charles Dumont, the imposter *bon vivante*. Dumont is sophisticated and knowledgeable about the finer things in life. He has the charm to pull off his scheme but crumbles under the pressure when Lundie swipes two painting as security for the check he has written.

William Bendix is funny as Larry Lundie. He is a flummoxed ape-man who wants to expand his vocabulary and become a fashion plate. He is dim but still can see straight to the point. He gets things done the old fashioned way, with muscle based on I.O.U.s. He offers to hire Dumont as a tutor about the finer things in life.

Ella Raines has a vampish quality to her. She is delightful but droll and seems to be off in a dream state. She encourages Dumont to seek his artistic muse and start painting again. Her younger sister, played by Patricia Alphin, owes a gambling debt to Lundie and this is the reason that Dumont has overextended himself.

Donald Curtis plays Bendix's henchman and exudes menace as he intimidates the younger Bradford daughter. Frank Jenks excels at playing wise guy, working-class types from the old neighborhood, although here, he is a rational font of wisdom to whom Charles Dumont won't pay any mind. Charles Kolb plays the gruff and stuffy society tight-ass that earmarked his career. Scotty Beckett and Nita Hunter are the children of the man of the house.

*In* Black Angel, *Martin Blair (Dan Duryea) is a successful song writer and cabaret pianist who harbors a dark secret that eventually destroys him.* 1946, UNIVERSAL PICTURES COMPANY, INC.

# Transformations

Dan Duryea shaded his characters with contradictory traits, eventually leading to a hybrid type that blended heroics with dubious motives. Two tragic heroes with villainous other halves are Martin Blair and Johnny Evans. Blair is a piano player whose hit song was playing the night his ex-wife, a nightclub singer, was killed in *The Black Angel*. June Vincent is the angel who leads him to a bleak redemption at his own expense during the investigation of the crime. In *Johnny Stool Pigeon*, Evans poses as a narc in order to earn a chance to go straight with Shelley Winters, the girl of his dreams. His redemption is anything but bleak, but his past is what makes him someone who lives on the dark side of the street.

*The Black Angel* is a nightmare that plays like a weird cabaret act with all of the thrills of an old pulp crime novel. Some of the hooks and clichés served up in this mystery are blackmail, the innocent man on death row, the persistent wife who tries to find the truth, amnesia as a part-time alibi for murder, and the helping hand of the victim's rum-pot, piano virtuoso husband.

Martin Blair (Dan Duryea) is the hard-drinking ex-husband of Mavis Marlowe (Constance Dowling), the victim in a murder that Catherine Bennett's (June Vincent) husband has been tried and convicted of. He is sent to death row to await execution while Mrs. Bennett enlists Martin Blair's help to clear her husband of the crime.

Marko (Peter Lorre), the sweaty, cigarette-smoking owner of The Black Angel club, becomes their chief suspect because Blair identifies him as the man who entered his wife's apartment building shortly before her murder. Blair and Catherine get jobs at The Black Angel as a piano man and his chanteuse, respectively. It is their way of keeping tabs on Marko, who, it turns out, is keeping tabs on them.

The movie asks if a murderer can be a hero if he turns himself in. It seems so only if he can turn back time. If not, then alcohol and amnesia are useful alibis until they cave in. That is when Martin Blair becomes a hero and a louse whose act of chivalry violates the Fifth Commandment.

His alcohol-induced amnesia is cured by the dry heaves, and a guilty conscience outweighs his upset stomach.

Alcohol frees Blair from his inner pain but imprisons him because of the dreams they inspire. Benders allow him to live in the past, but waking up returns him to his lonely present. Booze blends the past and the present to create a hellish future that creates the fog that enables him to commit the perfect crime. An alcoholic haze also allows him to recall a repressed memory that saves an innocent man from execution and forces them to trade places.

The solution lies in "Heartache," a song that can heal wounds or open them up. Who was playing the song the night of the murder, the victim or the killer? For one of them, it was a piece of passionate nostalgia. Its symbol is a brooch that becomes the real trace to the killer. Missing from the murder scene, it winds up being found by the confused mystery killer who becomes the guilty party when death row gives a rare reprieve to a lucky innocent man.

*Print ad for* Black Angel, *an intriguing film noir.* 1946, UNIVERSAL PICTURES COMPANY, INC.

Dan Duryea's Martin Blair is a complex character, a civilian detective whose investigation leads him to the face in the mirror. He has been destroyed by alcohol, but retains his brilliant talent for playing the piano. Blair has a fraction of morality left within him, because he is the one who saves Catherine Bennett's husband at a dear cost.

Blair is a classic tragic figure, a component of a mystery whose solution leads to his own demise. He is a man who is ruined by unrequited love, a sucker who surrenders his soul to a siren. His hit song, "Heartache," was written for his ex-wife who despises it, even though she recorded it with him. It is a tune Blair plays every night until he passes out at the honky-tonk bar where he works.

Martin Blair's courtliness is a disguise for love on the rebound in *The Black Angel*. Blair earns dubious honors in the hero category because he sacrifices himself for someone wrongly accused of his crime. Martin Blair sees that justice is served even though it means that he will be the main course. It is his offering of good tidings to Catherine Bennett.

The dizzy gent of *Black Angel* is a step in two directions when it comes to character labeling. He has the weak traits that make him vulnerable to a frame-up while being good-natured with a will to survive the nightmare.

*The dark side (Constance Dowling) to Martin Blair's (Dan Duryea) soul is a secret that will condemn him to die.* 1946, UNIVERSAL PICTURES COMPANY, INC.

Blair also has a nagging guilt so strong that it blocks out the details of the murder that he is trying to solve.

His angel inspires a loyalty in him that turns out to be a legal death sentence, something that never occurred to him when he was first awakened from a drunken slumber by the wide-eyed innocent blonde seeking help to clear her husband.

Constance Dowling exudes the bitchy sexuality of a woman who would ultimately be strangled by her own stocking. She has the face of a young Marlene Dietrich without the strong toughness to it. She plays it cool and mean, the way a blackmailer would if she thought her scheme would last forever. It's too bad she hedged her bets and lost her life because of unabashed arrogance. It was the night the doorman happened to look the other way.

June Vincent looks like a Veronica Lake clone. She has the same silky beauty that makes her at home in a drama with a cabaret setting. She is like a caged bird in her lackluster marriage but regains her freedom when she resumes her singing career with Blair. She is sultry without being tawdry, alluring without being cheap, and inviting without seeming promiscuous. It is her perseverance that gets the unofficial investigation underway.

Peter Lorre had a distinct personality that made him a marvel to watch no matter what type of role he was playing. He was diminutive, with a reptile's tortured face and eyes that popped when he spoke. He has a leering voice that was the hallmark of many voice impersonators' careers. In the movie, he is an obscene piece of putty in a tuxedo.

Broderick Crawford's police captain belongs to an age when cops could break constitutional amendments with impunity. He walks into a house without being invited and rifles a lock box without a search warrant while the owner points out the illegality of his actions. He also has the gumption to call the governor's mansion to rouse him from his sleep so that he can halt the execution of an innocent man.

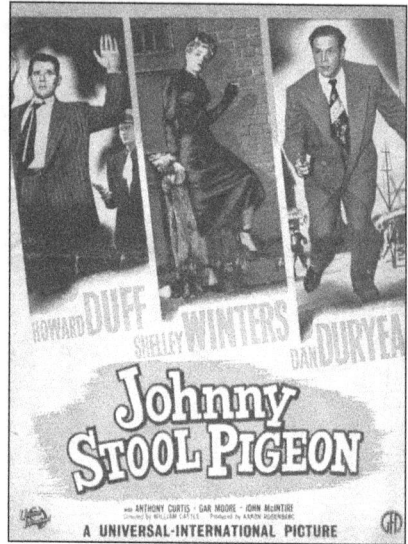

Movie poster for Johnny Stool Pigeon, starring Howard Duff, Dan Duryea and Shelley Winters. 1949, UNIVERSAL PICTURES COMPANY, INC.

Kirk Bennett (John Phillips), the man who is the cause of this noble campaign, is little more than a bewildered face who deserves to be wrongly convicted. He is married to a beautiful ex-singer and why he should want to cheat on her is a mystery that is never explained.

Wallace Ford is still playing the faithful sidekick at Universal, ready to put his life on hold if it means helping out a buddy in distress. In *The Black Angel*, he spends his life like a museum figure in the shadows, ready to come to life when his buddy needs him.

*Johnny Stool Pigeon* is an effective cops-and-robbers thriller with Howard Duff as George Morton, a cold hearted cop; Dan Duryea as Johnny Evans, a likeable Alcatraz inmate sprung for a special job; and Shelley Winters as Terry Stewart, a tarnished yet innocent *femme* in

Limbo. It's the story of two hard-boiled eggs and a tomato in a sting operation aimed at destroying an international dope ring with points of operation in Mexico, Tucson, and Winnipeg.

George Morton is a special agent whose mission is to bust a drug ring. His only chance of success lies in springing a con he once put away. Guilt and some latitude persuade the bitter inmate to aid the brusque cop.

*Johnny Evans (Dan Duryea) falls in love with fly girl Terry Stewart (Shelley Winters).* 1949, UNIVERSAL PICTURES COMPANY, INC.

Morton needs some underworld muscle so he secures a parole for a convict named Johnny Evans. They are a contentious pair posing as dope smugglers. Terry Stewart is an inamorata on the outs of the action and cuts herself in on the action when she plucks the strings of Evans' harp, thereby complicating the dope sting.

Evans is the stool pigeon of the title, but he is anything but a stoolie.

*Drug kingpin Nick Avery (John McIntire) protects his investments the old-fashioned way as Terry Stewart (Shelley Winters) wishes she could do the same.*
1949, UNIVERSAL PICTURES COMPANY, INC.

He may be an Alcatraz hood but he is the hero of the movie. He languishes in prison until the cop who put him away needs him to bust a dope smuggling ring. Evans is sprung into action to avenge the drug-related death of his wife. Freedom means nothing to him until he meets and falls in love with Terry Stewart, who brings out his inner gentleman.

Stewart is arm candy for one of the drug suppliers in Canada and she follows the men after they meet with the Canadian point of the drug connection. Morton is contemptuous of her but Evans takes a liking to her and makes it clear to the cop that if she goes, he will follow.

In *Johnny Stool Pigeon*, Johnny Evans is the only one who appreciates the power of a woman because absence makes the heart grow fonder. His

*George Morton (Howard Duff) believes that he has been double-crossed by Johnny Evans (Dan Duryea), who appears to have joined forces with low level thug Joey Hyatt (Tony Curtis).* 1949, UNIVERSAL PICTURES COMPANY, INC.

*A wounded Johnny Evans (Dan Duryea) is determined to warn Morton (Howard Duff) about a sudden change in plans by the drug smuggling kingpin.* 1949, UNIVERSAL PICTURES COMPANY, INC.

stint in Alcatraz makes him feel that way. It's something that makes him a hero. Evans is a caustic man when it comes to dealing with Morton but his heart is a-flutter when it comes to Terry Stewart. He plays the game with Morton in order to get his freedom.

Evans is really the guy who gets things done. His quick thinking and firm rough housing gets things done in Mexico, Canada, and the midwestern states. He is the one going undercover for the deal, too. He uses his name and reputation to set up deals but crosses the wires at the right time. His sense of righteousness is too much for Morton to take.

George Morton depends on Evans' underworld contacts to accomplish the bust. He puts his life in the hands of a man he sent to Alcatraz. There are several opportunities for payback and it seems that one of them ruins the scheme towards the end. Johnny Evans isn't so primal and has a wide streak of principle that seems to elude Morton. Quick thinking, good luck, and perfect timing get the job done.

Morton is self-righteous and smug, but he learns humility from Evans and Stewart. He looked down his nose at them at the beginning of the film but he could not have accomplished the mission without them. Johnny Evans and Terry Stewart are the ones who take the victory walk in the film's last frame. George Morton remains as bewildered as ever.

John McIntyre and Tony Curtis have supporting roles as criminals on opposite rungs of the ladder.

# Crime: Post Script (1)

To many *noir* lovers, Duryea has a bad reputation as an abusive cad, which came in part from the two films he made for Fritz Lang, *Woman in the Window* and *Scarlet Street*. In both films, he menaced Joan Bennett and dominated her with a creepy relish.

It was a type he would occasionally play again in his career and was a small addition to a larger scope of his characters, yet its impact on Duryea's image cemented his reputation as a larcenous opportunist. He repeated the odious physical oppressor in two other films, *Manhandled* and *Too Late For Tears*, both made in 1949.

Dorothy Lamour has a rooftop dance with Duryea in the former and Lizabeth Scott squares off with him in the latter. The seedy private investigator and the mobster vying to get his mislaid money back synthesize all of the traits Duryea imbued his trademark sleazeball characters with. The villains from the Fritz Lang melodramas come to mind and these two films are perfect matches for the earlier movies. An unpleasant connection to the Lang films is the anti-woman behavior of the villains. The private investigator has no qualms in framing an innocent woman for murder and the mobster plays rough with Lizabeth Scott to get his money back from her.

In *Manhandled*, Alton Bennett (Alan Napier) is a pompous author whose unfaithful wife (Irene Hervey) is bludgeoned to death with a cologne bottle. During the crime investigation, it is discerned that her jewels are missing from the murder scene. This brings Joe Cooper (Sterling Hayden), a wise-guy insurance investigator, into the crime investigation, much to the chagrin of Lt. Dawson (Art Smith) and Sgt. Foyle (Irving Bacon), two dumb detectives. Add Karl Benson (Dan Duryea), a tricky private eye, and Dr. Redmond (Harold Vermilyea), a wily phony psychiatrist, to the convoluted mess, and they add up to a clever murder frame-up for Merl Kramer (Dorothy Lamour), the pseudo-shrink's secretary.

The cops are not impressed with the forged credentials and blurry past of Miss Kramer, who has relocated from California to New York and used the credentials to gain employment with the fastidious fake psychiatrist.

Her situation isn't helped by Karl Benson, the former cop turned tricky private eye who is manipulating evidence against her, mainly because he has most of the stolen jewels hidden in his water cooler.

Benson is low-brow and obnoxious, a lazy detective who idles on his cot and sticks his used chewing gum wherever he wants to. He is also a sneak thief and he has made a haul that is ruined by the singer's murder.

Her death makes fencing certain items forbidden because of the heat they generate.

The wise-cracking investigator is relentless in keeping the bumbling cops off his trail. Benson settles for small cash for some spangles and baubles and covers his tracks by planting false clues that point to Miss Kramer. She has access to the shrink's files, including records of sessions with the husband and his murdered wife. This is enough to cast suspicion on Kramer's motives.

The odd angle of the transcripts is the husband's recounting of a recurring nightmare where he bludgeons his wife to death. The police deduce that this knowledge plus a desire for the jewelry pro-

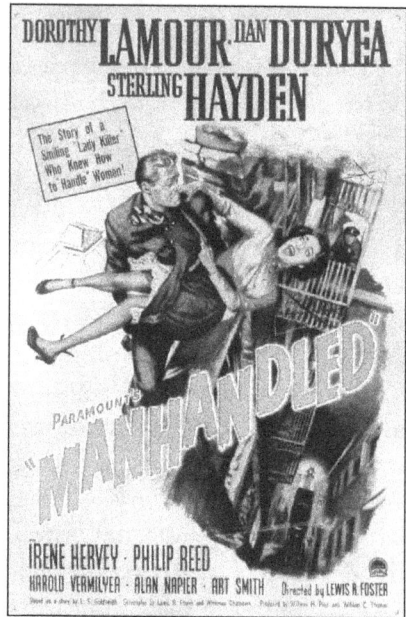

*Movie poster for* Manhandled. 1949, PARAMOUNT PICTURES INC.

vided motive and opportunity for the stranger with the forged past.

Joe Cooper is a brazen insurance investigator who won't take no for an answer and has a natural disdain for cops. He believes that Merl Kramer is innocent and he is suspicious of Benson, whose wise-cracking, gum-chewing arrogance trips him up because someone in Cooper's business is alerted to a fast-talking wise guy.

Kramer's boss is the real king of frame-ups, and nothing he can do can get him out of the one he made for himself. His attempt to regain the stolen jewels from the private eye (who hijacked them from him in a surprise assault) ends with his own murder.

*Manhandled* could have been a palpable crime *noir* if not for the feeble attempts at humor that belabor the action. Most of the script is solid, except for a couple of seams. A running gag about failed brakes is

*Joe Cooper (Sterling Hayden), Merl Kramer (Dorothy Lamour) and Karl Benson (Dan Duryea) are the three principal players of* Manhandled. 1949, PARAMOUNT PICTURES INC.

*Karl Benson (Dan Duryea) tries to divert Joe Cooper (Sterling Hayden) from the water cooler where he hid the stolen jewels. Lt. Dawson (Art Smith) gives him the once over.* 1949, PARAMOUNT PICTURES INC.

unnecessary as is an attempt to squeeze laughs out of Cooper's theory on the sleeping tablets that serve as an alibi for the husband/author.

The acting is good and would have been more effective without the strained attempts at humor. Sterling Hayden is his usual forceful and commanding self, propelling the action and plot development with his imposing personality. Dorothy Lamour acts like a comatose shrinking

*Karl Benson (Dan Duryea) bears false witness against his neighbor (Dorothy Lamour), strengthening Lt. Dawson's (Art Smith) case against her.* 1949, PARAMOUNT PICTURES INC.

violet, which befits a tired character trying to lay down roots in a new environment so she could send for her daughter.

Dan Duryea is exceptionally obnoxious, even by his own standards. The scheming private detective is as sleazy as his habit of sticking his chewing gum wherever he wants. Equally sleazy is Harold Vermilyea as the psychiatrist, once his veneer is stripped away. His scenes with Duryea are the highlights of the movie as they try to outwit each other. The best scene in the movie is a death scene where the roles are reversed and the shrink is killed with his own car.

Art Smith is mostly effective as the intrepid detective who is an imp with a Brooklyn attitude. His character is undermined by some of the comic bits that he has to perform but he is not nearly as inane as Irving

Bacon, the sergeant who is his sidekick. The sergeant's character is what nearly sinks the movie and is responsible for the lame attempt at humor that ends the film. The ending dampens any grim satisfaction from a closing where justice is served with a healthy dose of old-fashioned irony.

Old-fashioned irony is better served in *Too Late for Tears*, a low budget crime drama that is satisfying because of the sincerity of the leads, chiefly an amazing Lizabeth Scott. Scott had a hypnotic effect on her marks because of her intense eyes, deep-set voice and the kind of smoky moves that had a way of making things go in her favor, at least until this movie's finale demands a swift, clean penance that proves crimes of passion do not pay.

*Poster for* Too Late for Tears. 1949, UNITED ARTISTS CORP.

It was always crimes of passion with Lizabeth Scott, a dame with moxie during an age when being called that was a sign of respect or a thing to be dreaded by everyone except the mark that prevented itself from being erased. If the protagonist resisted her evil charm, he was considered the hero of the drama; if not, he painfully died in service of the woman who inspired misguided trust in her stooges.

That's the setup for Arthur Kennedy and Dan Duryea in *Too Late for Tears*, an ambiguous and convoluted thriller that delivers more character development and fateful exits than you would expect from a cheap drama of this sort.

Illicit fortunes always provided a great head start for movies about greed, where the accidental factor is an unhappy couple who unexpectedly receive a blackmail payoff for an underworld deal. This happens to Scott and Kennedy; they are taking a drive along a road when a suitcase of cash is tossed into their car by a vehicle driving in the opposite direction.

The mishap opens a new world for Jane (Lizabeth Scott) and Alan Palmer (Arthur Kennedy), not only because of the sudden riches, but because of their opposite reactions to the occurrence and how they want to deal with the money. He wants to turn it over to the police, but she has other uses for the money. For Jane, it is a way out of her boring and hopeless marriage.

Her plans are derailed when she is rudely reminded that the money already belongs to someone else, blackmailer Danny Fuller (Dan Duryea). He tracks her down and lays down the law about his money in an afternoon visit that includes a slap in the face for her and a rude awakening for him.

After their first drink, they become partners because of her quick thinking and the lack of resistance she shows to the idea of getting rid of a husband who has become superfluous due to his determination to turn the money over to the police. He is eliminated through an ingenious murder plot during a ride with his wife on a dark lake where the shadowy boat attendant is the only witness to the married couple boarding and alighting from the boat. The attendant does not realize that it is a case of bait and switch and, of the three participants, only two — Jane and Fuller — live to talk about it.

Shadows from the past haunt the lake as Kathy (Kristine Miller), Alan's sister, wants to search for her missing brother. She refuses to believe Jane's explanation that he deserted her to be with another woman. Kathy is aided by the sudden appearance of Don Blake (Don DeFore), who claims to be a war buddy of Alan's from their European tour of duty. The couple hound Jane until she is about to crack and even put Danny Fuller under surveillance. The blackmailer had become Jane's dupe during the commission of the murder and becomes the victim of his own farewell when he gets choked up during a toast to Jane.

Jane uses the sole proceeds of her good fortune to enjoy the decadent life of a rich American debaucher in Mexico, where she buys the company of young men and the servitude of maids and butlers. It is the conflicting philosophy of low hems and high heels that determines her faith as a slap in the face becomes nothing compared to a tumble through space.

*Too Late for Tears* is a dark, brooding thriller with seedy characters that add a dark dimension to the drama. Kennedy is a downbeat, honest dullard who gets iced in a crime drama triangle. Scott is deadly because of her insecurities. She kills because it is an easy way to deal with a problem. Duryea is protective of the secret that remains uncovered by the hush money intercepted by Scott and Kennedy.

Kristine Miller is sensual without being showy, a trait that could be a ruse or the real thing. Ruse is what comes to mind when Defore shows inconsistencies with his story. He becomes a hero in the end and takes off with Miller. The shadowy boat attendant is an unaccredited Billy Halop, former leader of the Dead End Kids, before he took a temporary hiatus from the film industry.

*Danny Fuller (Dan Duryea) is reunited with the blackmail money misappropriated by housewife gone bad, Jane Palmer (Lizabeth Scott).* 1949, UNITED ARTISTS CORP.

*Don Blake (Don DeFore) and Kathy Palmer (Kristine Miller) become acquainted when they search for her missing brother.* 1949, UNITED ARTISTS CORP.

*John Wheeler is the third of Duryea's Universal crime bosses in* One Way Street. 1950, UNIVERSAL PICTURES COMPANY, INC.

# Universal
# Crime Bosses

Duryea's crime bosses at Universal may have rough, but with one exception, they didn't slap around their women. They were soft on their molls in ways that made them vulnerable to challenges when the ladies decided to take a powder on them. Slim Dundee was the only one who had something going on in the shadows, but the other boss men took it on the chin when it came to their ladies. Such was the case with the trio of crime bosses when they mixed their women with confidence games, armored car heists, and clever employees.

Silky Randall is just what you'd expect him to be, a smooth con artist. His one hang up is the insane love he has for Shelley Winters. It makes him soft, and her hard-headed enough to derail a heartless scam in small town USA.

*Larceny* is Silky Randall's game as he masterminds stings that use Rick Mason (John Payne) as a front man. His latest scam is building a phony war memorial in a small California town. It all goes smoothly until his moll (Shelly Winters) upsets the balance because of her unbridled passion.

*Larceny* may have been a popular programmer but it had a serious undertone that made the movie jolting at times. Con men and smooth talkers were nothing new to drama but the two smoothies who cooked up the war memorial scam register with more conviction for their callousness. Rick Mason (John Payne) and Silky Randall (Dan Duryea) have just bailed out of a blown yacht-club hustle in Miami and have now set their sights on a small town that still reels from the combat death of a local hero.

Mason is a masterful and heartless masquerade artist who impersonates a fictional buddy of the local hero. He ingratiates himself with the kids at the youth center with a speech about honesty and giving the task at hand one's best. He is an instant hero with the kids, a welcome relief for Deborah (Joan Caulfield), the hero's widow and an object of deification for Charlie (Percy Helton), the froglike man who runs the youth center and directs all of its activities.

Mason's instant welcome allows him to become a popular man about town, especially when he sows the seeds of the memorial in the widow's sentimental reminiscences. The movie belongs to Mason, who presses the irony of being an upstanding, righteous, top-notch kind of guy. Everyone

*Silky Randall (Dan Duryea) lays the groundwork for a war memorial scam as Duke (Dan O'Herlihy) and Rick Mason (John Payne) wait to hear the details in* Larceny. 1949, UNIVERSAL PICTURES COMPANY, INC.

looks up to him and appreciates the way he has added a shock to the dull everyday type of sameness of their lives. Mason has them eating out of his hand and doesn't go soft until after he has the scam money in the form of a check.

His con is moving as scheduled until it is derailed by Tory, Randall's moll. She is an empty-headed, hot-blooded sex machine whose passion for Mason clouds her judgment and makes her the loose cannon of the gang. Silky sends her to Havana, but she makes a detour to the California coastal town to be near Mason. Tory is impulsive and reckless, possessing a tunnel vision that prevents her from seeing the bigger picture, an intricate high stakes scam that revolves around raising the investment money for building a war memorial.

*Tory (Shelley Winters) is a bold inamorata who does not think twice about cheating on Silky (Dan Duryea).* 1949, UNIVERSAL PICTURES COMPANY, INC.

*Tory's (Shelley Winters) unbridled desire distracts Rick Mason (John Payne) and eventually derails the war memorial scam.* 1949, UNIVERSAL PICTURES COMPANY, INC.

She is the spoiler and it is not just because of her impetuous behavior, it's also the effect she has on Silky. His jealousy may turn out to be well-founded but he lets it cloud his business judgment and that begins to foul things up. Another monkey wrench in the works is good old-fashioned love. It happens to the weary war widow who has become a living statue for the townsfolk to pity.

*The cops arrest Rick Mason (John Payne) and Silky Randall (Dan Duryea) while war widow Deborah Owens Clark (Joan Caulfield) seeks solace in her father (Walter Greaza).* 1949, UNIVERSAL PICTURES COMPANY, INC.

It is also Cupid's arrow for the con man when the little innocent melts his heart and ruins his chance for a clean getaway. Everything runs its course because of Tory's hysterical behavior. Her payoff is very funny because she creates the possibility of a new scam at her expense when she becomes a prop in the grifters' final gambit. The little innocent wins out and it's the paddy wagon for the con artists, the noble Mason included.

John Payne is convincing as the phony chum of the fallen soldier and eases into the confidences of the people who knew and loved his Army buddy. Joan Caulfield is the innocent small town war widow who conquers the con man with her wholesome sensuality.

Dan Duryea has a smooth smile and a hard tone of voice in a role that sets him up as the mastermind and sometime-player of the hustle team. Shelley Winters is the cloudburst that dampens the spirits of the two con men. Her electricity short-circuits the team and has every man scrambling for himself.

Dan O'Herlihy lends a dash of charm as one of the cultured hustlers. He is in for the long haul but backs off at Payne's request. This costs him a bundle but he does not complain or demand recompense. Dorothy

*Lt. Ramirez (Stephen McNally) prevents a drunken Steve Thompson (Burt Lancaster) from flattening Frank the bartender (Percy Helton) for refusing to serve him another drink in* Criss Cross. 1949, UNIVERSAL PICTURES COMPANY, INC.

Hart is wolfish as a receptionist on the make. She takes baby steps that she thinks are giant strides. Percy Helton displays his eccentric quirks as a big-hearted director of a YMCA-like organization.

Slim Dundee is a cruel gang boss and a keeper in *Criss-Cross*, a warped love story where Duryea's crime boss and Burt Lancaster's inside man cancel each other because of Yvonne DeCarlo's ill-fated spell.

Dundee is an extreme example of Duryea's abusers. He not only uses force, he keeps tabs on his wife and her ex-man in an armored car caper that has him blowing it all in the end with a double-homicide crime of passion.

In *Criss-Cross*, the ex-husband and current spouse of a confused femme fatale plan to double-cross each other and the woman they love prepares to betray both of them. It is a criss-cross, a double cross taken to the next level where more than two people plan to cut each other out of the lucrative haul of a successful heist.

The heist is an intricate armored truck robbery, something that has never been successful in the past. The twist is utilizing an inside man, someone with a thorough layout of routes and procedures. His name is Steve Thompson, played by Burt Lancaster.

*Slim Dundee (Dan Duryea) lays down the law to his girl Anna (Yvonne De Carlo) about ex-husbands and infidelity.* 1949, UNIVERSAL PICTURES COMPANY, INC.

Thompson is a man without roots and someone who lacks ambition. He has a past but no prospects for a successful future. He is a man ruined by the love for a woman who was his wife for seven months. He left California after the divorce and worked for a trucking outfit in Chicago, did construction work down South, and toiled in the Oklahoma oil fields.

He returns under the illusion of helping his aging mother with her responsibilities and overseeing the marriage of his younger brother. No one believes him, not even his mother or childhood friend Lt. Pete Ramirez (Stephen McNally). They know that he has returned to see Anna (Yvonne DeCarlo), his ex-paramour.

Thompson visits the Rondo, a nightclub that was the old hangout. It is the first in a series of missteps that end tragically for the three principal characters. The club is owned by Slim Dundee (Dan Duryea), a small-time gangster who runs a gang of two-bit crooks.

Slim has a placid face with a pensive stare. He speaks in a slow, deliberate monotone when he is angry, which is most of the time. He is rail-thin,

*Lt. Ramirez (Stephen McNally) breaks up a fight between Slim Dundee (Dan Duryea) and Steve Thompson (Burt Lancaster) while Vincent (Tom Pedi ) diverts the cop's suspicion from a planned payroll heist.* 1949, UNIVERSAL PICTURES COMPANY, INC.

but given an imposing presence by a jacket with padded shoulders. You know he means business because he likes to wear black shirts and white ties.

He has eyes for Anna and is insanely jealous and possessive. One thing leads to another after Steve and Anna meet again. That is where the double-crosses begin. It is the lovers' triangle trying to become a twosome with the payoff being the take of the armored car robbery. Dundee and Thompson plan to cross each other with Anna as the stable element in each other's plans. They base their success on who she will stick with and each man thinks that he is the taker. Both men are mistaken.

*Criss-Cross* is a tight crime drama where flashbacks, first person narration, and clever dissolves are used to make the action seamlessly flow from one scene to the next. The film was the second collaboration between Burt Lancaster and Robert Siodmak. The first one was Lancaster's debut film in 1946, *The Killers*, based on the short story by Ernest Hemingway.

The film was originally about a racetrack robbery as envisioned by the

*Slim Dundee (Dan Duryea) gives his prize possession (Yvonne DeCarlo) the eye while most of the gang gets his point.* 1949, UNIVERSAL PICTURES COMPANY, INC.

first producer, Mark Hellinger. He died before filming started and the project was in Limbo before Siodmak and Daniel Fuchs, the screenwriter, changed it to an armored car heist that takes second stage to the intense and ill-fated lovers' triangle.

Steve Thompson's plan for the armored car robbery can be seen from two angles; first as a way to get enough money for him and Anna to start a new life on the run, or it could be seen as Steve's way of talking his way out of being caught alone with Dundee's wife. It is more likely that his plan was hatched on the spot when Dundee and his men invade the privacy's of the Thompson family's home.

Anna gains the audience's sympathy throughout the movie by pretending to be a victim of unfortunate circumstances. She has been hounded by an amorous gangster since her divorce from Steve and she is threatened with a frame-up by Lt. Ramirez if she does not stay away from her ex-husband.

She shows her true, rapacious nature in the film's last scene when she tells Steve that she had planned to cross both him and Slim. Anna was going to leave town with the money because she believed that Steve would

*John Wheeler (Dan Duryea) has one way of dealing with insubordination in* One Way Street *as William Conrad and King Donovan (center, left to right) provide backup sidearm support.* 1950, UNIVERSAL PICTURES COMPANY, INC.

have to spend weeks recuperating from his wounds in the hospital and Slim would have to stay underground until things cooled off. Neither she nor Steve escapes the heat of Slim Dundee's passion-fueled revenge at the cottage by the moonlit sea. A walking stick and a smoking gun are the gangster's grim-faced nod to the electric chair. Steve and Anna become a Method Pieta.

In *One Way Street*, John Wheeler (Dan Duryea) is also soft on his lady, a Mediterranean beauty who abandons him for the greedily successful family doctor. Wheeler's tough guy authority is challenged by a minion who sees a soft heart as an invitation to take it all.

*One Way Street* is another U.I. crime parable set in Mexico. The gist is showing the senselessness of greed in the concrete jungle when nature's challenges are blessings to be appreciated. It is a road movie until the end, which is when it becomes a one-way street, and a slick, rainy one at that!

Poison and an antidote are an original variation on the bargaining power of an ambitious underling. In this case, it's the cultured Dr. Frank Matson (James Mason) who wants to take the boss's grand bundle, including his girlfriend Laura (Marta Toren), when she offers to go along

*Dr. Frank Matson (James Mason) and Laura Thorson (Marta Toren), Wheeler's moll, abscond with the boss' bounty from a robbery gone wrong.* 1950, UNIVERSAL PICTURES COMPANY, INC.

for the ride. John Wheeler, the boss, is powerless to get his button men to take out the doc because the physician leads him to believe that he has given him poison instead of medicine for a headache. A phone call will be the subscription for the antidote along with providing enough time for a safe getaway.

Laura and the doctor make strange bedfellows and road companions as

*Dr. Frank Matson (James Mason) and Laura Thorson (Marta Toren), try to blend in with local populace in Mexico.* 1950, UNIVERSAL PICTURES COMPANY, INC.

they elude Wheeler, the double-crossed mob boss. The time they spend in the small Mexican village is a purge for their big city mania. They become people of the soil and this is what upsets the balance that they seek.

Wheeler's persistent quest to track them down leads to a stand-off in Mexico City. Dr. Matson and Wheeler suffer from sardonic twists of fate. They survive each other, but succumb to themselves. Only Laura gets to wash her soul off in the rain.

James Mason had a restrained and cultured character that was more suited to a pedantic college professor with heartburn than to any character faced with a dilemma that could cost him his life. Mason played many such characters, and he did it with flair. Maybe it was his pained elocution or his stern and troubled expressions.

In *One Way Street*, he totally trumps Duryea by devising a powerful hook for a brazen swindle. It is sentimentality that brings him down, not a wronged crime boss or a determined woman. The epiphany of generosity eclipses the value of the dirty money. To be rid of it, Mason has to return it to its original abductor.

His second plan is more risky than the first and just as successful. Both encounters had to do with Duryea, who loses on both accounts. It was Mason's third plan — the intention of returning to a pastoral past with Toren — that did not pass the muster with fate.

Duryea's dependence on Toren is what brings him down. She was the daughter of one of his underlings and was brought to maturity under his watchful eye. She was molded and shaped into the type of woman he desired. His Pygmalion fantasy was a complement to wishful thinking, but losing the money and having his woman run out on him were the insults that became defiant blows to his empire. It's something that resonates with one of his men (William Conrad), whose double cross nets him more than the money.

Marta Toren picks up in *One Way* where Yvonne DeCarlo left off. She, too, inspires betrayal in a doctor played by James Mason. He has an ingenious ruse to keep Duryea's crime boss at bay, and only fate and circumstance bring down the doctor. The same cannot be said about Duryea's character. He is the only crime boss whose vulnerability sets him up for a payback for all the others' indiscretions.

Marta Toren has a Mediterranean charm that sizzles when she gets to Mexico. She understands the mendacious guidance of the itinerant priest, played by Basil Ruysdael. The priest is solid oak, a bulwark traveling through the jungle, spreading his faith and helping others. William Conrad is a wise guy with dreams that are more than he can handle. King Donavan and Jack Elam play quirky gangsters who make early exits because of greedy thinking and small minds.

# Shysters and
# Second Rate Ringers

Paddy rollers, vaudeville missteps, and drunken interludes notwith-standing, even the big bosses on the studio payroll cashed in their chips by the closing credits. It was that way until the Fifties when television softened Duryea's image with sympathetic roles that influenced some of his big screen roles. A kinder, gentler Dan Duryea still meant a conniver, a rake, and a ne'er-do-well in most cases.

Even when Duryea played heroes, their virtues were dubious and their manners somewhat seedy. If they championed a worthy cause it was because they were likely to reap a formidable profit with civic duty a coincidental afterthought. Duryea's heroes also chiseled, connived, and did all that they could to pull off a scheme.

The term 'hero' was often ambiguous when applied to any of Dan Duryea's protagonists. That is because these characters were virtuous by default, having to deal with characters with motives and sins more dis-reputable than their own. Usually, the heroics were at the behest of a beautiful woman or an intriguing set of circumstances. In the end, all that mattered was self-glory and a reward. It was all done with respect to breeding and circumstance, something that his devilish alter-egos on the range never understood.

There were even hints of chivalry in some of Duryea's characters. They were the slightly shady anti-heroes who performed noble services for damsels in distress. Think about Mike Reese, the duplicitous newspaper-man in *The Underworld Story* or *World for Ransom*, with an adventurer based on Duryea's television character in *The Adventures of China Smith*. That is why Mike Reese and Mike Callahan come up winners despite having been good guys in sordid crime melodramas.

They operate from more perspectives than most people could handle and that makes them mercurial personalities. They infuriate everyone they come in contact with, but always get the job done because their lives depend on it. They save the very systems that were trying to destroy them by taking out the enemy. Mike Reese bags a murderer and his gangster buddy, while Callahan takes down nuclear spies that threatened the free world.

Duryea's good guys are hard-boiled anti-heroes with soft insides. Their weaknesses make them repugnant, but all of them are redeemed by shouldering the responsibilities of victory and being given little from the spoils of its success. It is the defining deed that is the reward for these rapscallions with hearts of plated gold.

*The Underworld Story* is a B-movie Mulligan Stew whose ingredients are the staples of various subjects and genres. We have a newspaper setting with two sides of the business, the cynical and the idealistic. A gangster connection and the genteel privileges of old money are the other two worlds that come together courtesy of the press. The three worlds are the playing board for characters caught up in the murder of a publishing magnate's daughter-in-law.

There is the disgraced reporter fighting the system, the newspaper baron covering up a scandal in the family, an idealistic small newspaper woman publisher, a light skinned African-American female scapegoat, a spoiled dissolute rich kid, a boorish gangster trying to make the next notch a social occasion, and a DA whose wounded pride has it in for the disgraced reporter.

*A poster for* The Underworld Story. 1950, UNITED ARTISTS CORP.

Mike Reese (Dan Duryea) has fallen from the big time when a story he wrote leads to the shooting death of a gangland witness. Reese is blackballed and finds a way out of his shame when he invests in a suburban newspaper. The owner has a change of heart when she finds out who he is and the scandal that engulfs him. That changes when a newspaper publisher's daughter-in-law is murdered.

Reese's instincts kick in and pretty soon he moves into high gear and takes center stage in the running of the country paper. Catherine Harris

(Gale Storm) and "Parky" (Harry Shannon), her typesetter, are swept up by his enthusiasm and authority, but it does not take long until his dark side emerges again when he starts wheeling and dealing at the expense of others.

He uses his contacts at the big city presses and news wires to attract attention to the small town scandal. Reese devises schemes that make

*Mike Reese (Dan Duryea) is an amoral reporter who finds redemption in running a small town newspaper that cracks a local murder.* 1950, UNITED ARTISTS CORP.

him the center of attention, all the while pretending to help out the accused killer, Molly Rankin (Mary Anderson), a light-skinned African-American maid.

Rankin has been arrested for the murder of her mistress and Reese begins to exploit her by forming a citizens' committee on her behalf. Things begin to gain momentum when everything collapses because of Reese's hustling. Mike Reese connives with the defense lawyer on splitting fees, even it means sending Molly up the river. The DA exposes Reese's motivation of getting the reward money. This sours many people on Reese and he becomes a pariah in the small town, an outcaste just as if he were in the city.

He makes amends for selling Molly out when he finds a witness who can corroborate Molly's contention about leaving flowers on a bus. Suspects become apparent to Reese and he has a run-in with the gangster.

He arranges a meeting with E.J. Stanton (Herbert Marshall), the father of the real murderer (Gar Moore). There is a showdown with the publisher, his son, and Carl Durham (Howard Da Silva), the gangster.

*Mike Reese (Dan Duryea) shows small town newspaper owner Catherine Harris (Gale Storm) how they do things in the big city as typesetter Parky Parker (Harry Shannon) copies his style.* 1950, UNITED ARTISTS CORP.

Reese is roughed up but wins in the end. He is called a hero and even complimented by DA Munsey (Michael O'Shea) as he is loaded into the ambulance.

The onerous urban newsman Mike Reese in *The Underworld Story* saves an innocent woman from the electric chair by earning a stripe for his incredulous partner, a suburban newspaperwoman. Reese is a disgraced reporter whose weasel-like personality overcomes a struggling small town newspaper and forces it to become an influential scandal sheet when a grisly murder occurs in the community. He wheels and deals with the outside press organization and wrangles deals that count the suspect out so many times that she goes from a beloved victim to the public to a convicted murderer who deserves to burn.

Reese proves her innocence, exposes the real killer, and pulls off the ultimate scoop in slam dunking a press magnate into the crime section. He is wounded in bringing down a loathsome gangster who dealt himself into the power games of the rich and infamous. Reese is a hero, and even the DA who hates him has to give him the stamp of approval as his junior partner becomes a junior miss in her first ambulance ride.

*Mike Reese (Dan Duryea) grills Molly Rankin (Mary Anderson) so he can net the reward money. Catherine Harris (Gale Storm) and D.A. Munsey (Michael O'Shea) are appalled by his lack of civility.* 1950, UNITED ARTISTS CORP.

*World for Ransom* is really a China Smith movie even though the main character's alias is Mike Callahan. There were copyright problems with the owners of the television show so a direct reference to China Smith was avoided, but many things remained the same. The theme music was the same, as was the exotic Singaporean locale. We have the same producer of the television show and Don Siegal, who directed a couple of episodes. Douglas Dumbrelle was on hand as the dogged British colonial who had his suspicions about the legitimacy of the main player.

The star may not be called China Smith, but he dresses in white with a matching fedora and is tagged as a soldier of fortune, smuggler, and beachcomber. In *World for Ransom*, the colonials want to parlay these tags into charges of treason and murder as it concerns the killing of a British officer and the kidnapping of a nuclear scientist. The culprit is really Callahan's dubious friend, the erudite Julian March (Patric Knowles), an ex-British intelligence officer now in the employment of a nefarious nuclear saboteur, Alex Paderas (Gene Lockhart).

March is married to Frennesy (Marian Carr), Callahan's ex-sweetheart. Frennesy is the romantic mystery that gives *World for Ransom* one of its

*Mike Callahan is the big screen name of China Smith in* World for Ransom. 1954, ALLIED ARTISTS.

interesting angles. The adventurer tags after her like a wounded lover. He acts concerned about their love, but is really full of spite. Callahan is still in love with Frennesy and tolerates March only because he is the only link to his old flame. There is no hope for a reunion but Callahan is led along by Frennesy's mock interest in him. He sees a chance of reconciliation when he discovers that March in involved in the treasonous plot.

*Mike Callahan (Dan Duryea) confronts Frennesy (Marian Carr) about the disguise used for her husband's masquerade.* 1954, ALLIED ARTISTS.

Alex Paderas is a saboteur and blackmailer. He plans to auction the kidnapped scientist (Arthur Shields) to the highest bidder between Allied and Communist concerns. Nigel Bruce plays the colonial governor who gets to have a parley with Paderas, who drops by in an arrogant encounter with the colonials to deliver his demands. A monstrous nuclear weapon in the hands of the Communists makes the colonial governor quake, as do his subordinates. Somehow, Callahan becomes a prime suspect because of his friendship with March.

Only Callahan finds the courage to face the kidnappers, saboteurs, and traitors in an assault on their headquarters. Explosives and gunfire clean out the nest and the scientist is rescued. Did Callahan do it to clear his name? No. Was it because of loyalty to the freedom of the

Western world? No. Maybe it was because he was inspired by love. Not only that but it was for the cause of liberating the captive girl of his imagination.

Callahan exposes his long-time rival as a fake and tries to reclaim the love of his former sweetheart. It backfires and the captive girl remains enslaved. Her destruction is also due to love. The traitor was also the only

*Callahan (Dan Duryea) is surrounded by the traitorous March (Patric Knowles) and his saboteurs when he infiltrates the traitors' hideout.* 1954, ALLIED ARTISTS.

man who accepted her as she was. In the end, Callahan destroys her when he thinks that he has freed her.

In *World for Ransom*, Mike Callahan is a serious and morose China Smith incognito who tries to rekindle an old romance by destroying a subversive international nuclear espionage gang. He is also a noble scoundrel because he peddles his style in Singapore, where post-war etiquette rates him as above-board and honorable. He is a waterfront hustler with mercenary experience and is none other than the television character China Smith with another name.

In *World for Ransom*, the earthy adventurer is more serious and plays for bigger stakes than his television counterpart. Mike Callahan is playing a game where the fate of the free world is at stake. It's B-movie madness and mayhem with a ne'er-do-well who has the same look, dress, and mannerisms of China Smith because that's who he really is for all purposes except legal.

Duryea is more serious in this role on film than on television. He is more tormented, but that's because he is dealing with his life's love, Frennesy. He is caught in a strange world where she weaves gossamer dreams to give him hope. He is a third wheel, one that is more pitied than appreicated by March and Frennesy.

This odd relationship bears on the violent climax, when Callahan storms the compound and wreaks havoc with his grenades. He has liberated the kidnapped nuclear scientist and believes that he has freed Frennesy from the evil March. His heroic status is negated when he destroys Frennesy's world by killing her husband, whom she had loved more than him. There was never a past to return to, and this stuns Callahan. It is another tale to add to *The Adventures of China Smith*, only this time around you can call him *Callahan*.

*Nat Herbin (Dan Duryea) has conflicted emotions about his ersatz kid sister (Jayne Mansfield) in* The Burglar. 1957, COLUMBIA PICTURES CORP.

# Crime: Post Script (2)

Dan Duryea appeared in many independent films that were made off the beaten track of Hollywood. *Storm Fear* and *The Burglar* are two offbeat crime dramas that have heists as major plot elements. In the first movie, it is a bank robbery turned sour. The second film boasts a successful theft that creates its share of problems for the thieves.

Duryea's roles in the two movies are on opposite sides of the law. In *Storm Fear*, Fred is the hermit writer whose soul has provided respectability for his shotgun bride and bewildered son. He confronts a dark and angry part of his past when gangsters on the lam hide out at his desolate, snowy ranch after a robbery gone bad.

Nat Herbin is a down-on-his-luck burglar who hatches and pulls off a peculiar jewelry robbery with his gang in *The Burglar*. It is a successful theft even though it spells tragedy for the jewel thieves.

*Storm Fear* and *The Burglar* share a common claustrophobia aggravated by two sets of sociopaths that bet against house odds and lose. Both films are originals because they take familiar conventions and reinvent them through the unique lens of their directors, Cornel Wilde and Paul Wendkos, respectively.

*Storm Fear* is a delirious, paranoid nightmare set in a snowy mountain retreat. Elmer Bernstein's haunting score includes disturbing harmonica solos that add a wistful sadness to the snowstorm that hems everyone in. Fred (Dan Duryea) lives in isolation with Elizabeth (Jean Wallace), his frustrated Nordic wife and David (David Stollery), his pre-pubescent son. He needs the seclusion to write novels that no one will read.

Fred is a bitter and sickly man whose sense of honor is outdated and unappreciated. He married his hoodlum brother's lover after she gave birth to a child out of wedlock. His chivalry imbues her with respect she does not appreciate as she still harbors a secret love for her bandit lover, Charlie (Cornel Wilde).

Repressed desire turns into unbridled passion when Charlie shows up with his holdup gang. They seek the solace of the mountaintop retreat as a temporary hideout after a bank holdup goes wrong. One of the gang had been shot and captured while Charlie has been wounded and needs a day to gather his senses. It is a day that will turn into an eternity as tempers flare, old wounds are opened, and allegiances turn into betrayals.

The sickly Fred is pushed into the background as Charlie recuperates after his former lover removes the bullet. His gang: crazed gunman Benjie (Steven Hill) and dissolute showgirl Edna (Lee Grant) dominate

*A young boy (David Stollery) undergoes an identity crisis when there is a power struggle between virile Uncle Charlie (Cornel Wilde) and his weak father (Dan Duryea). Lee Grant, Jean Wallace and Steven Hill play different shades of gray.* 1955, UNITED ARTISTS CORP.

the household with their drinking and arguing. The person caught in the middle of this madness is David, a young boy who is on the verge of an early entrance into manhood.

The boy is going through adolescent changes and his only guide to maturity is Hank (Dennis Weaver), the understanding ranch hand who harbors a secret love for his mother. The ranch hand takes the child hunting and teaches him survival in the wilderness. It is the ranch hand who changes everyone's lives when he becomes the conquering hero by the film's end.

Uncle Charlie is a father figure to the child, a former shadow that gains substance as he learns more about him. The boy does not know that he is his real father and prefers his manliness to Fred's.

By the film's close, it is obvious that the sickly Fred is more of a man than any of the other male figures in the drama. He appears weak because the weight of his torment bogs him down. His physical sickness makes him less appealing than the ranch hand and his shabby appearance is no match for the unbridled sexuality of the gangster on the run. Added to Wilde's attraction is his dominance of the crazed gunman and the hare-brained

*David (David Stollery) bonds with Uncle Charlie (Cornell Wilde), not realizing that the bond is deeper than he thinks.* 1955, UNITED ARTISTS CORP.

showgirl. They are lunatics who set things on fire, a whirlwind duo who would have taken down the family if not for the power of Uncle Charlie.

Lee Grant is brilliant as the brash, drunk ex-singer. Her fur coat and the bottle are the things she relies on to get her through the botched robbery. Steven Hill is pushy and always wants to knock somebody around or snuff someone out. The boss keeps him in line until the odds change during the failed getaway attempt through the snowy countryside. A triple cross cancels out the trio and leaves two of them dying in the snow and the third a crippled convict in a hospital death bed.

Cornel Wilde gives an intense performer as Uncle Charlie, but his real accomplishment is his direction of the movie. Wilde's direction creates electricity out of the isolation by squeezing the characters until they pop.

Horton Foote wrote a screenplay based on a novel by Clinton Seeley. It is a nerve-wracking group torture session where Fred's frustration turns into martyrdom, Elizabeth becomes an earthy, closet gun-moll within the cabin configuration, Benjie is an arsenal about to explode, and Edna is the expendable dupe who becomes the fizzling fuse when she has served her purpose. She winds up with her fur coat and a fist full of cash but spending it on her back in the snow banks does not do her a whole bunch of good.

The hero of the movie is Hank, the honest ranch hand who observes the rules of social etiquette. He was always a surrogate father to the boy, teaching him about the great outdoors. The hero is the one who tracks down the convicts and rescues the boy from their clutches.

David Stollery is effective as the kid who gets to play the sensitive observer. He is held in check by the changes he goes through as he learns the lessons of manhood from his dad and Uncle Charlie. He is badgered by the gunman and intrigued by the bleached-blond nightclub singer who is fond of drinking and doing bits of her showbiz act to entertain him.

*A confrontation of emotions between former lovers played by Cornel Wilde and Jean Wallace.* 1955, UNITED ARTISTS CORP.

In the film's turbulent finale, his world is broken into many fragments, but when it is put back together again, it is rebuilt into a picture to his liking. Faux paw has been claimed by the snow when he tried to take a hike into the elements to find help to fight the gangsters. Uncle Charlie has been emasculated in the boy's eyes as he watches bio-dad die an ignominious death in a county hospital bed. The gun moll goes back to being Elizabeth, the Nordic queen, when she is rescued and freed by the new paw in town, Hank the heroic handyman, a safe and agreeable synthesis of Fred and Uncle Charlie.

Nat Herbin is *The Burglar,* a crime master done in by his own ingenuity. He was an orphan asylum escapee adopted by a burglar who gave him a conscience when it came to keeping a promise. It is this iron-clad adherence to a rule that makes Herbin plan and pull off a jewelry heist with a built-in escape clause that guarantees failure.

Before network news and cable television, newsreels were a way of conveying news, trivia, and the esoteric to the public. The newsreels were a dose of reality before the escapist fare of the main attraction. They were also a way for crooks like Nat Herbin to hatch their next heist.

Herbin is part of a movie theatre audience that enjoys the segment on Sister Sara, a fraudulent spiritualist who has swung a lucrative real estate deal

*Benjie (Steven Hill) asserts himself before he realizes that there is no longer a gang to command.* 1955, UNITED ARTISTS CORP.

from an eccentric millionaire. It is newsworthy because the miser did not believe in charity because he was a business man. The gimmick to the story is that Sister Sara bought the estate for less than two dollars, along with a diamond necklace for sixty cents. The necklace is the focus of Herbin's next job.

He uses his half-sister, Gladden (Jayne Mansfield), to case the mansion when she takes Sister Sara in her confidence after she travels miles to offer a fifty-cent donation. This impels the spiritualist to invite Gladden in for lunch and supper, which includes a guided tour of the palatial estate. Gladden later returns to the thieves' den with a carefully drawn layout of the house. All Herbin has to do is to plan the heist down to the split second because of inherent limitations in the set-up.

The heist is successful, but the necklace is so hot that they can't fence it. They have to lay low, which creates too much tension for them to handle.

They begin to grate on each others' nerves, making them prey to an outside peeper. The point that connects them to each other is Gladden. She is an immature but sexually charged waif who grew up in a lair of male predators and is the cause of the sexual frustration among the men.

Nat Herbin is ambivalent about his feelings towards her. He has a love/hate relationship with Gladden that dates back to their childhood. He

*Tension mounts among the burglary team. (Left to Right: Mickey Shaughnessy, Peter Capell, Dan Duryea and Jayne Mansfield.)* 1957, COLUMBIA PICTURES CORP.

desires her, but cannot consummate his lust because of a promise made to the man who raised him. This confusion is what destroys him.

A nasty guilt eats away at his insides and clouds his judgment because of Gladden. He is the genius that pulls off the plan and the fool that turns it into a failure. Herbin is steely resolve held together by weak rivets. It is not something that is lost on his anxious sidekicks, Baylock (Peter Capell) and Dohmer (Mickey Shaughnessy), two stooges with a weary sense of fatalism. They claim to have a need for money and success, but they are losers waiting to cash in on their failure.

Baylock is a bundle of nerves, a neurotic chatterbox. He is the ice expert, a ruined jeweler who can still price a load through a worn-out loupe. Bitchy and somewhat jealous of Gladden, he is puzzled by her presence in the group.

The petty thief has big dreams of retiring to South America. He is a three-time loser who can't wait to fence the necklace so he can fly away from a lifetime sentence. He even recites his dreams to the fantasy strains of samba music.

*Charlie, the crooked cop (left), has his eyes on the stolen necklace and is the major obstacle in what was the perfect crime, much to the dismay of Nat Herbin (Dan Duryea, right).* 1957, COLUMBIA PICTURES CORP.

Dohmer, a lascivious pig who likes to torment Baylock, can't take his eyes off of Gladden. He eats in his undershirt and moves his lips when he reads the comics. Brutal and gross, the ape-man underlies the sickness of the team. He thumbs a ride on the death express when he winds up stranded in a car dumped in the Jersey swamps.

Charlie (Stuart Bradley) is a crooked cop, the peeper who upsets the

*One of Duryea's best roles is Nat Herbin, the tortured thief in* The Burglar. *It is also one of Jayne Mansfield's best pictures.* 1957, COLUMBIA PICTURES CORP.

balance that sets the table for justice to be served on the Atlantic City boardwalk. He is more venal than the crooks that he exploits, if only because he has crossed the line that he is paid to obey. He is just as wily and careless as Herbin when he muscles his way into the gang and winds up accused of killing the mastermind.

Charlie romances Gladden and has his paramour, Della (Martha Vickers), hook Herbin. Della is the odd woman out, a cliché on paper, but made believable by Vickers. Her hard-luck story is convincing, even when accentuated by the strains of the depression oboe. Della is drained of everything except her last ounce of decency. She puts all the pieces together in the stadium hall after Herbin pays dearly for the necklace.

Paul Wendkos directed and edited *The Burglar* in a bleak, freakish, baroque style. The visual composition of his shots is perfectly balanced,

*Gladden (Jayne Mansfield) and Nat Herbin (Dan Duryea) find refuge in a House of Horrors before their plan finally unravels.* 1957, COLUMBIA PICTURES CORP.

*In the end, Nat Herbin (Dan Duryea) becomes the fall guy in his burglary heist. Gladden (Jayne Mansfield) and the police chief (Wendell K. Phillips) ponder the irony.* 1957, COLUMBIA PICTURES CORP.

gaining an extra dimension from the clever editing that keeps the action movie's pulse beat strong. The oboe concerto and a passage that becomes the leitmotif are cloying, but add to the characters' desperation. It is mood music for depression and despair.

Everything about the movie is low-rent, from the dreary settings to the spent characters. The look of the film is dark, even during the daytime scenes. It is an oppressive *noir,* one where the seagulls have the final say. Atlantic City is the perfect place for the plan to unravel. The beachfront standoff, the house of horror music-box tip off, and the carnival act showdown are masterfully handled.

"We the dead welcome you," is the greeting of the keeper of the dead as he welcomes Nat, Gladden, and Charlie the cop into his Atlantic City labyrinth at the end of the movie. The scene is spooky, chilling, and unnerving because it is Nat's big payoff.

Nat Herbin, the man with the patent leather name and gelatin heart, winds up in a real-life newsreel viewed by a curious crowd of Atlantic City revelers as they gawk at a pair of anonymous shoe soles in a police meat wagon.

It all happened because of a necklace that had been bought for sixty cents. It was a piece of jewelry that inspired dreams in people who hated their lives. Belief in what the necklace represented was what doomed the players. Its origin was false and tainted by the pretensions of a phony spiritualist. Everything about the necklace is cursed because Sister Sara is a fake who lives in the world of the dead.

# The Madness Factor

Imprisonment in the box is a state of being confined by extreme limitations and can happen in or out of prison. It is intense confinement of any sorts, which can be caused by time restraints when dealing with a crisis, limited choices because of diminishing opportunities, or guilty memories that create failure out of success. Hysterics are the payoff, and it happens to those who find themselves living inside the box.

Bill Cannon is a disintegrating man who has lost his wife and daughter and faces a life threatening crisis in *Chicago Calling*. Major Bill Rogers must clear himself in his estranged wife's murder while on leave in *Terror Street*. Failure to meet their deadlines will be the cause of their demise.

Bill Cannon and Major Rogers are as disparate as two people can get but they share a common goal and that is to beat the clock to solve a crisis that will make or break their lives. Confinement, the need to make life altering decisions, and a race against time are the things that unite them, along with being downtrodden men who still cling to a vague code of ethics. That is the sentence that puts each man in the box, and how he ends his gambit depends on whether or not he lands on a period, a question mark, or an exclamation point.

Alcohol is the demon that figures big in *Chicago Calling*. Bill Cannon (Dan Duryea) is an alcoholic photographer whose life has turned into a downward spiral. His wife, Mary (Mary Anderson), has tired of his failed attempts to reform and has decided to move to Baltimore with their daughter, Nancy (Melinda Plowman), in order to live with Mary's mother.

The situation becomes a crisis when the daughter is seriously hurt in a car accident outside Chicago. Cannon receives a telegram from his wife promising to call him at a certain hour to inform him of the outcome of an operation to save their daughter's life. There is no return address. His bad luck worsens when he receives a turn-off notice for his telephone. The drama hinges on his efforts to keep the service active so he can receive the news of the operation's outcome.

His drinking buddy, a charitable organization, and a finance company can't help him in his time of need. His only hope is Bobby (Gordon

Gebert), a little orphan boy whom he persuades to filch the money from his big sister. A change of heart has him convincing the boy to return the money.

His salvation is a kind-hearted phone service man (Ross Elliot) who lets him have one more call. It is in vain because the news is bad and that makes him suicidal, but his little buddy saves him from killing himself.

*Bill Cannon (Dan Duryea) and his lifeline, the telephone, in* Chicago Calling.
1951, UNITED ARTISTS CORP.

*Chicago Calling* could very well be a reality show chronicling the last days of a man on the verge of extinction. It has a *cinema verite* quality to it, mainly due to its blue-collar cadence and the low-key performances of the players. It is a peculiar movie whose merit lies in elements extraneous to the plot.

The premise is slight yet it turns the movie into a weird adventure and Duryea's performance only heightens the bizarre proceedings. He

*Mary Cannon (Mary Anderson) reassures her husband Bill (Dan Duryea) that she loves him after notifying him that she is leaving with their daughter.* 1951, UNITED ARTISTS CORP.

delivers a performance that is so ordinary that it makes it seem as if you are spying on his life as he runs into obstacles in his attempts to keep his telephone service running.

The odd characters, the gritty cityscape, and the main plot device — the telephone — are archaic by today's standards. They make the movie fascinating because it is like looking into another world. The best thing about the movie is its on-location filming. The Los Angeles slums are really as squalid as some of the street characters.

A drinking buddy, a pretty hash-slinger, a small boy and a dog, plus a kind-hearted telephone man, figure big in a small adventure at the end of nowhere. These are characters that nobody pays attention to, the work force that keeps the machinery going at the grassroots level during the post-war years. In this world, even the bureaucrats are odd, including the stoic banker, the hyena-like loan-man, and the kind-hearted zombie woman of the welfare office. They all provide a brick wall for Connor to bang his head against.

*Bill Cannon (Dan Duryea) and his little friend, Bobby (Gordon Gebert) try to get by a telephone company guard (Gene Roth) in* Chicago Calling. 1951, UNITED ARTISTS CORP.

In *Terror Street*, serendipity is the wall that Major Bill Rogers gets to bang his head against. Who says that all serendipity is the cause of good things and merits outbursts of song and merriment? Sometimes the smooth flow of events adds up to something painful with a message so deep that it takes a heavy loss to understand its meaning.

The original title of *Terror Street* was *36 Hours*, a title better suited for an understated film about a unique murder investigation. The movie is a British crime drama about lost love and smuggling that packs a punch and has plenty of spice. Duryea finds himself in the strangest situation when his military leave loses its hopeful impetus and turns into a countdown to a rope fitted around his neck.

He plays Major Bill Rogers, the main suspect in the shooting death of his wife, a woman he hasn't seen in a year because of a snafu. It was a snag that cost him his marriage and now robs the couple of a future. Major Rogers easily tracks down his wife, but is unsettled by her posh circumstances. Before he can get an explanation from her, Rogers is knocked out and his wife is shot dead by an unseen assailant. His furtive hookup with his estranged wife becomes a demented detour into a bum murder rap and a police dragnet out for him. He is the main suspect because he was seen fleeing the scene.

The plot hinges on the police's pursuit of Major Rogers and his attempts to crack the number-one suspect in his own investigation, a smug customs agent who had a closer-than-normal relationship with his wife. The dislike is mutual until fortunes changes and power plays succeed before fading away.

Duryea becomes a man on the run who is aided by Sister Jenny, a trusting soul who works at a local goodwill mission and ministers to his wounds when she finds him

*Pressbook cover for* Terror Street.
1953, NATIONAL SCREEN SERVICE CORP.

hiding in her apartment. She is trusting and not fearful, even allowing herself to forge his wife's signature to find out what is inside the mysterious safety deposit box.

Sister Jenny's assistance earns her a spot in the intrigue and she becomes pawn of the murderer, a smuggler with an urge to kill anyone who gets in his way. The smuggler is effete and obscene, a smug huckster hiding behind the clever front of customs agent.

The diamond smuggler is even seedier than the crooked customs officer. He speaks with a languid accent and fits in comfortably with the shadows of his forbidden basement, the oriental underbelly of his antique shop. The cartoonish menace adds spice to the finale as Major Rogers takes down the customs agent and the smuggler thanks to the misguided love of the lovelorn, psychopathic son of the customs man.

*Col. Bill Rogers (Dan Duryea) questions his ex-neighbor about the whereabouts of his estranged wife.* 1953, NATIONAL SCREEN SERVICE CORP.

*Slossen (Eric Pohlman, left) is a smuggler who has the goods on Col. Rogers (Dan Duryea) and a black market dealer.* 1953, NATIONAL SCREEN SERVICE CORP.

Smuggling is the crime that causes so much pain to the peripheral characters, including the major's wife. Her ill-fated heroics are not revealed until the end. It appears that she left him to live the high-life of a sophisticated escort. The truth is that she was hoodwinked into doing phony government work for the crooked customs agent, who used her and then neutralized her. The news offers closure for Rogers, who catches up with his other buddy on the tarmac to take off after their thirty-six hour leave has ended.

*Terror Street* is told in the typical understated British manner, but it moves well and reaches a satisfying conclusion with the clichéd smuggling den confrontation. The tear jerker finale is a mystery solved with old tears. It may seem cornball, but fits in comfortably with this small film.

*Maj. Redfern Kelly (Dan Duryea) is the power hungry head master of* Platinum High School. 1961, CINEMA ASSOCIATES, INC.

# Produced by Albert Zugsmith

Albert Zugsmith was a producer who wavered between the righteous and the profane during the 1950s. *Slaughter on Tenth Avenue* was made during his pinnacle, a period that also included *The Incredible Shrinking Man* and *Touch of Evil.* By 1960, he was ending his run as a producer for Universal-International and one of his last films for a major studio was *Platinum High School,* made for MGM. It still had his old stamp because it was a twisted and tormented overture in teen angst and military discipline.

Corruption, intimidation, and murder are some of the ingredients of the crooked hierarchy of these movies. A labor union and a military school are two settings where shady policies have claimed innocent lives and it takes the honest outsider to straighten things out.

In *Slaughter on Tenth Avenue*, Dan Duryea plays the counsel for the crooked labor union. He heads a murderous goon academy in *Platinum High School.* Richard Egan and Mickey Rooney are the troubleshooters. Egan is a green assistant district attorney investigating the shooting death of a dock foreman. Mickey Rooney is a concerned father looking into his son's death at the academy. He is an ex-Marine so it's not wise to try to strongarm him when he comes looking for answers and explanations.

Corrupt labor-union movies became Hollywood fodder after the Kefauver Hearings in 1951. *On the Waterfront* is the most prominent example of the genre, chiefly because of Elia Kazan's artful direction, Budd Shulberg's vivid screenplay, and Marlon Brando's passionate characterization of the washed-up pug who brings down a union boss.

The film unfairly overshadows other movies on the same subject. One neglected movie is *Slaughter on Tenth Avenue*, starring Richard Egan, Julie Adams, Dan Duryea, Walther Matthau, and Mickey Shaughnessy. It ranks among producer Albert J. Zugsmith's greatest achievements and tells the true-life story of fledgling ADA William Keating's attempt to bring justice to the docks when he handles the case of an honest pier boss' shooting.

Solly Pitts (Mickey Shaughnessy) is a rebellious longshoreman whose outspoken views about the union infuriate Al Dahlke (Walter Matthau), the union boss. The film opens with a meticulously-planned shooting of

*Solly Pitts (Mickey Shaughnessy) is confronted by 'Cockeye Cook' (Joe Downing) and "two of his meatballs."* 1957, UNIVERSAL PICTURES COMPANY, INC.

Pitts on the stairwell of his apartment building. His wife, Madge (Jan Sterling), cradles him in her arms as he tells her that, "Cockeye did it! Cockeye Cook and two of his meatballs!" It is a declaration that will rock the waterfront world of corrupt unions, silent dockworkers, and impotent law enforcement.

The only man strong enough to challenge the corrupt system is a green Assistant District Attorney named Kenneth Keating (Richard Egan). It is his strong moral conviction and naïve inexperience that make him take on the case of the people versus Al Dahlke.

Keating is new to the job and this is his first contact with the waterfront culture. He is confused and angered by his initial impression of the clique mentality even though he belongs to the kindred world of the coal miners. His father was a union man who would have cringed at a man like Eddie Cook (Joe Downing) and dealt with him much like Solly Pitts did, with venom and violent counter-gambits.

The layers of corruption and the people who operate on each level fill the movie with distinctive characters and interesting situations. Sgt. Varsnick (Charles McGraw), a hard-nosed, gravel-voiced detective turned

*Bride-to-be, Dee Paisley (Julie Adams) makes plans with her future husband to look at an apartment.* 1957, UNIVERSAL PICTURES COMPANY, INC.

gray-haired before his time, is Keating's guide through the underworld. He educates the ADA on the code of the dock people, but Keating ultimately has to find out for himself. It's not until he puts his life on the line that Solly's intimates begin to trust him.

Solly Pitts is as tough as he is honest, and tenacious enough to stave off death for a couple of days. He still subscribes to the code of silence that he reluctantly breaks after he is told that he will not live. He names his shooters, but rues that he will die a rat to his friends although Keating remarks, "not your friends."

Madge is just as rough as her husband, standing by his side and staring down her intimidators. She once dug a slug out of his leg with a kitchen knife and washed the wound with iodine. Nothing can sway her, from midnight peepers, shadowy tails on the street, or threatening phone calls. Not even being badgered on the witness stand can break Madge's spirit. She is determined to find justice for her fallen husband.

Benjy (Harry Bellaver) is Solly's best friend and saw one of the assassins leave the Pitts' apartment building after the shooting but he won't

*Assistant District Attorney Keating (Richard Egan) tries to talk Midget (Nick Dennis) into convincing Benjy (Harry Bellaver) to testify before the Grand Jury.*
1957, UNIVERSAL PICTURES COMPANY, INC.

cooperate with Keating. He metes out justice his own way, with two fists and a blackjack.

Midget (Nick Dennis) is a militant dock worker whom Dahlke calls "five foot nothing and all of it mouth." He tries to incite the longshoremen with a litany of honest dock workers who were murdered by Dahlke's men. Nothing can quell his anger, not even a beating and a dunk in the ocean by Dahlke's henchmen.

He despises law enforcement as much as he hates the union bosses. It is because he once spilled his guts to a crime commission in vain and was rewarded with a broken back. Keating stinks, according to Midget, who ultimately gives the ADA the ultimate show of respect in the film's final shot.

Unique characters, vicious shootings, and difficult investigations are part and parcel of every crime drama but the setting is what gives *Slaughter on Tenth Avenue* its extra charm and grit. The waterfront world of this movie is fascinating, from the supporting characters to the cityscape itself.

The hardscrabble environment is what makes the dock people unique. They have a code of honor forged by the will to survive. They not only

*Former District Attorney John Jacob Masters (Dan Duryea) taunts his former protégé Howard Rysdale (Sam Levene) and the green Assistant D.A. Keating (Richard Egan) about the lucrative benefits of private practice.* 1957, UNIVERSAL PICTURES COMPANY, INC.

have to deal with the natural element of the ocean but with the pier bosses and oppression by the dock union. Solly and Madge Pitts are the bedrock couple harassed by union thugs. Solly is shot and Madge is threatened by intimidation.

The buildings and the piers are characters in this waterfront drama, too, as are the lighting and shadows of the bricks and pipes, along with the breathtaking panoramas of the Brooklyn Bridge and the Atlantic Ocean.

Richard Egan is grim-faced and even-toned in his pronouncements. He can also fight, as he is from a coal mining town where many arguments were settled by bare knuckles. He is called to use his fighting prowess in the finale, when the film has the requisite labor riot scene with the protesters battling the head-busters brought in on the backs of trucks.

Julie Adams is the picture of smoldering sophistication. She is genteel and erudite yet supports the roughneck side of her husband's personality. Jan Sterling is the rough-and-tumble opposite; she has to be that way in order to survive the working class environment. Madge is honest and straightforward, a rock of support for her wounded husband.

Mickey Shaughnessy is magnificent as Solly Pitts. He is a stocky man

*Defense Attorney Masters (Dan Duryea) pokes holes in the testimony of the intrepid Lt. Varsnick (Charles McGraw).* 1957, UNIVERSAL PICTURES COMPANY, INC.

shot down by garlic-laced bullets and holds on to life while dying in a hospital ward. Walther Matthau is a highlight as a slimy rackets man whose protégée, Eddie "Cockeye" Cook, supervised the shooting.

Dan Duryea plays John Masters Tipton, a former DA who became a successful defense attorney. He is smooth on the outside and merciless inside a courtroom. He is representing the crooked union boss accused of murder and graft.

Charles McGraw is the tough-guy detective who knows all about the dock people. Midget is a pint-sized firecracker played by Nick Dennis. Tom Kennedy and Mickey Hargitay work the waterfront, as does Jack LaRue as Father Paul, who supplies the soul for the dock workers.

*Platinum High School* is another study in terror through intimidation. This time, the setting is a military academy on a remote island called Saber Island. The boss is a retired Marine officer named Major Redfern Kelly (Dan Duryea), and his henchmen are two ex-Marines who commandeer a squadron of maladjusted teenage misfits.

Major Kelly is a cool, calculating, and malicious headmaster whose

*Major Kelly (Dan Duryea), Steven Conway (Mickey Rooney) and Jennifer Evans (Terry Moore) enjoy a tense lunch with the academy faculty in* Platinum High School. 1961, CINEMA ASSOCIATES, INC.

motivation is greed. His academy is a high-priced reform school for rich juvenile delinquents. Twenty-four students at an annual tuition of $15,000 a year are enough to make him cover-up a lethal hazing.

Part of the curriculum is intimidating the locals, including a handful of civilians who run businesses on the island where the academy is situated. Saber Island may as well be Hell because it is an isle of the damned. Redemption comes in the form of Steven Conway (Mickey Rooney).

Conway is the father of a boy who died under circumspect circumstances at the military academy. The official explanation of the younger Conway's death is that it was due to his falling off a dormitory roof. Conway visits the school to get some insight and answers in his son's untimely death. Evasive answers and hostile cynicism are what the father receives, and it's enough to embroil him in a life-and-death struggle with the commander of the military academy.

In *Platinum High School*, the Major is the mania-driven headmaster at a boy's academy where everyone, from the staff to the distaff boating people, is cowered into silence. It all unravels when the boy's father comes

*Jennifer Evans (Terry Moore) is the personal confidante to Maj. Kelly (Dan Duryea).* 1961, CINEMA ASSOCIATES, INC.

to investigate his son's death. Major Kelly oversees a cover up of the death of Conway's son.

His students are a brown-shirt committee who protect their fearless leader. The main heavy is Hack Marlow (Richard Jaeckel), who supervises a group of thugs that includes Conway Twitty, Jimmy Boyd, and Harold Lloyd, Jr. The odd man out is "Crip" Hastings (Warren Berlinger), the

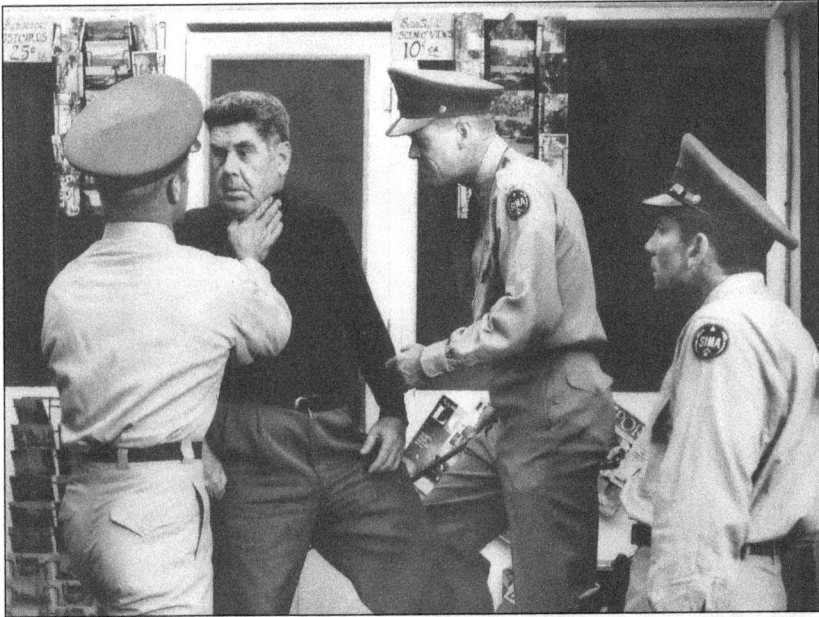

*Maj. Kelly (Dan Duryea) and Vince Perley (Christopher Dark) watch as Hack Marlow (Richard Jaeckel) strong arms Joe Nibley (Jack Carr), a deaf mute store owner.* 1961, CINEMA ASSOCIATES, INC.

object of ridicule, abuse, and ostracism.

Hastings is befriended by Conway. Together, Conway and Crip crack the academy's criminal code. Along the way, Conway has to pass several macho rites of passage to broach the mystery that smells of murder. It does not matter to him because he is a Marine. He first shows this in a bayonet confrontation with a henchman in Joe Nesbit's (Elisha Cook, Jr.) luncheonette.

He also has to deal with Jennifer Evans (Terry Moore), the Major's bitchy secretary, information gatherer, and compliant slave. She wavers in her loyalty as the facts bear against her boss/lover. Evans pays the price of betrayal when she swims with a different kind of shark in the film's final showdown.

One of Conway's strange allies is Lorinda Nibley (Yvette Mimieux), a mute country girl with the classic Daisy Mae look: blonde pigtails, revealing blouse, cut-off off jeans and bare feet. She runs the bait shop with her pa, a fat, bearded, dim-witted slob. It is a strange image of mute beauty and dumb beast, a perverse variation of the backwoods, country-bumpkin style of living.

*Harry Nesbit (Elisha Cook, Jr.) is an intimidated luncheonette owner who watches Vince Perley (Christopher Dark) combat ex-Marine Steve Conway (Mickey Rooney).* 1961, CINEMA ASSOCIATES, INC.

She and her father suffer intimidation from the brown shirts, who are led by Richard Jaeckel and Christopher Dark at their sinister best as cadets/teachers who inflict pain to ensure dedication to the school code. The code is broken in a final battle at sea between Conway and the Major in a yacht-versus-motorboat demolition race that nets the officer his *Gotterdammerung* chops.

Mickey Rooney and Dan Duryea play well off each other. They are two pros making the most of their pulp roles. Each character has the tenacious attitude earned by their respective stints in the Marine Corps. However, they are complete opposites not only in stature and demeanor, but in moral character, too. Each man is determined to get what he wants, but since this is impossible, confrontation means victory for one and total ruination of the other.

Warren Berlinger plays Crip Hastings, the witness to Conway's son's death by baseball bat in a hazing gone bad. He is threatened by a trio of thugs who only befriend him when Conway comes to the island. They turn on him again when they suspect that he is aiding the murder victim's father in bringing them to justice. His reward is being adopted by Conway at the end of the movie.

Elisha Cook, Jr. has a small role as the proprietor of a luncheonette that is a hangout for the major and his goon squad. It is a change of pace for Cook to be cowered into silence. Usually, he played the macabre creep who did the intimidating; now, he gets a taste of his own medicine.

Terry Moore and Yvette Mimieux play the only two women on the island. They, too, are opposites. Moore plays a school teacher whose reason for staying is a higher-than-average salary at her teaching position. She winds up as the major's secretary and scheming ally. Yvette Mimieux is the abused blonde beauty. In one scene, the sergeant tells the major that it would be wise to get her off the island. He cites that the recruits are tense enough as it is. She only turns them into tomcats sitting on a fence.

The major replies that "They're being trained for manhood. Where there's manhood, there's women."

This becomes evident when Conway stops two recruits from molesting her. She returns the favor by aiding him in his one-man assault on the major and his crooked recruits.

Van Alexander's military march theme-music was the antithesis of his big-band rock-and-roll soundtracks, but it still had the cadence of a juvenile delinquent's score. This film still had the requisite quota of sex and violence, even though drill and ceremony replaced stompin' the boards.

Some examples are the ambiguous death of a cadet, a one-on-one bayonet confrontation between Rooney and an officer, Daisy Mae's assault during her heroic scene at the end of the film, the secretary's swimming with the shark scene, and Duryea's explosive histrionics as he sails into the sunset. In this movie, murder and intimidation are the choice of decision makers as has always been the case with Zugsmith's sleaziest movies.

*In* Thunder Bay, *Johnny Gambi (Dan Duryea) is a hard-drinking, two-fisted oil rigger who is about to take a bath in black gold.* 1953, UNIVERSAL PICTURES COMPANY, INC.

# 16

# Sidekicks and Ciphers

During the fifties, Dan Duryea branched out into television. He had his own series, *The Adventures of China Smith*, and starred in its return to the air two years after it was originally cancelled. He also starred in many anthology series, dramatic shows, and comedy programs.

His first appearance was a tense, live-crime drama monologue on *The Kate Smith Evening Hour* (1952). He appeared on many of the premier anthology shows, such as *Climax, Studio 57, Schlitz Playhouse of Stars, The Ford Television Theater,* and *General Electric Theater.*

Dan Duryea was a flexible actor who was comfortable in either medium. He was able to fill-in the nuances of a solid supporting role or hold down the boisterous lead in an independent Western or pulp drama. Duryea also benefited from the character lines and rueful expressions that came from decades of experience. This gave the characters of his later years emotional depths and shadings that made him a durable supporting player.

Whether or not he was working in classic films or low-budget pot boilers, he gave an engaging performance. Duryea starred in independent movies, but also appeared in supporting parts, especially at Universal-International. He had been with the studio since the 40s and would stay in the 60s when it was owned by MCA. His supporting roles were done in addition to his independent movies and his numerous television parts.

The good-natured sidekick is a fair assessment of his parts in *Thunder Bay* and *Foxfire*. Of course, being Duryea characters meant there had to be some degree of ambiguity; in this case it was hard drinking and rash judgments.

Johnny Gambi likes the idea of trampling all over the Old World customs of a small Louisiana fishing village. He is drilling for oil with his partner, Steve Martin.

Doc is just as hard drinking as Gambi, but he is not nearly as ambitious, bold, or successful. He runs a clinic in a mining town. He is a sidekick to Jonathan Dartland, the enigmatic and super-strong lead, but he is far from being an asset.

Gambi and Doc are sidekicks to two leads who are mustering the forces of nature to create a legacy for themselves. *Thunder Bay* and *Foxfire*

*Macho man Teche (Gildbert Roland) orders a round of drinks to start a man-boasting contest between Johnny Gambi (Dan Duryea) and himself.* 1953, UNIVERSAL PICTURES COMPANY, INC.

deal with the water and the earth, but they share the common theme of the outsider who plans to tap into nature's reserves and make it his personal stake. Gambi will reap part of the rewards because he has a vested interest, but the Doc will become bone-dry because of his small dreams.

Taking over someone else's sovereign domain in the name of offshore drilling and becoming wealthy in spite of it is the story of Steve Martin (James Stewart), a two-fisted man who wants to rule the world and get something better. *Thunder Bay* is a passion play that serves as an apologia for the cherished myth of the individual with a vision that creates a new source of life while sacrificing the needs of a precious few for the even-more-precious many.

Martin and Gambi drill for oil and eventually find it, but not without cutting off the manhood of Teche (Gilbert Roland), the formerly respected resident male tough guy, and Phillipe (Robert Monet), the adoring sycophant who is swept away by a tumultuous sea that disagreed with their plans of sabotage.

Teche is an honest, hard-working man whose life is the sea. He belongs to a Louisiana fishing community that depends on the shrimp beds for its livelihood. He gambles, drinks, holds court, and wrestles at a sleepy,

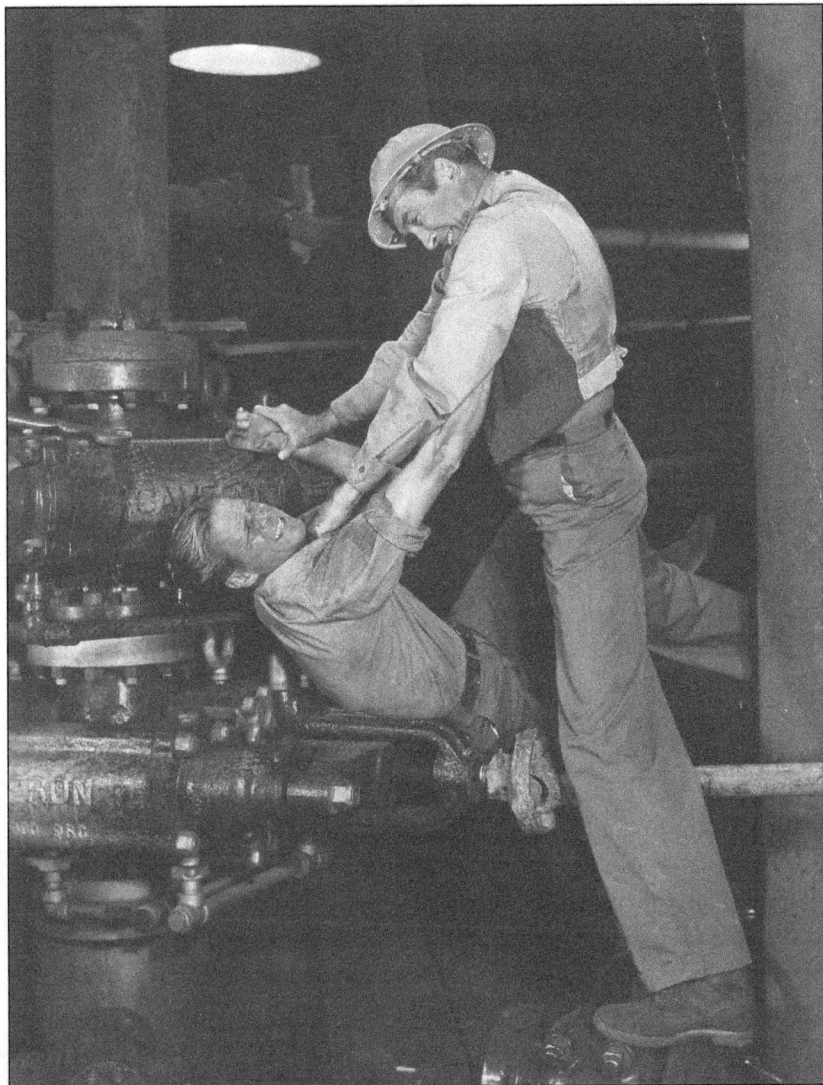

*Johnny Gambi (Dan Duryea) and Steve Martin (James Stewart) fight over different opinions regarding work habits. 1953,* UNIVERSAL PICTURES COMPANY, INC.

seafront club where the guitar player sings sad songs as drinkers argue with each other. His pleasant nature changes from tropical verve to a raging tempest when he leads the fight against the outsiders who introduce progress at the expense of tradition.

The ultimate insult comes from squiring the daughters of Dominique (Antonio Moreno), the inn keeper and town elder. He has resigned him-

*Teche (Gilbert Roland), Steve Martin (James Stewart), Johnny Gambi (Dan Duryea) and Francesca (Marcia Henderson) view nature's power in a gushing oil geyser.* 1953, UNIVERSAL PICTURES COMPANY, INC.

self to losing Stella (Joanne Dru), his oldest daughter, to the snobbish expectations of a college education, but to lose his younger girl to Johnny Gambi (Dan Duryea) in a sweep-me-off-my-feet deal is an ignoble insult. It results in the final rebellion of the male villagers against the oil rig. It's too bad it happens when Steve, Johnny, and Macdonald (Jay C. Flippen), their benefactor, hit pay dirt when the black gold explodes.

The geyser terrifies the village's men and they revert to their primordial instincts and flee. Their ancestors may have been intimidated by volcanoes and hurricanes, but they have to contend with a new aspect of nature.

The bulk of the spoilers' rewards belong to Steve Martin, who is unwavering in his insistence at sticking to the drilling target and getting the hostile residents to see things his way. Martin is there when the black gold changes the color of his life and the world of everyone around him. What saves Martin's hide is his accidentally coming across the revered beds of the golden shrimp.

Teche is led on to believe that he has discovered the coveted harvest, a ruse by Martin to let the man still think that he has primacy of his domain,

*Jonathan Dartland (Jeff Chandler) is a blue blood Apache who thinks that it is bad luck for his wife Amanda (Jane Russell) to visit the mine in* Foxfire. 1955, UNIVERSAL PICTURES COMPANY, INC.

never mind that Phillipe, his protégé, was swept away with the dynamite in a storm and that his former fiancé wed the impetuous Johnny Gambi, or that the college-educated bayou girl awards herself with the man of the hour. Macdonald gets a taste of his former greatness and a percentage of being a maverick who still knows how to gamble.

*Foxfire* is the eerie phosphorescent glow of a gold prospector's dream. It becomes the name of a mining company by the end of the film. The story line is a boy-meets-girl soap opera set in the desert. Jeff Chandler and Jane Russell are U.I.'s answer to Adam and Eve. They are as primal as the sunsets and rocky plains that make up the environment.

Jonathan Dartland is a mining engineer whose claim to fame is that he believed in what the foxfire told him, and Amanda is the insane society dame who falls in love with him. They marry on a whim and it is a bumpy ride once they leave the altar.

It is a clash of cultures that causes the friction. He a Boston blue-blood Apache and she is a spoiled eastern society girl who is used to getting

*Hugh Slater (Dan Duryea) satisfies his desire with Maria (Mara Corday), but does not appreciate her love for him.* 1955, UNIVERSAL PICTURES COMPANY, INC.

*Hugh Slater (Dan Duryea) is the alcoholic town doctor who falls in love with Amanda (Jane Russell).* 1955, UNIVERSAL PICTURES COMPANY, INC.

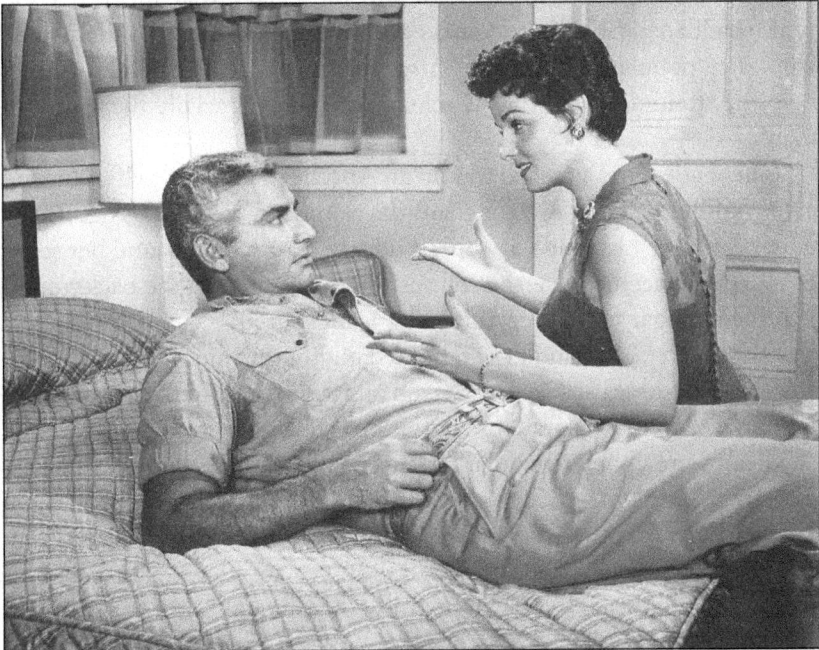

*Amanda (Jane Russell) tries to explain female independence to the traditional Jonathan Dartland (Jeff Chandler).* 1955, UNIVERSAL PICTURES COMPANY, INC.

what she wants. That makes him independent and emotionless, which conflicts with Russell's sentimental and romantic ways of doing things. Changes teach the couple things about each other and they reconcile just as he hits pay dirt.

It started when Dartland gave Amanda a lift after she was stranded in the desert when her car had a flat tire. He was returning from town where he picked up Doc after his friend had been out on a three-day bender. Seeing Amanda's bob cut, buxom manner, swivel-hipped capris, and high heels didn't hurt his incentive to be chivalrous. It is something that lights a spark in both men. Amanda invites the men to a party that her mother is giving that evening, setting the stage for a romance where the third wheel keeps spinning without even knowing why.

Amanda learns about racism when one of the town gossips visits and gives her the lowdown on Jonathan Dartland's quirks. The meddler assumes that there is a bond between the women because they are white. Comments like, "Once an Indian, always an Indian" or "they can never rise above their nature," peeve Amanda, who politely tells her guest that she would like to find out about her husband for herself.

Amanda gains further insight when she visits the reservation where her husband's mother lives. It is not only the squalor that affects her, she is also saddened by the listlessness and soulless existence of the people who once populated Colorado. Amanda's talk with Dartland's mother helps her to understand the Apache way of life, especially their ideal of manhood.

Independence is a crucial trait in an Apache man. To be self-sufficient is the fulfillment of an Apache man's development. This helps Amanda to understand her husband's aloofness; now he has to understand her sense of independence because she refuses to be relegated to the background. It is their cougar fight, everything else is incidental.

Dan Duryea is Chandler's inebriated buddy, the mining town's doctor who likes to do things with a slurred affect. He is adored by his beautiful nurse, played by Mara Corday, but he is oblivious to her charms. His daydreams are about Amanda. He thinks he has more finesse than the masterful Dartland.

Dan Duryea is there for comedic effect. He is annoying when drunk and cynical when sober. Too cockeyed to appreciate what he has in Corday, Duryea fakes himself out when he thinks he can take Andrea away from Chandler.

Mara Corday lives a hellish life in the mining community. She is still referred to as a half-breed, and this is cause for ostracism. It seems insane because she is beautiful and intelligent; even a buffoonish doc like Duryea thinks he is too good for her.

Frieda Inescourt is the befuddled mother, a society doyenne who is opposed to the strange marriage. Never mind that it starts with a gold mine and ends in a new town, she opposes the introduction of Mayflower blood to the lineage of the original Americans.

Barton MacLane is still playing the obstinate stick-in-the-mud, the business Philistine who can't see innovation even when it stares him in the eye. He is oblivious to the old myth about Indian gold and that is why he becomes a phantom by the end of the movie. He does not need to be drilled by a gangster to be removed from the scene. All he has to do is exit the screen gracefully with egg on his face.

*In* This Is My Love, *wheelchair bound Murray Myer (Dan Duryea) is a bitter ex-dancer who jealously clings to his wife and former partner, Evelyn (Faith Domergue).* 1954, RKO PICTURES, INC.

# The Fifties Weepers

By the end of the 50s, most of Duryea's best performances were seen on television. He starred in independent pictures but continued to work for Universal-International and made three movies for the studio between 1957 and 1960. One was *Kathy O*, a coy comedy about a child star, another was *Night Passage*, an excellent James Stewart Western, and the last was *Slaughter on Tenth Avenue*, a hard-core labor union drama produced by Albert J. Zugsmith. Duryea continued to work for Universal-International and appeared in many entertaining films for the studio during the 50s. He also appeared in many bizarre independent films that are brutal, cutting, and weird in their normalcy.

*This Is My Love* and *Kathy O* are different types of soap operas. The first film is an obscure oddity and fills the category for the whiners and the wimps, the drunken wastrels who think they deserve more than what they have. The second movie is an endearing comedy about a lovable husband who shills for a living and gets caught up in the world of Hollywood publicity run amok. It is a color film with a reigning child star of the time. The movies feature Duryea in secondary roles as impotent second bananas of various degrees. He is totally dependent on others in *This Is My Love* and totally overwhelmed in *Kathy O*.

*This Is My Love* is the story of how a typewriter and a wheelchair serve as crutches for two bitter dreamers who hate yet need each other for support in a world where they are secondary players. Vi (Linda Darnell) is a frustrated novelist on the verge of spinsterhood and Murray (Dan Duryea) is a vindictive former dancer who is confined to a wheelchair. They are in-laws whose common bond is Evelyn (Faith Domergue), Vi's sister and Murray's wife.

Their lives revolve around a diner that is the rock of their survival. Vi is a nanny and home attendant when she is not working the counter at the diner. She listens to Murray's put-downs and the children's inane chatter in between periods of writing her novel. She has a calm demeanor that is akin to that of a Buddhist monk, but beneath the peaceful surface is an active volcano about to erupt. When she finally erupts, Murray is dead and Evelyn is accused of murdering him with a lethal injection, the result of Vi spiking his medicine with poison.

*This Is My Love* is a turgid soap opera, a depressing descent into a whirlpool of passion, hatred, resentment, and frustration. There have been many lovers' triangles, but rarely has a volatile rectangle been explored in a cheap and tawdry way like love at the seaside café and hatred on the home front.

The female animal is represented by a waitress and an aspiring novelist and the man-beast is split into two species: the virile and the impotent. Faith Domergue supplies the fireworks, Linda Darnell applies the resentment, Rick Jason is the strong man, and Dan Duryea is the weakling in a wheelchair.

The haranguing is hair-raising at times and the romantic interludes are steamy because of Evelyn. Her wheelchair-bound husband screams, moans, and exacts guilt trips from his wife, a waitress who is bitter and frustrated until a male drifter steals her attention.

The real rivalry is between Vi and Evelyn. Murray is bitter and gripes, but he is powerless because he cannot move beyond his con-

*Dan Duryea plays an ex-dancer confined to a wheelchair in* This is My Love, *a strange and depressing soap opera.* 1954, RKO PICTURES.

fines. Vi desires Glenn, the gas station attendant with the steamy lines and dreamy eyes. He, in turn, desires Evelyn. Vi's jealousy inspires her to conspire against Evelyn by poisoning Murray and framing her for it.

The frame is successful in all ways but one and that is Vi's attempt to have Glenn to herself. He sees through her scheme and deplores her for it. It is his confrontational and condemnatory affront with her that causes her to break down and confess her guilt. It is an interesting resolution to a soap-opera dilemma. The useless husband and the unwanted admirer are eliminated, and all that remains are the couple in love.

Hollywood exposès tend to be dark shockers filled with terse comments on illusion, subservience, egotism, and blind ambition. The players are often repugnant characters, the antithesis of how they are

*Evelyn (Faith Domergue) meets and falls in love with Glenn Harris (Rick Jason), a slick, smooth-talking gas station attendant.* 1954, RKO PICTURES, INC.

*Vida (Linda Darnell), Evelyn's sister, and Eddie (Hal Baylor), her boyfriend, listen to Murray (Dan Duryea) make a frantic phone call to locate his missing wife.* 1954, RKO PICTURES, INC.

perceived by an adoring public. *Kathy O* is an expose, but it is tame and without casualties. A moral lesson is played out but it is sugary and not mocking.

Kathy O'Roarke (Patty McCormick) is a cumbersome, pig-tailed child star. She is distraught and becomes involved in an unwitting kidnapping plot when she runs away from the studio and holes up with the family of

Kathy O *(Patty McCormick) is a temperamental child star who undergoes a severe identity crisis.* 1958, UNIVERSAL PICTURES COMPANY, INC.

Harry Johnson (Dan Duryea), a Hollywood press agent. It is family fun and a useful ethics lessons for eight-year-olds.

She is an attitudinal child star who irritates everyone who has to deal with her, whether it is her co-star, press agent, or guardian. We get the impression that she is spoiled and hard to handle but by the end of the film we find out that she is stressed out because she is exploited by her surrogate stage mother Aunt Harriet (Mary Jane Croft) and the profit-minded studio.

The drama unfolds at the expense of Harry Johnson. It begins when he tells the child star to pour on the charm for Celeste Saunders (Jan Sterling), a journalist who is writing a profile of the girl for her magazine. It does not help matters that the writer is Duryea's ex-wife, who develops a rapport with the actress after they spend a day on a chartered fishing boat.

Kathy O and the writer realize that they fill the void in each other's lives and begin to resent how show biz politics are keeping them apart. Accordingly, they need each other to survive: the star needs favorable publicity and the writer needs interesting subjects. Both are being manipulated by the studio for the cause of a favorable public profile.

It all comes to a boil when Kathy O decides to run away. Harry spots

*Harry Johnson (Dan Duryea) is a Hollywood press agent who explains an ad campaign to the unappreciative Kathy O'Roarke (Patty McCormick).* 1958, UNIVERSAL PICTURES COMPANY, INC.

her on the street and squires her to his home, promising to contact Celeste, with whom the girl wants to live. She is distrustful of Harry because he represents studio politics. He is also leery of her because she is an accomplished actress who is rarely sincere. The common ground is Harry's home life, which is a fascinating and enjoyable mystery to Kathy O.

Harry's wife Helen (Mary Fickett) and their two sons are the ones who break the plastic bubble that the child star lives in. All it takes is a home-cooked dinner, pillow fights, and sage advice from mom to turn Kathy O into an average American kid. The only trouble is that Kathy O's disappearance is being treated like a kidnapping by the studio, police, and the news.

The situation is tenuous for Harry because he has to act normal with his co-workers, be level-headed with the police and rational with his wife. His resolution is to sneak the girl unto the studio lot at night and let the guards discover her. It is a successful plan until she is returned to her aunt and the intruding reporter begins to unravel the scheme.

All ends well, with Kathy O beaming for the camera.

*Lt. Chavez (Ainslie Pryor) suspects Harry Johnson (Dan Duryea) of having something to do with the child star's disappearance and wife Helen (Mary Frickett) hopes the cop does not find out that they are providing sanctuary for the weary star.* 1958, UNIVERSAL PICTURES COMPANY, INC.

Kathy O is *Father Knows Best* meets a heavily-censored *Bad Seed*. In fact, the deadening pace of the movie could have benefited from Kathy O striking out at the adults in a psychotic frenzy. There are no peaks and valleys to the movie so the viewer does not feel compelled about the plot or characters.

The sub-plot between revived feelings with the reporter and his ex-wife and how it affects his present marriage is more interesting than Kathy O's dilemma. Because of this tangent, Helen Johnson becomes the most interesting character in the movie.

She has a good life in Hollywood with a husband who has a seemingly glamorous occupation and two sons whom she adores. The stability of her world is threatened by the arrival of Sterling, who is still single and somewhat unhappy.

It's not just their time spent together because of Kathy O that upsets Helen; it is Celeste Saunders' job offer to her husband to work on her magazine in New York that pushes her buttons. Despite the threat to her home, Helen seeks a solution that will bring happiness to Kathy O and exonerate her husband of any wrongdoing.

Duryea does not have much to do in Kathy O. He is nervous and flustered most of the time, having the manic energy of a pinball in motion. He is perceived as part of the problem, another studio flack who looks at Kathy O as little more than studio property. It is his wife who changes his perspective and the incentives to change are the possible loss of his job and impending kidnapping charges.

Kathy O hates him from the start because he represents the studio's tyrannical control over her life. He only gets her seal of approval because he provides her with a window of opportunity when she is introduced to the wonderful world of his intimates, which not only includes his family but Celeste Saunders, as well.

*Col. Wyatt (Dan Duryea) and Jo McWerthy (Frances Gifford) share a tender moment in* Sky Commando *before a Young Turk comes between them.* 1953, NATIONAL SCREEN SERVICE CORP.

# The Korean War: Small and Big

*Sky Commando* and *Battle Hymn* are perfect examples of Duryea's appearances in both low-budget independent features and big studio treatments. Both films are about the Korean War, but one is a low-budget quickie stretched out with stock bombing footage and the other is a sweeping, colorful bio-drama of a heroic minister with a crisis of faith.

Both movies are examinations of conscience under duress. Right and wrong are debated while the fate of the lead player is held in balance. Duryea plays the lead role of Colonel Wyatt in *Sky Commando*. In *Battle Hymn*, he plays the resourceful supply sergeant. He chomps on a cigar and gets what is needed while leaving the worrying to the film's lead, played by Rock Hudson.

*Sky Commando* is a low-budget quickie about war and honor, snap judgments, and the military chain of command. It has the flat look of a dull documentary and uses stock combat footage to supply the thrills. The movie starts with a flying mission during the Korean War that becomes a flashback story set in WWII. The common point is Colonel Wyatt, a hated officer who has the courage to make on-the-spot decisions concerning life and death.

Two bombers head home after a successful combat mission when they receive orders to take two enemy bunkers with machine guns. It seems like a simple mission until they encounter four enemy MiGS. They radio headquarters to tell them that they don't have enough fuel to take out the bunkers and take on the MiGS. They will have to deal with the MiGS. Colonel Wyatt commandeers the mike and orders them to complete the original mission. Over and out!

Only one of the flyer returns to base. The other flyer ejected from his aircraft and parachuted behind enemy lines. This eats away at the survivor because the downed pilot was his brother. He is hospitalized and vents his spleen to Ol' Poppy, a beloved vet. Ol' Poppy has heard accusations about the Colonel before and he does not hesitate to defend his old friend. This includes the story that becomes the crux of the movie.

It seems that Wyatt had always had to contend with animosity because of his unpopular life-and-death decisions during combat. During WWII, his main detractor was Hobbie (Mike "Touch" Connors), a junior officer who hated Wyatt because of something he did during a flying mission.

After a raid, Wyatt realizes that they don't have enough fuel to make it back to the base. The only dead weights that can be jettisoned are literally two dead soldiers. They were along for the ride so they could receive a proper funeral and burial. It is when Wyatt gives the orders to dump the dead pilots that the survivors become enraged with a seething hatred for their commanding officer.

Hobbie is one of them and he spends the rest of the movie trying to bust Wyatt. It takes a long, hard lesson of keeping a clear head during combat to make Hobbie realize that Wyatt is truly an honorable man. He realizes the guilt and pain that Wyatt has to deal with and knows that his soul is made of scar tissue.

The bedridden soldier takes the story in stride and becomes relieved when he discovers that his brother survived the bailout. The young pilot is added to the list of soldiers who learned to respect the veteran for the stalwart leader that he is.

*Sky Commando* may be a low-budget cheapie that is over shortly after it begins, but it is worthwhile because of the principal actors. Dan Duryea and Frances Gifford were veterans by the fifties and Touch Connors had yet to become a television star, so their presence gives the film its interest. Add to that two vets like Selmer Jackson

*Tempers flare when Col. Wyatt (Dan Duryea) orders his crew to jettison two dead flyers to lighten the load that will conserve fuel so they can make a safe landing.* 1953, NATIONAL SCREEN SERVICE CORP.

*Lt. Lee (Mike "Touch" Connors) and Col. Wyatt (Dan Duryea) see things from clashing perspectives.* 1953, NATIONAL SCREEN SERVICE CORP.

and Morris Ankrum as two generals and you have a curiosity piece, a movie that is not great shakes, but has redeeming value to keep it off the junk heap.

*Battle Hymn* is the screen story of Dean Hess, a combat flyer who became a minister after he accidentally bombed a German orphanage during World War II. The twist to the saga is that he leaves his Ohio church to return to active duty in Korea so he can teach a squadron of flyers how to fly combat missions. It is a tale of redemption, Hollywood style! — which means that it has its mawkish moments as well as courageous scenes.

Minister Hess is a man plagued by doubt, one who bogs down his sermons with guilt instead of hope. He is haunted by the thirty-seven orphans he unintentionally killed and believed that being a minister would alleviate the guilt. The film loses no time in touching on the tragedy with a powerful flashback. The accident was due to a faulty trigger mechanism that released the bomb once the original target was past. Informed of the bombing by a propaganda broadcast, 'Killer' Hess visits the site and is devastated by the destruction. What makes the situation more difficult is that it took place in his grandmother's hometown.

Five years after the war, doubt still clouds his judgment so he takes advantage of an Army recall program and volunteers for active duty as a senior USAF advisor/instructor pilot. His mission is to train the ROK (Republic of Korea) Army to fly F-51D Mustangs,

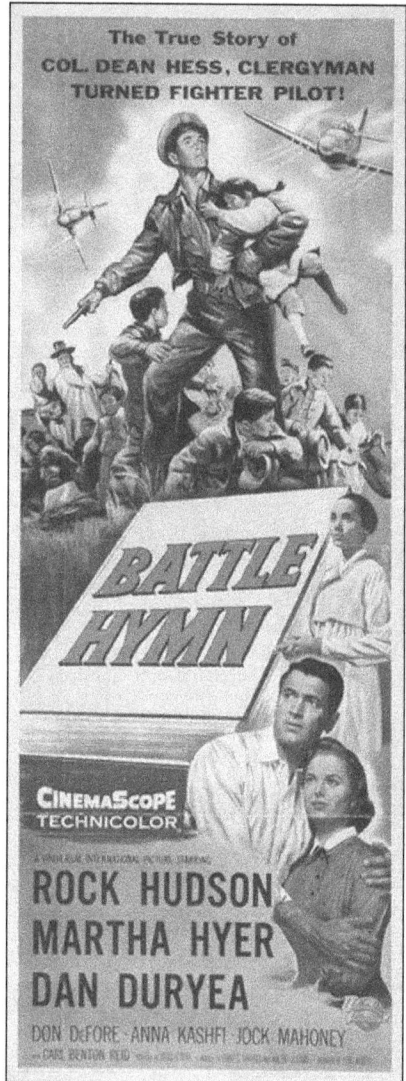

*Insert for* Battle Hymn. 1956, UNIVERSAL PICTURES COMPANY, INC

nothing more. This is the irony that creates the conflict in the story when the enemy soldiers begin to broach the airfield and threaten the village.

Hess arrives in Korea and finds that his airbase is a rundown strip that was built by the Japanese during World War II. The American troops are rag bags who are killing time by doing nothing because they are separated from the action. Hess changes this by imposing strict military discipline,

*En Soon Yang (Anna Kashfi) explains social conditions to Sgt. Herman (Dan Duryea) and Col. Hess (Rock Hudson).* 1956, UNIVERSAL PICTURES COMPANY, INC.

a step that is necessary in cleaning up the base to make it acceptable for the planes that will shortly arrive. This does not sit too well with Captain Skidmore (Don DeFore), his old battle buddy from the previous war.

Training turns into actual combat when the flyers spot a convoy of enemy soldiers and obliterate them. There appears to be one fleeing vehicle that is neutralized, but it is discovered to be full of refugees. This opens up old wounds for Hess, who berates Skidmore for disobeying orders by engaging in combat. Skidmore does not want to hear about guilt because he accepts accidents as being a part of war.

"You win or you die," says Skidmore, adding that if "you go soft…you're one step away from being dead."

It's when Hess speaks with Lieutenant Maples (James Edwards) that he begins to get a spiritual perspective on the contradictions of life that are woefully spelled out in a war. Maples is a spiritual person who accepts the Bible at face value and reluctantly accepts that God has a plan for everyone, even if the individual does not perceive it.

From that point onward, the challenges mount for Hess. He has to find a humanitarian solution to the orphans who have been flooding the base for meals. His authority is undermined when it is discovered that he is a minister. Things look bleak when enemy troops move closer to the encampment.

His solution to the orphan problem is to convert a bombed out Buddhist temple into an orphanage. He regains the men's trust by proving that he can still engage with the enemy. Hess felt comfortable being a trainer, not realizing that he would have to engage in combat. The rest of the movie shows just how wrong he is. His biggest challenge is to safely move over four-hundred orphans after the base is bombed and the orphanage threatened. He accomplishes this with the last-minute aid of a group of cargo planes who airlift the orphans to the island of Cheju.

*Battle Hymn* is a departure for director Douglas Sirk and producer Ross Hunter. They usually helmed glossy soap operas for the studio. This film breaks away from the heavy dramatics and improbable plot twists, possibly because it is based on a true story. There were deviations in the script. For instance, the real model for Kashfi's character was older and did not die in the war, and the strafed refugees were fleeing on a boat rather than a truck. Otherwise, it is an uplifting and engaging film, truly inspiring and emotional.

Russell Metty's cinematography is breathtaking, which was the case with all of his films because of the mastery of his craft. The dogfights are impressive and powerful. The music is a variation of Japanese martial music mixed with American folk tunes, such as "The Battle Hymn of the Republic."

Rock Hudson is perfect as the square-jawed, broad-shouldered leader of men. He successfully portrays the conflicts Hess must have felt as a minister turned warrior. Hudson shows the subtle changes in his thinking as his challenges help mold him and give him back his confidence.

*En Soon Yang (Anna Kashfi) and Col. Hess (Rock Hudson) simulate domestic bliss during the Korea War. 1956, Universal Pictures Company, Inc.*

Anna Kashfi has a quiet reserve as the woman who is the mother spirit to the orphans. She carries on her charitable work until her heroic death during the air raid that caps the film's drama.

Dan Duryea is wonderful as the wily, cigar-chomping Supply Sergeant Herman. He is able to secure any ration or supply under the most arduous conditions. The sergeant is always cheerful and supplies a sorely needed sense of humor.

Dan DeFore plays Hess' old war buddy, someone who offers the audience a glimpse of Hess during the previous war, when he was known as 'Killer' Hess. He is at odds with Hess throughout the whole movie until he is mortally wounded during a heroic two- man mission towards the end of the film. His deathbed revelation is a touching moment and is not overdone or mawkish.

Philip Ahn plays Lun Wa, an elderly ivory carver who is a font of wisdom for Hess. He stays on to aid the orphans because he is needed. He seems to have all of the answers to Hess' questions and appears to be an angel whose wisdom is a salve for the wounds suffered in war.

James Edwards is Lt. Maples, a flyer who unintentionally strafes a truckload of orphans. He is an impressive character, one of the few

*Col. Hess (Rock Hudson) heroically transports an orphanage to safe passage during a bombing raid.* 1956, UNIVERSAL PICTURES COMPANY, INC.

African-Americans shown in war movies of the fifties. His only stereotypical moment is singing "Swing Low, Sweet Chariot" when trying to comfort the orphans after a devastating air raid.

Martha Hyer plays his faithful wife, who remains steadfast in her love for him as he confronts his inner demons in Korea. Alan Hale, Jr. plays a garrulous mess sergeant and Jock Mahoney is a major who adds his farmland charm to a couple of scenes.

Lieutenant Colonel Hess was the technical adviser to the film. Hudson wore Hess' Navy-issued gold flying helmet with the United Nations emblem. Hess got it from a downed Navy pilot who crash landed at the Korean airfield. He donated his profits from the film to help the orphanage that he helped found in Korea.

# The Prairie Dogs and Town Bosses Club

Dan Duryea created an impressive Western portfolio over his career, amassing a list of credits that included prairie men, gunslingers, and town bosses. Duryea's sagebrush villains were the western forebears of their urban crime brethren. Few of them rose to be the crime boss of the range, but even the big men who did failed to escape ironic twists of fate when they lost the opportunities to save their hides.

Duryea's first Western bad man was in *Along Came Jones* (1946), starring Gary Cooper. His last gunslinger was in *Incident at Phantom Hill* (1966). That's twenty years of terror and marauding, a repetitious loop of dying in the dust. No one can beat the good guy and that includes the legion of Black Bart roles Duryea played throughout his career. The only one who got away was Mr. Denton in the *Twilight Zone's* episode of *Mr. Denton at Doomsday*. He is aided by a magic potion that the others do not possess. That is why they wound up on Boot Hill and Mr. Denton didn't. He got to live in *The Twilight Zone* and that was television.

In the movies, it was a requisite for the Black Bart villains to return to the dust. It all ended in the dust that created the gunslinger in the first place, and that includes the variations on the gunslinger, such as the maverick marauders or town bosses, the gunmen made good and gone respectable. They owned the towns that they once terrorized but still managed to die the gunslingers' death.

In *Along Came Jones*, Melody Jones is mistaken for Monte Jarrad, a gunslinger, and he encounters all sorts of trouble and awkward situations when he and George Fury (William Demarest), his sidekick, arrive in a town called Payneville. Jones matches the description in the wanted poster and also has the same initials as the killer bandit. It is a mystery to Jones why townsfolk defer to him but his false pride turns to fear when gunmen and a posse hunt him down.

The real bad man is holed up in the house of his showgirl sweetheart, Cherry de Longre (Loretta Young). She sees a formidable dupe in Jones and plans to use him as a diversion to the boyfriend in hiding. Trouble starts when she falls in love with Jones, starting a feud between him and the real bad man. The rivalry ends in a classic Western shootout.

*Along Came Jones* is a good-natured spoof of Westerns, where the strong,

*Title lobby card for* Along Came Jones *starring Gary Cooper and Loretta Young.* 1945, INTERNATIONAL PICTURES.

silent, lawman romances a petticoat beauty while contending with a ruthless Black Bart. It does not hurt that the star of the movie is known for playing lone hero types. Gary Cooper is the laid-back Melody Jones, and he spoofs his image well. He gets plenty of support from a humorous William Demarest, a seductive Loretta Young, and a villainous Dan Duryea, who creates his first Western bad man in the role of Monte Jarrad.

The movie may be a Western spoof but it is still Duryea's prototype gunslinger. It's a stagecoach that he robs at the beginning of the movie, passengers that he shoots, and that is Gary Cooper and a posse that he shoots it out with in the finale. Gary Cooper may have been spoofing himself, but Dan Duryea was carving a new niche in his cast of characters.

Cooper and Duryea are a study in opposites, even though they are both tall and lanky. Cooper is tentative and self-effacing and Duryea is

*A wounded Monte Jarred (Dan Duryea) is as dangerous as a cornered wild animal.* 1945, INTERNATIONAL PICTURES.

*George (William Demarest) and Melody Jones (Gary Cooper) take what they believe is their last stand.* 1945, INTERNATIONAL PICTURES.

blunt and ruthless. This creates a riveting rivalry between the characters. Loretta Young is leather and lace as the frontier woman whose hardness is softened by Cooper's lanky heroics. Her character once loved the outlaw because he was wild in his youth. The wildness was supplanted by meanness, and this change is what causes the rift between them.

Loretta Young possessed a strange sex appeal that was a blend of

*Monte Jarred (Dan Duryea) keeps a tight rein on Cherry (Loretta Young) in* Along Came Jones. 1945, INTERNATIONAL PICTURES COMPANY, INC.

gawkiness and eroticism. It was an unusual blend, along with presenting the illusion of helplessness mixed with total control.

William Demarest is humorous as the hero's sidekick. He is tough and funny, mainly because he is bewildered by his saddle sidekick. Demarest provides comic relief, but he is also there for the final showdown, lending moral support even though he was wounded by the bandit.

*Along Came Jones* was adapted by Nunnally Johnson from Alan LeMay's novel, *Useless Cowboys*. Stuart Heisler directs the film with a light-handed manner in a dark and foreboding atmosphere. It takes a special talent to blend humor and drama, and Heisler achieves the balance by providing a humorous satire that is also an earnest Western.

The next step in the evolution of the prairie gun man is the town boss. That takes economic power backed up by showdown dexterity. Beauvais is the first character to take the next step in Duryea's Western bad man's climb to power. In *River Lady*, Beauvais wears the fancy suits and smokes the finest cigars while wheeling and dealing, but he still knows how to kill a man and has not lost his killing instincts.

Beauvais is not yet the town mayor but he is a player nonetheless, and he goes for the catbird seat in *River Lady*. Duryea plays a morally cor-

*A magazine ad for* River Lady. 1948, UNIVERSAL PICTURES COMPANY, INC.

rupt wannabe town boss who does not come up to Yvonne De Carlo's river lady snuff. She is being wooed by a hero played by Rod Cameron, a do-right kind of guy who is Duryea's main headache.

*River Lady* is a rousing, Technicolor, romantic tale of the logging industry, business ambition, and hostile takeovers. It is a moral story of integrity versus chicanery and the perils of using each trait as a means to an end. Machiavelli would have been proud of the four main players as they do what they have to in order to get what they want: power and respectability. Are they victims of Darwinian circumstance, or agents of Christian free will? It does not matter because as in all contests there are two clear-cut winners and losers when the movie rolls its final credits.

Sequin owns the *River Lady*, a floating saloon and gambling den. She is a heavenly angel for the loggers who will gladly spend all of their hard-earned wages in her den of iniquity once their season is over. Her popularity is an empty mark of distinction for her.

She dreams of being a lady of leisure because she is angry about being avoided by proper women. Sequin does not like to be considered cheap and desires social prestige and economic stability. The only way for her to live on the largest house on the hill is to settle down and marry Dan Corrigan, a logger who thinks like an executive.

Corrigan loves Sequin, but he would rather stick to the outdoors

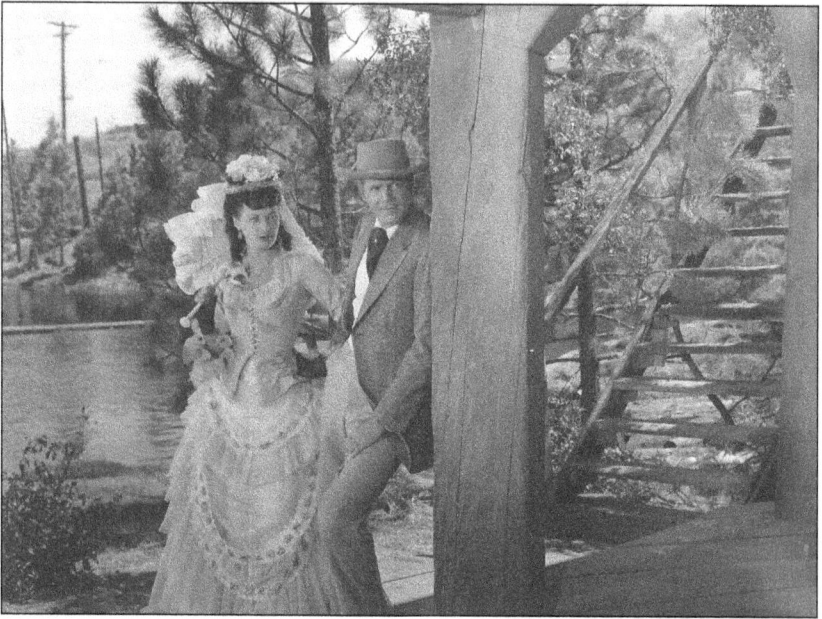

*Jim Beauvais (Dan Duryea) has big dreams for Sequin (Yvonne De Carlo) and himself.* 1948, UNIVERSAL PICTURES COMPANY, INC.

because he does not mind being a river rat. He knows that Sequin wants to domesticate him and he is cynical because he has seen too many men worked to death because of ambitious women. They don't see eye-to-eye because he wants to be one thing and she wants him to be another. He is honest with himself and believes that Sequin is delusional about her dreams of becoming a society lady. She is offended when he tells her that all the money in the world won't make her a refined lady. She says that he learned everything he knows about women in kindergarten. Opportunity knocks the day H.L. Morrison, the owner of a small mill, arrives to seek financial support from Sequin. His business is being squeezed by the dastardly Beauvais, a front man for an emerging logging syndicate. Beauvais informs Morrison that the days of the small mills are over and that he had better sell his business while the price was right.

This disturbs Morrison and he offers Sequin a percentage of his mill if she will offer some clout against the syndicate.

Sequin agrees to purchase 49 % of Morrison's mill if he will offer Corrigan an executive post without telling him that Sequin is responsible for his new opportunity. This is Sequin's attempt to civilize Corrigan and lay the plans to a successful life as a power couple.

*Jim Beauvais is Dan Duryea's first suave Western villain.* 1948, UNIVERSAL PICTURES COMPANY, INC.

Corrigan is reluctant to accept Morrison's offer because he still likes the outdoors. He relents because he does not want to look a gift horse in the mouth. His new career will enable him to marry Sequin to fulfill her dreams, not knowing that they have turned into a scheme. Things fall apart when he meets a woman who is as manipulative as Sequin.

Stephanie Morrison is the boss's daughter. She has just returned from

*Dan Corrigan (Rod Cameron) warns Jim Beauvais (Dan Duryea) about getting in the ways of his big dreams.* 1948, UNIVERSAL PICTURES COMPANY, INC.

school and is dismayed to find that her arrival coincides with the end of the logging season. She considers the loggers an uncouth lot, but is won over by Dan Corrigan when he saves her from the clutches of a Swede. She had been accosted by him on the docks when the loggers arrive to vent their pent-up passion.

Chivalry is an aphrodisiac for the society woman, and she develops a rapacious appetite for Corrigan, making her intentions clear at a picnic in the countryside. Stephanie shows that a society dame can wrestle in the mud when she learns of Corrigan's impending marriage to Sequin. She spoils the plans by informing Corrigan of Sequin's deal with her father.

Corrigan is infuriated that his good fortune was financed by Sequin's wealth. He confronts Sequin and calls off the wedding, prompting her to threaten him with financial ruin. This is Stephanie's chance to move in for the kill. Stephanie takes advantage of the rift between Corrigan and Sequin by offer a shoulder to cry on when she visits a hard-drinking Corrigan in the local saloon. He wakes up the next morning with a hangover and a wife.

Stephanie proves that she is as tough as she is conniving when she lives the frontier life with her new husband. He has promised her the house on the hill but only after he has earned it on his own. His brainstorm is to create a new syndicate with the independent miners who are about to be taken over by Beauvais and his clique.

Corrigan and Sequin are now bitter enemies and she gives her support to Beauvais, who is thrilled because he desires her. He constantly reminds her that they are two of a kind and that she will never be the school type that Corrigan likes. Sequin gives him insider information on a logging deal Corrigan has engineered that will mean a resounding financial success if the timber can be delivered on schedule. It is a pretty big "if," because Beauvais plans to sabotage the deal by creating a logjam.

The logjam creates the violent climax of the movie when the two opposing forces collide. Beauvais is aided by the bitter Swede who is aided by his buddies and confidants. It looks as though Beauvais will succeed until the confrontation boils down to a fight between him and Corrigan. If Beauvais does not stop Corrigan from dynamiting the logjam, he will be ruined. It turns out worse for him because he loses his life in the explosion that frees the timber.

The final scene has Sequin making a last ditch attempt to win back Corrigan with a passionate apology. He does not forgive and forget, reminding Sequin that he is married, even though his wife will step aside if that's what her husband wants. By the movie's end, the new syndicate is born, Corrigan and Stephanie will have the life that Sequin sought, and the *River Lady* sails away to her next destination.

Al Jennings of Oklahoma *(Dan Duryea) is a lawyer who turns to banditry when the Fates conspire against him.* 1951, NATIONAL SCREEN SERVICE CORP.

# Heroes
# and Desperadoes

Universal-International excelled at making crowd-pleasing, story-book-costume dramas that were a compendium of old Hollywood's used storylines redone in Cinemascope. One crowd pleaser was the romantic adventure triangle made up of a mysterious Robin Hood figure and a desirable, exotic, and quixotic dark beauty hampered by a wily and con-niving ex-partner out to benefit from a perceived double cross in the past.

*Black Bart* and *Al Jennings of Oklahoma* are two righteous gentlemen whose honor forces their hands at playing dishonor as their vocations. They have points to make and lose their grips because of the "true love and let's settle down" factor. This is what softens them up and brings them down. One goes down in flames, and the other rises from the ashes.

*Black Bart* has Dan Duryea as a new kind of banker, one who steals from the rich and invests it in the birth of a new banking system. All it takes is nerve, a fast horse, and a lucrative target: Wells Fargo and its payload routes. The new kind of banking believes in establishing credit with someone else's money. It is especially satisfying because Charles E. Boles, aka Black Bart, and his friendly lawyer, Clark (John McIntire), have declared themselves fair competition for Wells Fargo's payload.

The story unfolds as three thieves decide to go their separate ways to prevent the law from capturing them. Charlie, Lance Hardeen (Jeffrey Lynn), and Jersey (Percy Kilbride) go their separate ways after agree-ing to meet at a secret location so they can split the money. Charlie trusts his buddies to do the right thing by holding on to the money and bringing it with them for the split. They do not possess the honor their ex-partner has and decide that a two way split is preferable to a three-way bargain.

In time, Charlie becomes the respectable businessman, Charles E. Boles. He reverts to a life of crime when Clark, his cunning lawyer, comes up with a scheme to rob Wells Fargo of their gold shipments. He does all of the planning and Boles does the night riding as Black Bart, a masked desperado with a flowing cape.

A change in fortune occurs when Lola Montez (Yvonne DeCarlo) arrives in town for a series of performances. They develop a two-sided relationship; the first is when Black Bart robs her stagecoach and the second is when Boles falls in love. She is dismayed to learn that Boles

*Title lobby card for* Black Bart. 1947, UNIVERSAL PICTURES COMPANY, INC.

is the notorious bandit that stole her jewels, but love softens her anger. However, she gives him an ultimatum if he wants to wed her: either give up his life of crime or lose her.

He does not mind settling down because he would be foolish to risk their future because of his criminal behavior. His decision is complicated by the arrival of his former partners, who blackmail him into committing a series of robberies so they can collect a commission.

The careers of Charles E. Boles and Black Bart collide and cancel each other out. A shootout at a bonfire is fate's way of saying things are even between him and his ex-partner and that love conquers all.

Is it Lola Montez the dancehall queen, or Lance Hardeen, his former partner in crime, who brings down Black Bart? It is too easy to say a little of both or blame it on one of them. The final draw is Black Bart's

*Black Bart (Dan Duryea) robs dance hall star Lola Montez (Yvonne De Carlo) of her jewels.* 1947, UNIVERSAL PICTURES COMPANY, INC.

*Black Bart (Dan Duryea) and Lance Hardeen (Jeffrey Lynn) face their final showdown with the law.* 1947, UNIVERSAL PICTURES COMPANY, INC.

responsibility because he tried to satisfy both his past and his future simultaneously.

He does not owe Hardeen a thing and could have increased all that he had by sharing it all with Lola Montez and freezing out his phantom past. Black Bart and Lola Montez are a power couple in the making, the king and queen of a burgeoning gambling town.

*Lou Costello takes a break from filming* The Wistful Widow of Wagon Gap *to pay a visit to the set of* Black Bart. *Producer Leonard Goldstein seems jaded while star Dan Duryea takes an interest in Lou's scratch sheet.* 1947, UNIVERSAL PICTURES COMPANY, INC.

Bart's fidelity to the past and his generosity to the former partners who betrayed him are his own undoing. They are small time by their own making, which is why they belong to the past. With Lola by his side, Black Bart could have driven Hardeen and Jersey Brady (Percy Kilbride), the third gang member, out of town.

They would have had no choice, especially since they were already under suspicion by the sheriff. His ex-partners felt wronged because they had lost out the first time around. They tried for a second piece of the action. That was when it all fell apart, the former partners bonding again in a blood ritual called the shootout.

For them, hoof-and-mouth disease is a desert treasure and a lucrative side job that buys respectable dreams for low down criminals. Black Bart and Hardeen square their differences in a fiery showdown with the law and only Lola Montez lives to benefit from it, this being just another colorful tale to add to her legend.

*Black Bart* presents Duryea in a unique light as a romantic Robin Hood of the open West as he robs Wells Fargo and pays homage to a wealthy entertainer played by Yvonne DeCarlo.

Dan Duryea has the smooth moves and prairie lightning that it takes to play a genteel bandit. He is the sharp and sophisticated businessman and the prairie outlaw who plunders Wells Fargo.

Yvonne DeCarlo is the seductive Lola Montez. She is a dance hall queen with the power to make things happen on her own terms. Black Bart courts her love with his gallant, devilish commissions, but winds up going up in flames himself.

Jeffrey Lynn is the interloper who messes up things when his small ambition threatens the strange empire of his former partner in crime. It didn't matter to Lynn that he was the one who first double crossed Duryea.

Percy Kilbride is the third wheel who rode into the sunset, living in a cell to tell the tale of Black Bart. Kilbride would later hit pay dirt as Pa Kettle in the famous Universal-International "Ma and Pa Kettle" series.

*Al Jennings of Oklahoma* is a proud child of the old South, someone whose adversities inspired him to reach for the stars. Twisted fate and bad luck intervened, inspiring him to become a desperado instead of a brilliant lawyer. His fortune changed in 1863, a turning point for the South in the Civil War. The Union Army forces the Jennings family to flee their plantation while their father, a Confederate Major, fights the war. The film picks up years later to show the Major serving as a judge while his sons practice law.

Al Jennings' luck takes another turn for the worse during a trial when he observes his older brother, Ed (Ed Millican), being insulted by lawyer Tom Marsden (John Dehner) during a trial. Al disrupts the trial by demanding an apology, and when he does not receive one he punches the lawyer in the nose. A free-for-all ensues, including punches thrown by Ed and Frank (Dick Foran), his other brother. The judge will not tolerate disrespect in his courtroom, even if it does involves a case of old-fashioned Southern honor.

The judge levies one fine after another at the Jennings brothers, but his punitive action is nullified by Al Jennings' brilliant legal mind. He points out the illegality of the fines or the lack of jurisdiction involving the punitive damages. The judge finally settles on contempt of court, a charge that Al cannot deny.

Later, Mardsen seeks retribution for the slight and shoots Ed Jennings as the man is playing poker at the saloon. The murderer is arrested by Marshal Slattery (Stanley Andrews), but later released on bail. Al visits him at his ranch to seek retribution by having him make a

*Al Jennings (Dan Duryea) rides to the home of Tom Marsden (John Dehner) to get a written confession from his brother's murder.* 1951, NATIONAL SCREEN SERVICE CORP.

written confession. He is forced to shoot the lawyer in self-defense, but is framed by false testimony by one of the victim's ranchers.

Jennings goes on the lam with his brother Frank and they are forced to start a life of crime. The marshal leads a posse and corners the brothers, who are outwitted by an ingenious bluff tactic. The men make a one-horse getaway and find refuge at The Diamond B Ranch, run by Fred Salter (Harry Shannon), a shady cattleman. To avoid being turned in for ransom money, the brothers become long riders who do some night raiding. One of their sidelines is cattle rustling and they ride the back country and strike with sudden precision. The brothers have no choice to stay with the long riders because Shannon blackmails them, using their wanted poster as a hedge.

Al Jennings starts his notorious career with that first night ride and builds a reputation when he leads the gang in raids against a stage line that connects remote railroad communities.

An eventual split occurs when Jennings is recognized by Hanes (John Ridgely), a railroad detective, during a payroll robbery. Another incentive for the split is Al's fear that Slater will turn him in for the reward money, which has increased.

The Jennings brothers flee to New Orleans where they lead respectable lives as shopkeepers. Al turns a former acquaintance with a woman he saved from a runaway carriage into a budding romance. Her name is Margo St. Clare (Gale Storm), and she is a Southern belle who leads Al to the altar at a respectable pace until their plans are ruined by the railroad detective, who recognizes the brothers. Ridgely organizes a posse to subdue the brothers, but they are thwarted when Margo St. Clare aids their escape.

They return to the Diamond D Ranch and use it as a headquarters to pull one more robbery. They bribe Mrs. Slater (Helen Brown) into letting them use their place. It takes money to make up her mind because she is bitter that her husband has been imprisoned for being a rustler mixed up with the Jennings brothers.

Her cooperation is just a front for betrayal because she plans to trade the Jennings brothers for her husband's early release from prison. Marshal Slattery hunts them down and arrests them without the proper jurisdiction. The judge coerces the jury into making a deal that he ignores when he sentences the brothers on charges his court is not sanctioned to uphold.

Frank is given five years and Al is sentenced to life in prison. However, improprieties in the arrest and trial of Al Jennings impel President Theodore Roosevelt to pardon him. The narrator informs the audience that Al Jennings returned to Oklahoma and resumed his career as a lawyer. He became one of the leading proponents of statehood for Oklahoma.

Dan Duryea exudes charm and sophistication as Al Jennings. He is an American patriot fighting for the rights guaranteed by the Constitution. Duryea plays it hot and cold. He possesses a mean temper that cannot be quelled when his ire is raised. This is displayed throughout the movie when he cannot have his way. He is always bickering with an authority figure because it is either his way or the highway.

The turning point in his life comes when he will not accept that his brother's murderer is free on bail. Murder is not an offense that allows bail and the only reason Mardsen is released is because he is a town bigwig. This does not sit well with Jennings, who shoots him in self-defense when the lawyer tries to shoot him after he refuses to write and sign a confession to the murder.

Gale Storm plays Margo St. Clare, a society dame of her time. She desires Al Jennings, but feels that he is socially inferior because of his

*Margo St. Clare (Gale Storm) stands by Al Jennings (Dan Duryea) after his conviction.* 1951, NATIONAL SCREEN SERVICE CORP.

underworld activities. Ironically, it is the same criminal behavior that creates the allure.

Margo plays hard to get while leaving openings for advances and praise from Jennings. She is not thrilled by his attention but does not discourage him from making overtures. It is she who first makes the suggestion that he set up shop in New Orleans, something Jennings considers unappealing at the beginning of the movie but reconsiders when he is on the lam. Margo may be frills, buttons, bows, and corsets, but she stands by Jennings, not only by aiding him to escape from the detective, but by attending his trial.

Dick Foran has always been a tower of strength. In this movie, he is Al's older brother. He sticks by his brother's side when he becomes a desperado and does not abandon him when the net tightens and he is caught.

Frank Jennings tempers brother Al's irrational emotionalism. Frank may be quiet, but he stills rides with his brother and shares in the danger. He is a quiet thinker, one whose rationality adds logical perspectives to Al's grand plans.

Raymond Greenleaf plays Judge Jennings, the family patriarch. He is a respected jurist who fought valiantly in the Civil War. Ed Millican and Louis Jean Heydt are the other Jennings brothers, Ed and John, respectively. Harry Shannon is the shady cattleman, John Dehner is the unscrupulous lawyer, and William "Bill" Phillips is his ornery henchman. John Hamilton and Myron Healey have small unbilled parts.

*Whitey Harbin (Dan Duryea) is a sarcastic, trigger happy gunslinger who feels threatened by the presence of the Utica Kid (Audie Murphy) in his gang in* Night Passage. 1957, UNIVERSAL PICTURES COMPANY, INC.

# The Hired Gun

The hired gun was a man without a past who had a mean reputation for gunning down people and taking things over when he had a mind to. It took more than a sheer arrogance and a fierce bloodlust to make a good gunslinger. He had to have a quick wit, a sardonic philosophy, and a keen way of getting things done. If that meant bribery, murder, and mayhem, then so it was because all his hoods had a bloodthirsty gang at their beck and call.

Dan Duryea's high standing as one of the movies' premier Western bad men cast him against many popular screen heroes. He was the foil to James Stewart in 1950's *Winchester '73* and *Night Passage* in 1957. John Payne faced off with him in *Rails into Laramie* and *Silver Lode* in 1954. Audie Murphy was aided and abetted by him in *Ride Clear of Diablo* in 1954 and *Six Black Horses* in 1962. He made it rough for Tom Tryon in Disney's 1959 *Texas John Slaughter* tele-movie and a Universal TV remake of *Winchester '73* in 1966. He also stuck around in between to needle Tony Young in *He Rides Tall* and *Taggart*, two retro-oaters made by Universal in 1964.

Monte Jarrad was Duryea's first Western gunslinger and he had to square off against Gary Cooper in *Along Came Jones*, a Western satire spoofing Cooper's tall-in-the saddle image. It took four years before Dan Duryea got back into gear as a Western villain the memorable character of Waco Johnny Dean in *Winchester '73*. The 1950 Western classic relates a captivating story about the rifle's history as it passes hands, usually after violent confrontations. It stars James Stewart, along with Shelley Winters, Rock Hudson, Charles Drake, and John McIntyre.

*Winchester 73* is an episodic movie that tells the stories of the people who temporarily own the rifle that built the West. The violent vignettes range from the heroic to the tragic as the rifle passes hands from one owner to the next. Some of the people whose lives are changed by the rifle include two brothers on opposite sides of the law, a rebellious Indian chief inspired by the Battle of Little Big Horn, a gun merchant (John McIntyre) whose admiration of the rifle costs him his life, a petty criminal who is not man enough to own it, and a wily gunslinger whose sarcastic humor makes him the last laugh.

The story starts in Dodge City, where Wyatt Earp is hosting a shooting contest for the rifle, a top of the line Winchester 73, one of a thousand perfect in every respect. Other men who own a perfect Winchester 73 are President Grant and Buffalo Bill Cody.

*Poster for* Winchester '73. 1950, UNIVERSAL PICTURES COMPANY, INC.

The two top contenders are Lin McAdam (James Stewart) and Dutch Henry Brown (Stephen McNally), two men who hate each other and have a score to settle. It's not until the story gets underway that we find out that the men are brothers and Dutch is guilty of patricide.

The brothers compete in overtime until Lin wins, but Dutch steals the rifle. He does not hold it for long because he trades it for a cache of guns that a merchant has promised an Indian chief (Rock Hudson). The gun merchant, in turn, loses it to the Indian chief, who wants it because of the efficiency of the repeating guns used against General Custer at the Battle of Little Big Horn.

The Indian chief is killed in a raid on a Cavalry camp and the rifle is given to a civilian (Charles Drake) who fought bravely in the battle. He, in turn, is killed by Waco Johnny Dean, who reluctantly turns it over to a partner-in-crime, Dutch Henry Brown. The rifle ultimately winds up in the hands of the rightful owner, who settles his vengeance in a desert shootout.

Gimmicks such as the rifle passing hands have often been used to tell an episodic story. It takes a credible script and expert direction to make the story a success or else it descends into paperback-novel

*Lin McAdam (James Stewart) is the rightful owner of a Winchester '73 that affects the lives of everyone who possess it.* 1950, UNIVERSAL PICTURES COMPANY, INC.

commonalities. *Winchester '73* works because it has several things going for it. Lin McAdam is a likeable lead because he is a decent man with a moral mission. He is brave without being foolhardy and kind without being weak. He earns respect and has no problem showing it. His sidekick is a likeable fellow, too. He is an experienced frontier man and reflects all of the admirable qualities of the leading man.

The story is multi-textured because the only thing in common with the characters is the rifle. They all have different lives that depend on survival on the prairie. The Indian chief wants to live free on the home of his people. He believes that the white man is a devil who is stealing what does not belong to him. He is inspired by Chief Crazy Horse and will do what he can to acquire the repeating rifles.

The gun merchant is a low-down cuss because he will sell his guns to anyone who has the money. He does not care that the Indians are fired up at Chief Crazy Horse's success at Little Big Horn. He does what he has to do to survive.

*High Spade Frankie Wilson (Millard Mitchell) is McAdam's sensible weather-beaten sidekick.* 1950, UNIVERSAL PICTURES COMPANY, INC.

The young couple acquires the gun through default, but it costs the young man his life when he tangles with Waco Johnny Dean. He is a crazed outlaw who lives to kill and takes what he wants without asking. He is part of a plan to rob a bank and had acquired the rifle through force.

The man he hooks up with is Dutch, who immediately reclaims his gun. It does not matter for either man because they will be killed in the course of the robbery. The man who shoots both of them is Lin McAdam. He gets to show his shooting prowess, not only in town with Waco Johnny Dean, but on a mountaintop when he has a unique gun battle with his brother. Fate is the underlying theme of the movie and it proves that everyone engineers their own death. It is how a man dies that determines his worth. James Stewart is excellent as the trail beaten cowpoke staking his evil brother. Stephen McNally plays his part well as the oily, snake-like villain. Charles Drake is jelly as a coward who dies while wearing an apron. Shelly Winters is sexy and touching as the saloon girl whose life changes for the better because of her hair-raising ordeals. Jay C. Flippen is a wizened Cavalry sergeant who can add one more gunfight with the Indians to his legacy and Tony Curtis is one of his young charges.

Dan Duryea sinks his teeth into Waco Johnny Dean. He is boldfaced, boisterous, and bad to the bone. He loves shootouts because they make

*Waco Johnny Dean (Dan Duryea) is a psycho with a hair-trigger temper.* 1950, UNIVERSAL PICTURES COMPANY, INC.

him feel alive. There is no hesitation in killing a man, because that's what he does best. As is the case with prairie gunman, there is always one more cowpoke that is faster on the draw. He is the righteous lead who cuts the bad man down to size in public. The last laugh is on Waco Johnny Dean because he ran out of laughs of his own.

Seven years later, Whitey Harbin becomes Waco Johnny Dean's kin-

*Lola Manners (Shelley Winters) is a vanquished dance hall queen who is given protection against the prairie elements by Lin McAdam (James Stewart). 1950,* UNIVERSAL PICTURES COMPANY, INC.

dred spirit when he gets his chance to have a showdown with James Stewart. He also has the added thrill of a gunfight with Audie Murphy. Harbin wins one and loses the other.

In *Night Passage*, a single bloodline with mixed alliances provides the conflict for Grant McLaine (James Stewart), a soft spoken accordion man with the aim of a hawk. He has been hired by the railroad bosses to safeguard a payroll shipment from Whitey Harbin's gang. The robbers have been targeting the railroad as of late and the lack of funds is causing unrest among the rail splitters.

The Utica Kid (Audie Murphy) rides with the Harbin Gang, making things difficult for McClaine because the gun man is his kid brother. The disgraced railroad man was fired for allegedly colluding with The Utica Kid on a previous robbery. The railroad is desperate and needs McLaine's services once more when Harbin pulls three successful robberies of payload runs.

*Night Passage* is a lyrical Western because it shows the West at a time when it was about to be transformed into an urban empire. The movie shows the way the railroads changed how business was conducted and how the mining towns were taken over by the new conglomerates, namely the banking system.

However, the film's final confrontation takes place in an empty mining camp and it's an old-fashioned showdown between good and evil. It is a unique place to have the final confrontation and provides for an exciting finale. The sprawling canyon and the empty coal chutes dwarf the men shooting it out with each other. There is death and redemption, but not without losses. Reputations are restored and new alliances are

*James Stewart and Audie Murphy plays brothers on opposite sides of the law in* Night Passage. 1957, UNIVERSAL PICTURES COMPANY, INC.

made, all signed with outlaw blood and sealed with the sweet music of an accordion that went up in smoke.

*Night Passage* is entertaining and awesome in its portrayal of the great outdoors. The empty mining camps are like wounded giant canyons and the fertile prairie countryside are the new points of interest staked out by the new invaders. Its ledger sheet and bank balances dictate the law of the new West, and the old frontier vets are now hired guns and ranchers.

James Stewart is fantastic as the lanky accordion man with the lightning draw from the hip. Audie Murphy is charming and upright as the Utica Kid, a man caught in the middle of alliance and allegiance. Dan Duryea is slovenly and brazen as Whitey Harbin. He has a hair-trigger temper and it works against him in the final showdown. Dianne Foster is energetic as the woman who loves the Utica Kid. She is as tough as the merchants she sells her boxed lunches to, and she rides across hostile territory to see the Kid.

Elaine Stewart is the ice block that makes men sweat, whether it is in a sumptuous railroad car or a grimy bandit hangout in an abandoned mining camp. She plays the odds with her high-minded temperament

*Grant McLaine (James Stewart) is a lanky accordion man whose music livens a mining camp that has not been paid in weeks.* 1957, UNIVERSAL PICTURES COMPANY, INC.

and almost loses more than her cool in the final match between hero and villain.

Jay C. Flippen is railroad power, a fading field man who was kicked upstairs and fears that he is losing his grip on power. This is his last chance to show that he can supervise a successful payload run. Hugh Beaumont is an aggressive assistant to Flippen, a sidekick who is not above seeing things the way he thinks they should turn out. He has visions of being top man because he thinks that Flippen is soft and Stewart villainous. Herbert Anderson is a traitorous underling. His duplicity comes as a surprise and he pays dearly for being untrustworthy. Brandon De Wilde is a young boy caught up in the bandit life. He is mentored by Murphy, but rescued by Stewart. Jack Elam is one of the outlaws whose draw can't match his mouth when he challenges Stewart to a face off.

*Grant McLaine (James Stewart) cautions Charlotte Drew (Diane Foster) about pursuing her love for the Utica Kid.* 1957, UNIVERSAL PICTURES COMPANY, INC.

*Whitey Harbin (Dan Duryea) serenades Verna Kimbal (Elaine Stewart) while The Utica Kid (Audie Murphy) harmonizes.* 1957, UNIVERSAL PICTURES COMPANY, INC.

*McCarty (Dan Duryea) in a reflective mood in* Silver Lode. 1954, RKO
PICTURES, INC.

# The Road to City Hall

The next step in the evolution of the gunslinger is the shooter with a grand plan. Besides a being a quick draw, this takes intelligence. Few prairie gunmen can think beyond the showdown or make it to the cat-bird seat.

Beauvais was a smooth sharpie who tried and failed to rise above his nature and become a player in *River Lady*. Years later, Ned McCarty is a gunslinger with a grand plan in *Silver Lode*. Shanessy also has a plan — and the catbird seat! — in *Rails Into Laramie*. McCarty and Shanessy may be the same person on different rungs of the ladder, but they still wind up falling off the same way as Beauvais.

In *Silver Lode*, McCarty tries to pull the wool over a town's eyes through deception and this backfires because he does not have a real backup plan. His only backup is two gunmen, and their extra firepower proves to be useless. Shanessy is a gunman who finally makes it to the catbird seat in *Rails into Laramie*. He also wants a cut of the new railroad system besides pieces of the town he lives in. Shanessy has the same razzle-dazzle that McCarty has, but he has boosted it up a couple of notches. He, too, has two gunmen at his beck and call, plus the wife of his former best buddy.

The happiest day in a man's life is his wedding day. Imagine having it turned into a funeral march seconds before the nuptials start. In *Silver Lode*, this is Hank Ballard's (John Payne) dilemma when he becomes the victim of a phony Federal Marshal's clever plan to have him arrested and extradited for a crime he did not commit.

In the course of this fateful day, Ballard sees all of his friends and would-be in-laws turn against him and he has to outgun a whole town turned insane by mob justice. It takes the love of two women: his former flame and his would-be bride, to save him.

Hank Ballard has his world turned topsy-turvy when McCarty (Dan Duryea) rides into town accompanied by his gunmen. He is a marshal with a warrant for the arrest of Payne, who is accused of shooting a man in the back and absconding with $20,000.

Duryea interrupts the wedding ceremony when he arrives with his men, setting off a wave of indignation. Most of the townsfolk cannot believe that such a popular and law-abiding citizen could be guilty of murder. There is a small group of dissenters who have blind faith in the federal agent and have their doubts about Ballard's integrity. Before the movie is finished, the whole town tries to hunt him down to kill him.

The mass lunacy is caused by a series of circumstantial evidence that builds until everyone is armed and taking aim at Ballard. This is because McCarty is a masterful instigator. He knows how to play the townsfolk and does a masterful job in subverting their opinion by rallying their support.

First there is the marshal's arrest warrant, something that the local judge validates when it is brought before him for authentication. The second is the sheriff's murder and Ballard holding the smoking gun for all to see. The third is Ballard's mad attempt to bolt for his life and the last is his brazen attempt to engage his former friends, family, and colleagues in armed shootouts.

*Silver Lode* has textured layers that have logical buildups to the final confrontation in the bell tower of a church. It ends with the marshal being shot through the heart when his bullet ricochets off the bell. Profuse apologies from his hunters are rebuffed by Ballard, who reminds everyone that they spent the whole afternoon trying to kill him.

*Poster for* Silver Lode. 1954, RKO PICTURES, INC.

John Payne should be given a lot of credit for successfully portraying this type of hero. He is a swashbuckler in reverse, an anti-hero who is fighting his pursuers by trying to elude them. The life he is trying to save is his own and that is the chivalry of self-preservation.

Payne successfully shows the transformation of a respected town figure into wily prey using his primitive wits to survive. He shows the gradual breakdown of the civilized man into a cornered animal. It is the saving grace of the church that restores the humanity to the animal, not only the one that was hunted, but the ones below who conducted the hunt.

*McCarty (Dan Duryea), flanked by Mitch (John Hudson) and Kane (Alan Hale, Jr.), warns Hank Ballard (John Payne) about the perils of resisting arrest.*
1954, RKO PICTURES, INC.

Lizabeth Scott is the faithful bride-to-be whose conviction is shaken only when she sees her man holding two six guns with the dead sheriff lying at his feet after the townsmen break down the barn door. They refuse to believe that the marshal killed the sheriff. It is at this juncture that the crowd turns on Ballard and he becomes a hunted man, especially after he uses the murder weapon to make a quick getaway.

Dan Duryea is ambivalent as the lawman trying to bring in his man. He has hatched the perfect scheme, but the only drawback is the mark who is an innocent man with a strong moral character.

Ned McCarty hides behind this veneer in *Silver Lode*. His character arrives in a cloud of prairie dust, a lawman appearing out of nowhere. He has two deputies to enforce his flowery speeches about justice, and one can believe that he might be breaking the commandment about telling the truth. He also has the strangest timing of any lawman trying to bring in a fugitive.

Duryea gains the town's support only after the sheriff is killed and it appears that Ballard shot him. He has their support until the end, when a wire from San Francisco exposes the marshal as a murderer and a rustler. This becomes apparent after one of his henchmen tells Ballard that Duryea killed the man who forged the arrest papers. It is also oblivious after Ballard tries to barter his life for his property.

Dolores Moran is Dooly, the bitter saloon girl who harbors a grudge against Ballard because he dumped her for the richest girl in town. Her anger isn't strong enough to make her turn her back on her ex-lover. She is the one who forces the telegrapher to forge the first letter that states what the real telegraph corroborates when it finally gets through.

Emile Meyer is the sheriff who believes in Ballard's innocence, but has to obey the warrant. Before he dies, he points to Ballard with his eyes bulging and gasps for air, making the townsfolk believe that he was identifying his killer. They can't imagine that he was trying to declare Ballard's innocence.

Morris Ankrum is the supportive future father-in-law who turns into a vicious hunter after he sees the sheriff die in front of him. His apology is rebuffed by Ballard when he climbs down from the bell tower.

In *Rails into Laramie*, Duryea gets to play the gunman who makes it all the way up to being town boss. This time around he does not have to deal with a church bell but with railroad steel, instead. A certain somebody is still a headache. What makes this different is that somebody is a friend from the past who is currently working for the U.S. Cavalry. The movie is a take on how railroad justice trumps town-boss politics in the new West. Duryea's town boss still comes out on the short end of things.

*Rails into Laramie* is a short, quick-paced Western that illustrates the importance of the railroads in building the post-Civil War United States. The railroads were not only a way of linking remote regions but in building commerce, the backbone of the nation. That's why the federal government is perturbed when there's trouble in laying rails down in Laramie.

The President orders a general to send in his top sergeant to clear up the trouble. The trouble is that Sgt. Harder (John Payne) is reluctant to go because efficiency and mobility are not his strong suits unless he's motivated. He likes to drink, fight, and frolic like a private, but orders are orders and the brig is still the brig. That much is a sobering thought and that is his motivation. Another incentive is receiving a captain's commission after spending several years traveling up and down the non-commission chain of command because of busts and infractions.

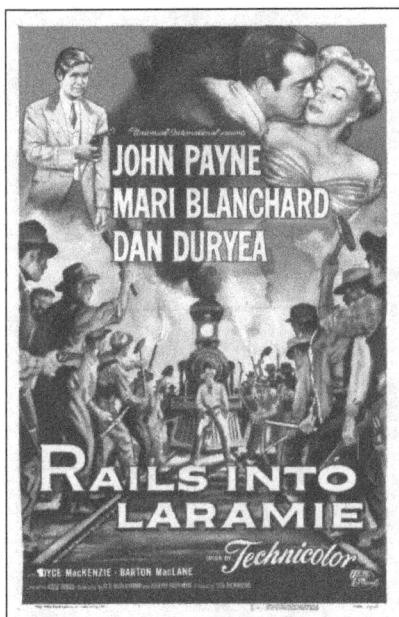

*Poster for* Rails Into Laramie. 1953,
UNIVERSAL PICTURES COMPANY, INC.

Sgt. Harder arrives in Laramie and finds that an unofficial work strike has halted the progress on laying the rails. There is no particular reason why the men won't work, but pretty soon it becomes apparent that Jim Shanessy (Dan Duryea), the unofficial town boss, is behind the work stoppage. Harder and Shanessy are old war buddies and this tickles the town boss pink because he thinks that his old buddy will throw in with him. It soon becomes obvious that their attitudes and philosophy are just as divergent as the paths their lives have taken.

Shanessy has married Helen (Joyce MacKenzie), Harding's ex-sweetheart ,but there are no hard feelings. She is just window dressing for Shanessy's real hanky-panky, and that's keeping the rails out of Laramie. Helen uses her old charm to sway her former lover from pressing her husband. Her wiles soon wear thin and are not enough to prevent Harder from turning the heat up on Shanessy.

Lou (Mari Blanchard), the dance hall queen, is Shanessy's business partner. They rule the town and keep themselves free of law and order because they foot the bill for it. Everything changes with the arrival of Sgt. Harder. Lou is one of the dominoes that falls in the wake of the sergeant's two-fisted approach to solving the government's problem. She is impressed with his integrity, and how he can't be bought, intimidated with force, or seduced through temptation.

Shanessy is aided by two ornery henchman, Con Winton (Myron Healey), a smooth talking dandy and Ace (Lee Van Cleef), a sadistic,

trigger-happy gunslinger. They assist the boys in subverting the rail splitters who have been fired by the new marshal in town. They plot against
the government agent by wreaking havoc. They dynamite mountains
to block rail travel in and out of Laramie, cut the telegraph lines to
break down communication, and destroy the work camp to prevent new
laborers from moving in. The insurrection comes to a head when Ace

*Sgt. Harder (unseen) sets his sights on gunslinger Ace Winton (Lee Van Cleef)*
*while Jim Shanessy (Dan Duryea) enjoys a drink.* 1953, UNIVERSAL PICTURES
COMPANY, INC.

murders the marshal (James Griffith) as he rides to Colorado to deliver
a message to the General.

The murder causes Lou to throw in with Harder and Shanessy is
arrested. The townspeople are cynical because arrests and trials have meant
nothing in the past because of rigged juries. Lou's brainstorm is using
the newly framed suffragette laws to empanel an all-female jury, which
enrages the men folk.

Shanessy is tried, convicted, sentenced, and imprisoned, mainly due
to Lou's vote on the jury. Helen helps Shanessy escape by smuggling a
gun into the jail when she has a last meeting with her husband. Shanessy
escapes, exacts his revenge on his former partner, and confronts what

he tried to avoid through the whole movie: a serious showdown with his former buddy.

He makes a break for it by hijacking the railroad and high tailing it out of town. What good can that do when he is not the hero of the movie? Harder rides his horse and catches up with the train in an old-fashioned Western style. He and Shanessy engage in a fist fight as a train approaches from the other direction.

*Sgt. Harder (John Payne) and Lou (Mari Blanchard) seal a deal with a kiss.* 1953, UNIVERSAL PICTURES COMPANY, INC.

Harder emerges victorious, not only because he subdues Shanessy and resumes the building of the railroad; he also becomes betrothed to the wounded Lou, promising to return to Laramie when his hitch in the Army is up.

*Rails into Laramie* is an enjoyable programmer. It is entertaining because everyone, from the players to the technical crew, performs their jobs well. It is an assembly-line film, but one that is done properly and that is why it is enjoyable. Jess Hibbs was a prolific director at Universal-International and was adept at directing in various styles, including costume dramas, film *noirs* and Westerns.

John Payne was a strong leading man, but he never achieved the popularity that he deserved. He handled himself well and created sympathetic roles out of flawed characters. Payne's Sergeant Harder is a good-time Charley with a strict code of honor. He may be a bar scrapper, but he is not corrupt.

Dan Duryea is slick as ever as Shanessy. He is smooth-talking, well-dressed, and oily in his machinations. Shanessy is married to Harder's ex-paramour and is partners with his future lover.

Mari Blanchard is a dance hall queen who plays the godmother to Duryea's godfather. Payne splits them apart and town politics changes when she throws her lot in with Payne. Blanchard had a sultry voice that matched her come-hither look. She pretends to be intimidated by the film's villain, but she pulls her own weight when push comes to shove.

Joyce Mackenzie is the opposite as the good-girl gone bad through association. She is like the crime boss's moll who ignores the source of her wealth. Her corruption is laid bare when she smuggles the gun to her husband in prison.

Myron Healey and Lee Van Cleef play their usual, shifty, knuckle-busting sidekicks. Harry Shannon, Ralph Dunke, and Barton MacLane are three power brokers who are flustered by the new marshal's methods. James Griffith plays a marshal who is a heroic wimp who finds courage and is shot dead because of it. Charles Horvath has a colorful part as Pike Murphy, the blustery railroad foreman and Shanessy stooge.

*A classic western showdown between the villain (Dan Duryea) and the hero (John Payne).* 1953, UNIVERSAL PICTURES COMPANY, INC.

# Stock In Trade

Dan Duryea had the Western bad man patented before long. That does not mean that he was strictly repetitive, because he also added a twist or a turn to each character to make him new and unlike any of his forebears. That is true from when he started to play a series of prairie mad men to many of the heroes-in-residence on Hollywood's best Western back lots.

A distance of eight years presents two different hired guns who become Audie Murphy's strange benefactors. In *Ride Clear of Diablo*, Whitey Kincaide still has the hair-trigger temper and maniacal laugh, but has now developed a sardonic sense of humor. Eight years later in *Six Black Horses*, Frank Jesse is a philosophical gunman. In both cases, he assists Audie Murphy in his mission and pays dearly two times around.

*Ride Clear of Diablo* stars Audie Murphy as Clay O'Mara, a Denver railroad surveyor who returns to town to avenge the murders of his father and brother by cattle rustlers. This is not an unusual theme for a Western, but it is certain plot oddities that make this movie unique. The viewer is aware from the get-go that the sheriff and his father's lawyer are the culprits. They are also the men who offer guidance to Clay O'Mara while actually trying to set him up for the kill.

It is their plotting against O'Mara that creates the drama because their efforts are turned against them. O'Mara convinces the sheriff to deputize him so he can investigate the murders. Meredith tells the sheriff in private that a way to throw O'Mara off their track is to send him on a bounty hunt for a notorious killer. They tell O'Mara that he was involved in the murders and can give him additional information.

It is a mistake to hire O'Mara to track down Whitey Kincaide, an outlaw wanted for murder. What they didn't bargain for is that the gun-slinger would bond with O'Mara and help him with his mission. That is what makes the movie unique: the strange detours, alliances, and frictions.

O'Mara confounds his benefactors by apprehending Kincaide and bringing him back alive. Along the way, the reluctant lawman and amoral gunman bond in a strange and uneasy alliance. This happens because Duryea's mercurial mad man is the Joker without makeup.

Whitey Kincaide is constantly laughing, snarling, scheming, and causing mayhem. He actually becomes the sidekick of the lawman who was ordered to bring him in dead or alive. They complement each other. Whitey Kincaide is won over by Murphy's honesty, but still does not grant him a free pass.

O'Mara still plays by Kincaide's rules. This is what earns him the

*Title card for* Ride Clear of Diablo. 1954, UNIVERSAL PICTURES COMPANY, INC.

criminal's respect. Kincaide also hates the crooked town officials. He is really setting them up. It is a case of the sober and the straight arrow contrasted with the amoral and impulsive.

Kincaide is impish in the way he strings O'Mara along and then leaves him alone to fend off a jam. This haphazard shooting gallery is how they wind up in a final shootout that starts in town and ends up in the mines. It's the sheriff and the lawyer versus the lawman and the gunslinger.

Kincaide's genius is to control the rivalries and direct them to a final standoff. Unfortunately, it is a warped Mexican standoff and the last laugh again is on him. Nevertheless, the crooked sheriff and lawyer are brought down and O'Mara is victorious.

Clay O'Mara is the only one who gets to go home as the winner. He has got it all, including Laurie Kenyon (Susan Cabot), the sheriff's niece.

*Clay O'Mara (Audie Murphy) falls in love with Laurie Kenyon(Susan Cabot), the niece of a murderous sheriff.* 1954, UNIVERSAL PICTURES COMPANY, INC.

*Whitey Kincaide (Dan Duryea) warns Kate (Abbe Lane), the dance hall queen, about giving away his whereabouts.* 1954, UNIVERSAL PICTURES COMPANY, INC.

She is an odd love interest for O'Mara. There is a sardonic in the way she moves and speaks. She plays the sheriff's niece and fiancée of the lawyer.

Laurie is clueless to the dirty deeds that the dirty dogs in her life have been committing. Her only emotional moment is falling in love with O'Mara from the get-go. Laurie falls for O'Mara like a ton of bricks, but is calm and reserved when told of the circumstances of her uncle's and fiancée's deaths.

*Whitey Kincaide (Dan Duryea) is an ornery cuss who can roll a cigarette while staring Death in the eyes.* 1954, UNIVERSAL PICTURES COMPANY, INC.

Susan Cabot plays her role with a somnolent nonchalance. She not only fails to be too upset upon learning about her uncle's — the sheriff-duplicity but remains unperturbed when he is killed in the last shootout. Still, Susan Cabot on any level is still mystical and she lends a dark, almost somber tone to her scenes.

Duryea gives Whitey Kincaide some admirable traits, but only so in respect to the rules of the outlaw. He still likes to pit parties against each other in life and death situations. Kincaide also alters the odds by aiding Clay O'Mara.

By doing so, he cancelled out the policies of the assured lawyer, the nervous and guilt-ridden sheriff, and Jack Elam and Russell Johnson as vicious gunmen. Abbe Lane plays a sultry saloon singer who steams things up with a song and some attitude.

In *Six Black Horses*, Ben Lane (Audie Murphy) and Frank Jesse (Dan Duryea) trade away pieces of their destinies when they cross paths on a fateful day in the desert. Jesse prevents a band of mustangers from lynching Lane, whom they mistake for a horse thief. They ride into town and are later offered a dangerous job that

*Poster for* Six Black Horses, *a retro oater with a gold standard.* 1962, UNIVERSAL PICTURES COMPANY, INC.

will be a way for them to abandon their dreadful pasts and start fresh lives…if they survive the mission.

Ben Lane can stop being a cow-poking drifter when he buys a spread to call his own. Frank Jesse can stop killing for a living when he hangs up his gun belt and finds a place to spread out with a woman to keep him warm. All they have to do is to escort Kelly (Joan O'Brien), a wealthy enigmatic woman, across Indian Territory to reunite her with her husband.

Kelly is bitter and angry, which has made her a reckless benefactor. The deal she makes with Lane and Jesse is fraught with danger and there is no guarantee that it won't be a suicide pact with three scalps hanging on a Coyotero lance.

Kelly may have persuaded the men to escort her to DelCobray so she could be reunited with her husband, but it is really a ruse to kill Jesse. She holds him responsible for murdering her greenhorn husband in a gunfight. She wants Frank Jesse to be killed on the desert trek.

Along the way they are stalked by hostile Indians and confronted by a gang of ornery scalp-hunting pale faces. There is a gun fight at a mission

*Ben Lane (Audie Murphy) and Frank Jesse (Dan Duryea) are two diverse personalities whose destinies cross paths in* Six Black Horses. 1962, UNIVERSAL PICTURES COMPANY, INC.

and face-to-face encounters with angry Coyoteros. The men turn on each other when the stakes change because of Kelly's hidden intentions.

The real terms of Kelly's deal become irrelevant because killing Frank Jesse is not an option. Lane knows that he and Jesse have been deceived, but it does not matter to him because he has found someone to share his life with. Ben and Frank are no longer partners when Ben tries to call

*Ben Lane (Audie Murphy) and his best friend share a meal while Frank Jesse (Dan Duryea) wishes he can share Charlita's dance moves.* 1962, UNIVERSAL PICTURES COMPANY, INC.

the deal off. He wants to find a safe passage for Kelly, but Jesse is intent on escorting her to the original destination and collecting his fee. This leads to a final showdown and a new beginning for Ben Lane and Kelly.

Audie Murphy re-channels his man-of-few-words cowpoke for Ben Lane. He tames a wild buck, saves a dog from a crooked fight, calls an Indian's bluff, and is quick on the draw when his life depends on it. It is Lane who becomes unhinged when he falls in love with Kelly.

Joan O'Brien is the stunning if inscrutable beauty that has a tantalizing mission for them. Frank Jesse deflates her bravado when he shows her that they are two of a kind. She slept with men for money during bleak times and he killed for money as a matter of course. He didn't remember the faces of the men he killed and he asks Kelly if she could remember the faces of the men she slept with.

Her silence is a negative and Jesse tells her that is the reason that she is no better than him because "that's how we made our way." Kelly is manipulative and self-hating in the end. It takes a sincere cowpoke to melt her heart and the betrayal of his friend to turn it into love.

Dan Duryea's eloquent portrayal of an aging gunslinger at the end of his line prevents the movie from being a routine Western. Duryea had the Western heavy down pat by now, but he still found a way to create a unique character with nuances that created a gray area out of stark good and evil.

In *Six Black Horses*, Frank Jesse is a seasoned gunslinger, one who lives by collecting silver for shootings that he deals with in escapes into whiskey terrain. Frank Jesse is a blend of noble and venal traits. He has an iron-clad rule to never do an honest day's work unless it is absolutely necessary. Jesse became a hired killer by choice, not chance. It was an easy way to earn money, something that is not as clean-cut as it seems because of his conscience. He drinks away much of his pay trying to forget the men he has killed. Still, he swears by the profession as evidenced when he tries to persuade Ben Lane to earn a living by the gun.

Jesse is a hired gun with a sense of righteousness that does him no good in the end. Jesse saves the life that will take his and his road to riches is mined by a golden-haired assassin whom he calls Ma'am. He hedges his bets on mortality and delivers an elegant treatise on the art of dying. It includes how a man ought to have a proper funeral procession with six black horses drawing a black, spangled hearse. It is something that he gets in the long run and it is a powerful epitaph to his unique character.

Harry Keller's direction is adequate and Burt Kennedy has written a script full of great lines, even if he has pilfered his script for *Ride Lonesome*. George Wallace (Commander Cody) is the ill-fated leader of a pack of scalp hunters, and Charlita still has her fire in a small role as a cantina dancer.

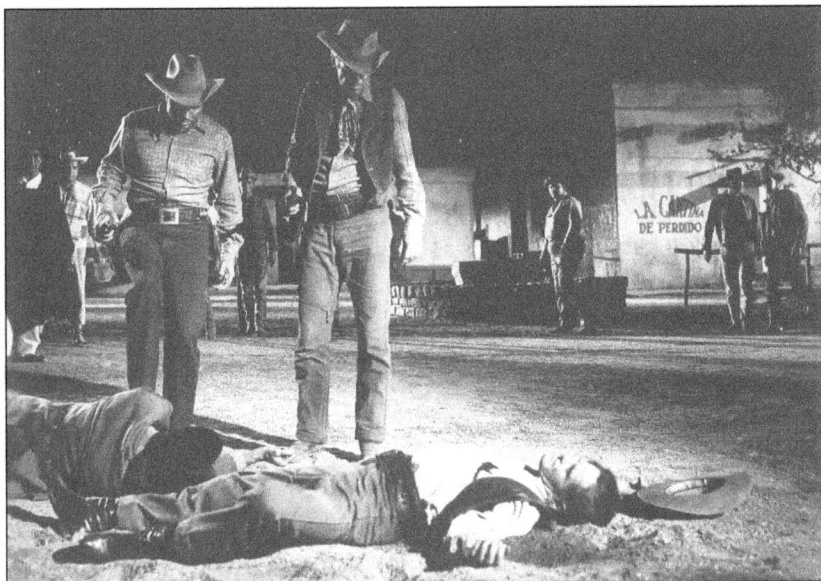

*Ben Lane (Audie Murphy) and Frank Jesse (Dan Duryea) examine the corpses of the strangers who tried to ambush them after they rode into town.* 1962, UNIVERSAL PICTURES COMPANY, INC.

*Frank Jesse (Dan Duryea) takes great amusement in telling Kelly (Joan O'Brien) that they are two of a kind although Ben Lane (Audie Murphy) disagrees.* 1962, UNIVERSAL PICTURES COMPANY, INC.

*Jason (Dan Duryea) is a cynical saddle tramp who hires out his gun to hunt down* Taggart. 1964, UNIVERSAL PICTURES COMPANY, INC.

# The 60s
# Retro Cowboy Star

Universal Pictures was still making old time Westerns during the early 60s, a time when television was gaining popularity over a medium whose dwindling popularity saw the last of the 40s movie emporiums close or become sub-divided in a phase that preceded the creation of the multiplex theaters.

In the 60s, at a time when even the television Westerns had supplanted big screen showdowns were riding into the sunset, Universal pushed a new movie cowboy hero and he was played by Tony Young. Young was the star of *Gunslinger*, a television Western, when he was pegged to star in big screen Westerns for Universal. He had a firm speaking voice with precise diction and had good posture, bringing a soap opera actor's technique to the great outdoors.

Tony Young made a convincing, righteous lawman because he was made of wood and could outdraw any gun. Young starred in two Westerns for Universal, *He Rides Tall* and *Taggart*. Dan Duryea played his nemesis in both movies. Bart Thorne and Jason are twin villains, split visions of Frank Jesse, the philosophical villain in *Six Black Horses*, the first film in Duryea's twilight gunman phase.

*He Rides Tall* is an apt title for a movie about a man who has to create order out of chaos and put his life on the line during a crisis that threatens the hopeful turn his life has taken. Morg Rocklin (Tony Young) is a marshal who will be turning in his badge and gun to get married to Ellie (Madlyn Rhue), his sweetheart. What should be his last day on the job turns into a nightmare when he winds up at odds with Josh McCloud (R.G. Armstrong), a powerful cattle baron and the man who raised him. The Marshal shot the cattle baron's son in self-defense in a saloon showdown. In doing so, the marshal also rekindles an old feud with Bart Thorne (Dan Duryea), McCloud's foreman, a man he once sent to prison.

Thorn is an arrogant opportunist. He doesn't care if people are aware that his smile is phony or that he grates on their nerves. His laughter is mocking and his speech is labored. He considers obnoxiousness to be a virtue and thinks that he is doing people a favor by paying attention to them. It is all a prelude to ruining his mark.

He talks a drunken cattle baron into ordering his doctor to perform

*Morg Rocklin (Tony Young) assures his wife Ellie (Madlyn Rhue) that nothing will go wrong on his last day as sheriff in* He Rides Tall. 1963, UNIVERSAL PICTURES COMPANY, INC.

surgery on the hero's gun hand, then rustles the baron's cattle, barters the baron's wife when an Indian brave declares that it is either his life or hers, and instigates a cattle stampede that kills the baron who pursues him. His *coup de grace* is taking over a town in a midnight siege. It all ends with him crawling on his belly like a dying snake as the hero rides tall.

*He Rides Tall* plays like a cowboy *noir* because it is dark, harsh, and dreary. The obvious example is the final showdown in the sparsely-lit town. The dark shadows and razor thin highlights are hallmarks of the film genre, but there are also other elements that form a kinship. The puritanical righteousness of the hero and the amoral sociopathic behavior of the villain are severe contradictions. Cruel deaths and ironic plot twists are the other touches that make this film a strange, deranged crime drama.

Tony Young is the stoical hard boiled lawman ready to turn his badge in for love. A crisis interferes with his plans and he has to deal with a life-and-death situation in a short amount of time. Young is a wax-figure cowboy who can withstand the heat of a high-noon showdown. He gets

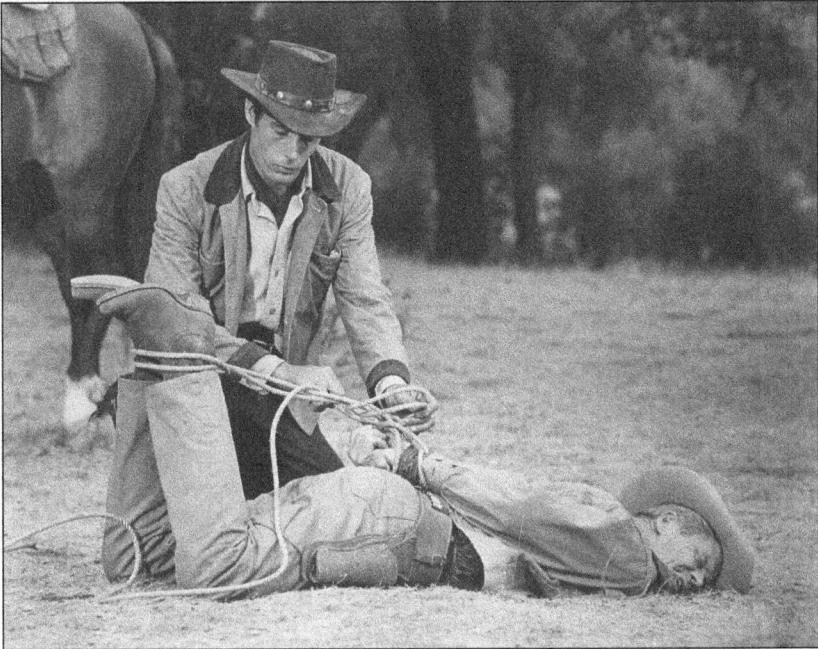

*The only way for Morg Rocklin (Tony Young) to trust nemesis Bart Thorne (Dan Duryea) is to hog tie him.* 1963, UNIVERSAL PICTURES COMPANY, INC.

the job done during a time when movie Westerns hardly caused a ripple.

Madlyn Rhue was a distinguished television and movie veteran who gave many fine performances in Warner Bros. shows and many other comedies and dramas. She was married to Tony Young when they made the movie.

She delivers a solid performance as the saloon owner and bride-to-be. She, too, is tough and made to last, as evidenced in the scene when Thorne takes over the town and temporarily has the upper hand in her business.

Duryea plays Thorn as an opportunist who only thinks of himself. His charm is a thin veneer for a strong ego. He is really flattering himself when he compliments others. He looks people in the eye, says something charming, and cancels it out with a mocking laugh. He intimidates the weak and grovels before anyone stronger than himself. In the movie, only two people dominate Thorn: Morg Rocklin, the hero, and the Indian who demands — and gets! — his purloined woman.

Jo Morrow is feisty, torrid, and restless. She can plan a get-rich scheme on paper, but does not have the wits to make it all happen. She becomes someone else's trophy in a hair-raising scene.

*Morg Rocklin (Tony Young) recuperates from an operation under the watchful eye of Dr. Sam (Joel Fluellen) as Bart Thorne (Dan Duryea) examines the gun hand rendered useless by a scalpel.* 1963, UNIVERSAL PICTURES COMPANY, INC.

R.G. Armstrong gives a robust performance as a hard-edged cattle baron confined to a wheelchair. He is the backbone of the movie and his unraveling provides a storyline for the other characters to make their claims. Duryea and Morrow take him for all that he is worth. Rocklin gives him the respect due to a foster father and Dr. Sam keeps his conscience straight and that is a blessing to the doctor.

The surprise performance of the movie is Joel Fluellen's portrayal of Dr. Sam. He comes from a long line of faith healers. His grandfather was a witch doctor in the Congo, his father was a shaman on the plantation, and he was an assistant surgeon during the Civil War. The doctor is the voice of reason and supplies a conscience for the movie.

*Taggart* is a shop-worn Western with some merit, namely a couple of nice bits by old vets such as Dan Duryea, Dick Foran, Emile Meyer, and Bob Steele in a small part. Tony Young is still deadpan, monotone, and stone-faced as the hero, but this time, he's in color. Jean Hale gives a strong performance of a pioneer woman, the daughter of a displaced rancher acted by Dick Foran. His scheming wife is played by Elsa Cardenas, a

*Bart Thorne (Dan Duryea) romances Kate McCloud (Jo Morrow), a rancher's wife, before he sells her out to an Indian brave.* 1963, UNIVERSAL PICTURES COMPANY, INC.

Latina vamp from old-school central casting. She uses her torrid charms to get what does not belong to her, only to be destroyed by when her warped desires exact a deadly price.

The movie's theme is the quest for power and the people who work for it through sanctimony and sweat versus those who expand their bases through violence and intimidation. It is a tale of carving out a niche in a new country where the rules had more meaning than what was stated in books and declared in courts.

*Taggart* begins with a standoff between settlers and a land baron because of the difference between court decree and the power of coercion. Ben Blazer (Emile Meyer) is a grumbling town boss who does not take kindly to squatters. Neither does his son, a hot head who raids a settlement camp with his father and kills the couple and their handy man, leaving the son with a head wound and a motive for revenge. Blazer is critically wounded and escorted back to town.

The next scene is one of the highlights of the movie, because it is well done and sets up the premise for story of the hunt. It depicts the hero and villain in their defining moments, one achieving one-on-one justice for his parents' murders and the other exacting blood money from a dying man whose dreams of power will mean nothing before the day is over.

Ben Blazer lies dying while former silent screen comic Eddie Quillan ministers to him as a country doctor. The old man is comforted by his son when Taggart, the survivor of the raid, enters the room and challenges the young man to a duel. The kid is feeling his mettle, which becomes cold to the touch when he draws and loses.

*Tony Young plays* Taggart, *a young cowpoke out to avenge the murder of his parents.* 1964, UNIVERSAL PICTURES COMPANY, INC.

His violent death agitates Blazer, who almost passes out but holds on until the sheriff comes to perform his duty. The doctor attests to the fairness of the draw when asked by the law man for an account of the shootout. The sheriff escorts Taggart out and lets him free when he finds out his family name. The corrupt law man sympathizes with the young man when he realizes that his parents were the settlers who were brutally murdered at the behest of Ben Blazer.

Taggart's departure is followed by the arrival of Jason (Dan Duryea) and two other hired guns played by Tom Reese and David Carradine. They have come to hear the dying man's terms of employment. A petulant Jason is told by Blazer that it will take three men to take down Taggart. That is why he is offering the men five thousand dollars apiece to kill Taggart.

Jason, ever the pragmatic gunman, seeks a guarantee of payment because he gets the dying man to realize that the deed will be accomplished after he has succumbed to his wounds. Blazer assures him that his promise is validated by documents held by his lawyer. Jason's nagging hastens Blazer's death and he is off to collect his fee, trying to outwit the two other hired guns.

After Carradine makes an early exit and Reese is put to sleep in the desert, it will be Jason versus Taggart in a game where the winning stakes are five thousand dollars or the freedom to live a normal life. Taggart

*Stark (Dick Foran) and his daughter Miriam (Jean Hale) protect their gold mine from all stray wayfarers.* 1964, UNIVERSAL PICTURES COMPANY, INC.

becomes the mark of Jason, a hired killer who is also a philanderer, gold stealer, and leering panderer. They star in a chase that uses clichés, stock footage, and cardboard sets to make things exciting.

The usual things keep the action going: heroics, revenge, gold fever, duplicity, and Apache attacks. One thing that the movie relies on is stock footage of stunt men dressed as Indians careening off their horses after having been shot.

Like any chase movie, motives and momentum are gained by alternating between the scenes of hero and villain doing the things that help define their labels. In one scene, Taggart is kind and generous to a widow (Claudia Barrett) who reluctantly resorts to being a show girl in a woebegone cantina run by veteran character actor Peter Mamakos. In another scene, Jason shoots Tom Reese's gunman to put him out of his misery after he is wounded in a showdown with Taggart. He rides away leaving the dead man at peace with the desert sun.

The movie goes from one type of survival movie to another when Taggart stumbles upon a strange type of squatter, Stark (Dick Foran), a displaced rancher living in an abandoned mission with his young wife Consuelo (Elsa Cardenas), and Miriam (Jean Hale), his slightly younger daughter.

The secret to his eccentricity is his discovery of gold in a nearby cave. Stark has mined sacks of it and is guarding his turf until the Apache uprisings die down and he can make a safe getaway with his family and fortune. Stranger still is the arrival of Jason, who claims to be a bounty hunter in search of Taggart. This does not sit too well with Stark and his daughter and the gunman is viewed and treated with suspicion by Stark.

Jason's response is to make a cuckold out of over-the-hill tough guy Stark by treating him like an impotent sugar daddy who lives in an abandoned mission divided by his colluding, insatiable young wife, and strong-willed independent daughter.

Consuelo is the flame that will light Duryea's way through the desert, regardless of cattle stampedes or Indian uprisings. It is Consuelo and the gold that adds spice to this Western when she motivates Jason with promises of a promising cut of her fortune.

Elsa Cardenas plays the schemer two ways: as an over-the-hill beauty when filmed in bad lighting and breathtakingly beautiful in naturally lit sequences. Her voice goes from being strident and whiskey-coated to soothing and seductive. She is the movie's broad-stroked baddie because she is ready, willing, and able to collude with any man to double-cross her mature husband and rob him of his gold reserves.

It takes a bold and brazen nut to like Jason to accept an offer of riches with a getaway that will inevitably include an encounter with marauding Apache warriors. Such a conclusion means more to Consuelo than it does to Jason until he is indirectly undone by an Indian raid in the grand finale.

Jason has faced Indians many times by the end of the film. The first time is in a chance encounter between him and Taggart when they inad-

*Jason would not be a bona fide Duryea villain if he didn't romance someone's wife (Elsa Cardenas).* 1964, UNIVERSAL PICTURES COMPANY, INC.

vertently wind up aiding a pioneer couple in a mountain standoff with a war party. Jason also deserts an Army wagon train when he rides away with Consuelo's stolen gold and survives. His last stand with the gold is at an army fort where he is trapped because of an Indian raid. The end of the chase is a frantic shootout where a wounded Taggart shoots Jason to death. For all his bravado, the gunslinger throws up his arms and is done with everything as he hits the dust. No matter how hard he tried and how many people died because of it, Jason was still outmaneuvered by Taggart in the final showdown.

*Dan Trask (Dan Duryea) is the mayor of an underground south-of-the border town for desperadoes on the lam.* 1959, WALT DISNEY PRODUCTIONS

# Town Boss Requiem

Dan Trask and Bart McAdam are two town bosses on opposite sides of the law. Trask is the boss of an outlaw town south of the border and McAdam is a big shot in Dodge City. They both have to deal with Tom Tryon in two different ways. One does it at Disney in 1959 and the other plays it for Universal TV in a 1966 remake of one Duryea's best Westerns.

As Texas John Slaughter, Tom Tryon is cut from the Charlton Heston cloth of heroism. He is tall, broad-shouldered, and square-jawed, with few words to spare and a clear-cut sense of right and wrong. That is why he makes the perfect Texas Ranger.

His Ranger skills are admired by his cohorts, but not by his fiancé. She fears that the violent lifestyle will claim her husband-to-be. Slaughter believes in the ideals of law and order, knowing very well that blood may be required to make things work.

The conflict between Slaughter and his woman is one of the things that occupy the Ranger's time. Another growing point of his interest is to avenge the shooting death of his buddy during a bank robbery by the Bardo gang. Slaughter miraculously avoided being shot when a quick getaway was required by the gang.

The bulk of the movie deals with the Bardo Gang's reign of terror. They are run by a married couple, the twist being that the wife (Beverly Garland) is the brains of the outfit. That is the only unique point of the movie. Beverly Garland gives a good performance as Addy. Lyle Bettger hides behind his trademark pearly whites and the gang is the generic group of outlaws along for the excitement and money.

They rob banks that run in a pattern that will take them to the Mexican border. It is when a captured gang member spills the beans that the Texas Rangers realize that they are heading towards Sandoval, a safe haven for outlaws.

The outlaw town is run by Dan Trask, a debonair leader. The Texas Rangers will impersonate the Bardo Gang. Slaughter's fiancé will play Mrs. Bardo, much to the consternation of the Texas Ranger.

Trask entertains the false Mr. and Mrs. Bardo with a charm that nets him more than he bargained for. It costs him a duel at dawn and this coincides with the masqueraded Rangers taking over the town before destroying it with dynamite booby traps.

Trask becomes a memory as his army of outlaws is blown to kingdom by Ranger Slaughter and his wife, plus the Ranger recruits who posed

*Texas John Slaughter (Tom Tryon) confers with fellow Rangers on how to bring down the Bardo Gang.* 1954, 1959, WALT DISNEY PRODUCTIONS

as the Bardo Gang. It was a fast paycheck for Trask, who got to throw a fancy silver cup at the mariachi band in his hacienda after his come-on was rebuffed and he was challenged to a duel.

It is more than can be said for Trask in *Showdown at Sandoval*. He is the town boss who does not get to give a death speech when he is gunned down by the hero. He already gave his speech the night before when he tried to bewitch the hero's wife at dinner.

Dan Duryea plays Dan Trask, a debonair outlaw who runs Sandoval, a safe haven for outlaws south of the border. Trask, for all his charm and tall talk, is taken down by Texas John Slaughter in an old-fashioned gun duel. It happens at the end of the movie, which centers on a Texas Ranger's hunt for a murderous band of outlaws called The Bardo Gang.

Trask owns an outlaw town south of the border in *Texas John Slaughter: Showdown at Sandoval*. The town boss makes his appearance during the second half of this Disney outlaw tale. Beverly Garland and Lyle Bettger dominate the first half as the Bardo gang, vicious bank robbers. They are chased to Sandoval by the Texas Rangers. The outlaw town is run by the charming but reptilian Trask.

*Trask (Dan Duryea) romances Texas John's sweetheart Adeline Harris (Norma Moore), who is posing as an outlaw along with her fiancé.* 1959, WALT DISNEY PRODUCTIONS

*Winchester '73* was remade nearly two decades later as a television movie by Universal when it was owned by MCA. Dan Duryea had a supporting role as the father of the villain, a part that was not in the original. In fact, very few elements from the original were in the remake, including the insightful character studies and artful direction.

In the remake, Tom Tryon plays the Jimmy Stewart role and John Saxon is the villain originally played by Stephen McNally. In this movie, they are cousins. Duryea has a supporting part as the villain's father. He is the one who starts the drama when he holds a public shooting contest with one of the original Winchester '73s as the prize. It comes down to

blood kin, two cousins named McAdam. One is a sheriff and the other
has been released from prison after serving a six-year sentence for bank
robbery.

The unique rifle is the crossing point that tells the story of death on
the open plains. The rifle keeps changing hands because its uniqueness
causes a pattern of death that makes the action of the movie progress. The

*Lin McAdam (Tom Tryon), his uncle Bart (Dan Duryea) and cousin Dakin
(John Saxon) covet the cherished Winchester '73, the rifle that will change their
lives.* 1966, UNIVERSAL TELEVISION.

other motive is revenge for the murder of a loved one. It was all over the Winchester '73, which is how Saxon wrongfully gained possession of the rifle after he shot his uncle to wrest it from him. Paul Fix is the father of Lin. They have their ways of hunting down the killer. McAdam does it through the law, and Rawhide does it according to the bloodlust code.

Tom Tryon gives it his best shot as the sheriff. Tryon is a somewhat

*Uncle Bart (Dan Duryea) supervises a shooting contest that pits Lin McAdam (Tom Tryon) against his outlaw cousin Dakin (John Saxon).* 1966, UNIVERSAL TELEVISION.

ragged version of his earlier, rugged tough-guy stuff. He is still broad-shouldered and lanky in the Gary Copper sense of style, but he appears ragged around the edges with a somewhat desperate look in his eyes. His voice is squeaky, but he is still tough enough to make everything turn out in the long run.

John Saxon is bitter and tries to spit venom as the villain. He mainly scowls and grimaces. He has an attitude of his own making, but still likes to blame everyone for his misery. He is a formidable villain but is ultimately defeated by the anger that has clouded his thinking.

Dan Duryea gives a sensitive performance as the villain's father. He does what he can to gain the respect of his son, even if it means losing the respect of others. Bart McAdam, Dan Duryea's character, is the most complicated character, mainly because of his unwavering love for his wastrel son.

His blind devotion makes him a weak man, but he is more three-dimensional than the other characters with the exception of Meridan, a cynical croupier played by Barbara Luna. Her sour disposition makes her an earthy character with plenty of sex appeal. It is a shame that she is kicked out of town when she pulls a derringer on a boisterous gambler. Luckily for the viewer, she joins the action later and goes along for the ride.

John Dehner is dry and wily as a card sharp and gun runner. He acquires the Winchester '73 by beating a desperate Dakin McAdam at a couple of hands of table-stakes poker. He is brusque and erudite, but those qualities are not enough to stay alive in a gun deal turned rotten. John Drew Barrymore is sharp and straight to the point as the Preacher. He was a cellmate of McAdam's for three years and has filled up on Bible quotations. He is droll with his wit and calculating with his decisions. The Preacher is also a cadaverous undertaker who thrives on the commission of crimes.

Jack Lambert is borderline insane as Scots. He is a heavy drinker and handy with a dagger. He speaks with a thick Scottish brogue and can square off with the best of them. He is headstrong, but not tough enough to butt a wagon wheel. John Doucette plays a tavern owner who keeps wise guys in tow with his rifle. Doucette was always the frog-voiced bulwark who played a brick wall you didn't want to run into.

John Hoyt plays an Indian brave who mistakenly believes that owning the Winchester '73 will make him immortal. He plans to achieve great things with the repeating rifle and stake a greater claim than that of Chief Crazy Horse. Joan Blondell has a small part of LaRouge, an over-the-hill dance hall queen who owns a saloon in some jerkwater town where McAdam and his gang plan to rob the local church of its gold and silver icons.

It's impossible to compare the remake from the original because many of the unique elements are missing in the updated version. Most of the characters are stock figures and it's impossible to care about them because they lack personality. The rifle also does not have the intense charmed quality about it, either. There is no sense of the foreboding and eerie luck that is associated with it.

There is little tension between the card-playing gun dealer and McAdam. The same goes for the confrontation between the gun dealer and the Indian brave. In the original, the Indian chief needed the repeating rifle to help his tribe fight a winning battle against the Cavalry. In the remake, the brave wants to advance his standing with his newfound shooting prowess.

There is no interesting saloon singer like the part played by Shelley Winters. Meridan is interesting, but she does not have much to do. It is Barbara Luna's beauty and mystery that add an allure to the character, nothing that is written for her. She is still one of the film's highlights.

There is no climactic raid on a Cavalry encampment. Instead, the warrior just harasses a wagon of poor Mexicans making a pilgrimage to the shrine of St. Jude that McAdam and his gang plan to rob. There is no Waco Johnny Dean to speak of although we still have Dan Duryea, more mellow and obliging than ever.

The most noteworthy part of the film is the ending, when the gang robs the church. The robbery and the final shootout are impressive. The movie stands on its own as an entertaining Western, one of the early made-for-television films. It just can't compare with the original because the primary theme has been blurred and made secondary to wooden characters.

*Dan Duryea as Getz, the mysterious lone rider who aids Jerry Brewster (Thomas Hunter) in his quest for revenge in* The Hills Run Red. 1967,
UNITED ARTISTS CORP

# Twilight Gunslingers

Dan Duryea created some poignant Western villains late in his career when he appeared in several retro-oaters and shoestring prairie tales. *The Bounty Killer*, *The Hills Run Red*, and *Incident at Phantom Hill* are the sunsets of Duryea's Western villainy. The movies are low-budget films filled with Western legends who had seen better days, but Duryea's performances are powerful enough to broaden his Western villain portfolio.

In *The Bounty Killer*, Willie Duggan is a city slicker who goes West and becomes corrupted by the bounty tradition in a tale full of irony and hopeful desperation. Getz is not who he appears to be, but that does not change his heroic code, the one that forces him to lend his protective aid to a cowpoke with a motive for revenge in *The Hills Run Red*. He appears throughout the movie as a laconic outlaw whose support of the film's hero is an obstacle to the chief villain, played with manic relish by Henry Silva.

The villain in *The Incident on Phantom Hill* is Joe Barlow, the last of Duryea's gunslingers and a man to be reckoned with. He is freed from a prison sentence for masterminding a payroll robbery of cavalry officers that ended in the death of several troops. Barlow is needed as a guide to the loot he stole, but he has ulterior plans other than re-claiming his freedom.

Willie Duggan, Winnie Getz, and Joe Barlow are worthy additions to Dan Duryea's Western bad man credentials, adding seasoning and subtle touches of humor and regret to the shady, shifty high-plains gunmen of previous decades. Duggan, Getz, and Barlow have that wily country charm and psychopathic need to deceive and deter their adversaries while riding the range with a clear conscience because that's what the system decrees.

The *Bounty Killer* begins when city slicker Willie Duggan (Dan Duryea) is saved from barroom intimidation by Johnny Liam (Rod Cameron), a gunfighter who salvages Duggan's honor by shooting a loudmouth in a barroom confrontation. The haranguer is tough by the city slicker's standards, but he is a boorish loudmouth to others. This still does not sit well with Liam, who is having a drink to relax.

The gunslinger challenges the loudmouth to a draw and this petrifies the wise guy. He pleads for his life as Liam counts down from five after telling the man that he better draw when the countdown is complete. Willie Duggan watches in horror as Liam guns the man down.

A drink with his savior leads to a debate of principles between Duggan and Liam. Killing is a way of surviving says the gunslinger, but the city slicker remains undeterred or grateful for six-gun justice even though his life was saved by it. This is the beginning of the big change in Duggan's life.

Much of Duggan's change is motivated by meeting Carole (Audrey Dalton), the dance hall queen with the heart of gold and Luther (Fuzzy Knight), a jovial, land-bound sailor. She dreams of returning home to start a fresh life and he wants to build a wind ship, a Conestoga wagon with a sail for propulsion.

Their dreams inspire Duggan to become a bounty hunter. The mealy-mouthed nice guy turns into a hired gun after he and Luther survive a showdown with a gang of ruthless killers. After the shock wears off, they realize how easy it is to kill. This is the path Duggan decides to take to help finance the dreams of his friends.

*Poster for* The Bounty Killer. 1965, EMBASSY PICTURES CORP.

It is ironic that his final bounty on-the-house is Johnny Liam, who is enraged when he discovers that Duggan has killed three of his buddies for the bounties on their heads.

This zany premise lays the framework to show Duggan's disintegration into a depraved maniac. Duryea is a fearsome hired gun until alcohol wears him down. He is reduced to a bitter drunk lecturing a group of townsfolk about the art of killing as he waves his gun at them. It is the gun that brings him down, not only because of what it has done to others, but because of what it has done to him.

A dissolute Duggan still retains enough social bearing to woo Carole, the only woman he has loved, when he runs into her again at the end of the film. It is all for nothing as he becomes a losing part of the vicious circle that he has drawn for himself.

*The Bounty Killer* may be a low budget Western with Audrey Dalton and a cast of mostly over-the-hill Western vets and cheap sets thrown in, but it has redeeming values in a couple of good performances, some clever lines and plot development, and an ironic twist ending that seems existential and sappy at the same time.

Dan Duryea is very good as Willie Duggan. His performance is what

*The Bounty Killer draws a bead on two members of the Clayman gang.* 1965, EMBASSY PICTURES CORP.

makes this film memorable. It is characteristic of Duryea to elevate an otherwise unmemorable film into something to watch because of his performance. Duryea has done this throughout his career and he gives an earnest account of a cultured Easterner's devolution into a Western-plains bounty killer.

Duggan is laughable at the beginning of the movie, when he is a tee-totaling dude being harassed by a loudmouth in a cantina. By the end of the movie, he is a cold-hearted plains killer whose forgiveness comes from a whiskey bottle. The only people he cares for are the Captain and Carole. They are like his family and it is because of his dedication to their dreams that he becomes a bounty hunter. The Captain's wind wagon and Carole's dreams of going home are enough to make Duggan put himself in harm's way and tarnish his name with a repugnant reputation.

Audrey Dalton actually pulls off playing sexy and wholesome at the same time. She gives her cantina numbers the heat they need to get the drinks flowing and also lays on the cornpone when she expresses her desire to return to the open ranch. That is where Duggan sees her again at the film's end when he is on the lam from a posse pursuing him for the accidental shooting of a sheriff.

*An over-the-hill Johnny Mack Brown is about to take his last ride into the sunset thanks to an errant shotgun blast.* 1965, EMBASSY PICTURES CORP.

Fuzzy Knight returns from yesteryear's Saturday matinee to play Luther, a jovial, land-bound sailor whose dream is to build an airship. He is enthusiastic but also addled, so it is somewhat amusing to see him tied to a tree, being tormented by Mike Clayman (Buster Crabbe). The blade man throws his knives at Fuzzy, whose popeyed dismay adds more humor to the scene because the shots of the blades hitting the tree around his head have a weird, Claymation-like effect to them. It's too bad for Luther that Clayman's bullets are more to the point.

Buster Crabbe is to be commended for staying in great shape more than thirty years after he gained fame as the movie serial versions of comic strip heroes Flash Gordon and Buck Rogers. Mike Clayman is a tough posse boss who doesn't mind throwing torture and intimidation into his moments of rest and relaxation, but even his knives are no match for Duggan's draw.

Richard Arlen has a supporting role as Carole's father. He disapproves of her friendship with Duggan and chases him off the ranch after the gunman tries to find shelter there from being captured by the posse. Arlen earned his place in film history by starring in the first picture that won an Oscar, 1927's *Wings*, a silent movie directed by William Wellman.

Despite serious setbacks to his health and a film career that ended with appearances in the B-movies of the 40s, Arlen appears to be in great shape. It is plausible that he would chase away his daughter's shady suitor.

Excepting Dan Duryea, Buster Crabbe and Richard Arlen, *The Bounty Killer* is a mausoleum of forgotten Western heroes: Rod Cameron, Fuzzy Knight, Bob Steele, Red Morgan and Johnny Mack Brown are the matinee idols taking a final bow. Tom Kennedy, Grady Sutton and Eddie Quillan are funny men blending in to give straight support.

*The Hills Run Red* is one of the many prairie ghosts of a million desert revenge dramas. Duryea's ambiguous gunman and Henry Silva's villain in black breathe life into this choppy and violent shoot-em-up tale of vengeance.

*The poster for* The Hills Run Red, *a spaghetti western.* 1967, UNITED ARTISTS CORP.

Dan Duryea and Henry Silva recreate their unique brand of villainy for *The Hills Run Red*, a spaghetti Western that is dangerous to the palette. Duryea is Getz, the itinerant hired gun lending a hand to Jerry Brewster (Thomas Hunter), a righteous stranger who seeks revenge on a former partner for a double-cross. Henry Silva is Mendez, the marauding Mexican bandit in black whose scowls and laughter mean one thing: ornery sadism.

Nando Gazzolo is Seagall, the traitorous ex-partner who became a greedy land baron after he escapes with the loot from a botched robbery. It was mutually agreed upon that one of them would be bait for the posse while the other safeguarded the loser's share until he got out of prison.

Instead, Seagall uses the money to build a fiefdom, lets his ex-partner's wife die in penury and has allowed his only to be raised as an orphan. Revenge is the theme and Brewster does what he can to eliminate a gaggle of minions before he gets to Seagall.

Nothing much goes on, except for a lot of mendacious laughter by Mendez and furrow-browed assistance from Getz. A couple of pop tunes about optimism do not add any-thing to the film; even a scenic prairie panorama is wasted. There are the usual Western elements, but they are used to no avail. The only redeeming value is Duryea and Silva walking through their parts.

Winnie Getz is laconic, but always there to lend a helping hand to the hero. In the end, Getz twists his personality and bestows a gift on the hero that restores his public respect. Getz is a tough old bird who uses dynamite to fight rebels in the final's shoot-'em-up finale. He also turns solid citizen in a scene that shines the cavalry's brass, much to the advantage of Brewster, who starts a new life as a man with a star.

*Henry Silva plays Mendez, a sadistic high plains drifter in* The Hills Run Red. 1967, UNITED ARTISTS CORP.

The star in the dust is Henry Silva, who milks his high-noon scene for all it's worth. He spits laughter throughout the whole movie, so it's not surprising that he bombards his nemesis with a gaggle of yuks every time he gets plugged and revs up for more misery. This scene was a dream for the editor, because he cut the different reactions from several angles before focusing on his death in the dust. The sombrero in black can trade so many laughs for his leaden pain before becoming another crazed marauder biting the dust.

The *Incident at Phantom Hill* is the story of the massacre of a cavalry troop and the theft of the gold bullion they were escorting. Captain Matt Martin (Robert Fuller) reluctantly accepts a suicide mission to retrieve the gold. He is duty-bound to do so because his brother was the com-mander of the massacred outfit. His other burden is using Joe Barlow (Dan Duryea), the convicted ring leader of the rebel marauders, as a guide through the desert.

He is aided by a motley trio of dubious qualifications traveling incognito. Adam Long (Tom Simcox) is a survivor of the raid and is driven by guilt; Dr. Hannaford (Linden Chiles) is a dazed Civil War surgeon who is along for the ride; Krausman (Claude Akins) is a quiet giant who carries a music box and likes to kill Indians; and O'Rourke (Noah Beery, Jr.) is a jaunty, whiskey-drinking bloke who wears a derby hat.

*A poster for* The Incident at Phantom Hill. 1965, UNIVERSAL PICTURES COMPANY, INC.

A dance-hall queen with a Parisian motif named Memphis (Jocelyn Lane) becomes the mission's jeopardy factor. She is a hotter-than-the-sun type of stunner who is being kicked out of town for moral reasons by the sheriff. He insists that Captain Martin take her along for the ride as a way of ignoring the objectionable presence of the Confederate rebel Barlow.

The sheriff does not realize that the true nature of their mission is to go through

Indian territory; neither does Memphis. This scenario is what gets the indentured servant Barlow to thinking and scheming to find a way out. Freedom is the promise of helping find the gold, but that is not enough for Barlow. He wants the gold and he will appeal to Memphis' bold sense of independence to help him get it.

She knows that he is a phony and will sell her out, but that is what she would do to him. They need each other to get the gold out of the desert. An even split would be for one of them to be eliminated. Neither can stand Captain Martin and they use each other to take him down.

Barlow almost succeeds in duplicating his success at Phantom Hill. He absconds with the gold a second time after he picks off the doctor and the Irishman. He escapes with Memphis, leaving Captain Martin and Krausman to fight a band of attacking Indians.

Krausman loses his music box and appetite for killing Indians and Captain Martin escapes with his life. He tracks Barlow, Memphis, and the gold to a cliffside hideaway. The requisite showdown occurs over Memphis and the gold. Barlow fights a mean battle, but loses his smirk when he is felled by a fatal bullet. Captain Martin avenges the *Incident at Phantom Hill.*

The ads declared that *Incident at Phantom Hill* was TV's famed frontier fighter Robert Fuller's first starring role. The star of *Wagon Train*

*Joe Barlow (Dan Duryea) loses his cool with Memphis (Jocelyn Lane), the banished dance hall queen.* 1965, UNIVERSAL PICTURES COMPANY, INC.

*Joe Barlow (Dan Duryea) taunts a rooster with the money he plans to spend on getting blind drunk.* 1965, UNIVERSAL PICTURES COMPANY, INC.

*Joe Barlow (Dan Duryea) serves as a guide on a suicide mission in Indian territory to reclaim stolen government gold.* 1965, UNIVERSAL PICTURES COMPANY, INC.

and *Laramie* gets top billing in a revenge tale where "a woman's fury was deadlier than Apache arrows and a man's gold fever hotter than the desert sun!"

That woman was Jocelyn Lane, an English actress who made her American film debut in *The Sword of Ali Baba* and later appeared in *Tickle Me* with Elvis. She is a dancehall girl of questionable moral character, forced to become the flame that lights the way for the ragtag band of suicide troops.

Duryea dusts off the vicious cowboy routine for this movie. He has a few original tricks left up his sleeve. His character is still odious and is not above trying any means necessary to thwart the soldier boy and make off with the gold a second time. His character is a sweet talker who makes big promises to Memphis, who is unimpressed by his shenanigans and double-dealing. He stills dies a gunman's violent prairie death.

Noah Beery, Jr. plays O'Roarke, an Irishman with a merry disposition. It is the dreaded whiskey that is the death of him and he bites the dust without wetting his whiskers. Linden Chiles is a bitter doctor disillusioned by horrors of The Civil War. He is serious and wracked with so much guilt that his death in an Indian raid seems like a just penance for his self-induced loathing. Claude Akins is Krausman, a silent, Indian-hating brute who lets his music box do the talking for him. He pays a stiff price for all the Indians he has killed and part of it is never being able to be comforted by his music box again.

# A Western Perspective

One way to appreciate the variety and textures of roles that make up Dan Duryea's Western credits is to contrast two of his characters that are separated by a considerable length of time. A decade's span shows an evolution of maturity and diminution of power in men who once survived the frontier boom because of the instincts that finally made them go bust.

The General and O.E. Hotchkiss are men who wear their law on their holsters. They are driven by a mania separated by various degrees and time spans. A timid bookkeeper becomes the power-hungry General in *The Marauders* (1955). O.E. Hotchkiss is a near-sighted, elderly deputy to a hired lawman in a frontier railroad town in *Stranger On The Run* (1967), an allegory of the changing turn-of-century West.

In *The Marauders*, Corey Everett (Jeff Richards) is a mysterious stranger who strikes a rock in the desert and finds water. He digs a well and this doesn't sit too well with John Rutherford (Harry Shannon), the land baron who wants it all. Now that a well exists amid the rocks, Rutherford is upset with the squatter so he organizes a band of mercenaries to displace the man and lay claim to the whole canyon.

Rutherford believes that the squatter has a small army aiding his occupation. The cause for alarm is ill-founded because Everett has cleverly placed rifles at windows and ridges that make his cabin seem like a garrison. This starts a range war that will end long after the land baron and his pacifist son are killed in the first encounter with the bearded stranger.

Mr. Avery (Dan Duryea) is the catalyst of the violent campaign that follows. He is a numbers man who gets his hands dirty. Avery is Rutherford's sickly book keeper, a timid man who was prevented from serving the South in the Civil War because of respiratory problems. Guilt inspires him to wear the Confederate uniform of his fallen brother as he serves at Rutherford's right hand. It is Mr. Avery who keeps the quest alive when he morphs into the mission's leader when Rutherford is felled in the first battle with the stranger.

Mr. Avery becomes The General and he is ruthless in his battle with the bearded outsider. Reckless ambition blinds him to the enormity of the task. Anyone who crosses him dies. A steady gun hand rules the ragamuffin regiment led by the pointed Hook (Keenan Wynn). He has tamed the band of outlaws that once worked for Shannon and has Hook under his thumb to keep the others in tow. Occasionally the mercenaries try to overcome Avery, but he rebuffs them and they eventually get the picture as they decline in number because of failed assassination attempts.

*Poster for* The Marauders, *an unusual and intriguing Western about Mr. Avery (Dan Duryea), a timid book keeper who becomes The General, a maniacal land grabber.* 1955, LOEW'S INC.

The General dreams of taking over Rutherford's spread. He uses greed to keep his mercenaries in line. All he has to do is smoke out the stranger and his army. It's this mistaken belief in the phantom army that defeats the General. There is only one man, and he is aided by a wife and son abandoned by a well-meaning husband who sought the General's aid. The man winds up being tortured to death by the General for telling the truth that it is only Richards and his wife and son.

The battle commences and the General and his army are outwitted by the stranger, the woman, and the boy. Booby traps and vantage points decimate Hook and the mercenaries. The General without his army is nothing more than a bookkeeper with a mean temper. There is a final flare-up in the desert between the stranger and the General, who dies in the dust still applauding his plan with his dying breath.

Dan Duryea pulls out all stops as the timid bookkeeper turned megalomaniac commander-in-chief. His confederate uniform is no longer a pathetic affection, but a bold statement. He is as adept with a gun as he is with a ledger. Hook and his platoon are stared down every time they try to take him on. Duryea effectively becomes tough enough to boss around a gang of thugs and make them risk their lives in a final assault on the stranger.

*Hannah Farber (Jarma Lewis) watches as The General (Dan Duryea) asserts his authority over The Hook (Keenan Wynn) and Ramos (Peter Mamakos).*
1955, LOEW'S INC.

Jeff Richards is the bearded stranger, a brilliant military strategist who takes on the General and his army. He is the one who ambushes them when they mount their last attack. Richards' well is the base of power that cost Rutherford and the General their lives. Jarma Lewis is stern prairie righteousness. She has contempt for her husband and the stranger when they battle Rutherford and the mercenaries. They are effective in changing the odds because Rutherford and his peaceful son are killed. The General takes over, but he and the mercenaries lose their licenses to kill in the second attack on the outpost.

Keenan Wynn is the Hook, the foreman of the killer roustabouts. He likes to confront the General and make power grabs but is always defeated and put back in his place. Being punked-out by the General makes it easy for Hook to keep his sidekicks in line. Wynn is vicious and mean and takes down everyone except the General.

*Stranger on the Run* is a lyrical swan song to the turn-of-the century West, an era when the railroad barons became the new conquerors of the West, wresting power from the cattlemen. The railroad town supplanted the cow town and the businessmen with derby hats gained the power to

*The General (Dan Duryea) tries to impress Hannah Farber (Jarma Lewis) with his Southern hospitality.* 1955, LOEW'S INC.

knock off a ten gallon hat and let it roast in the sun of a one-horse town.

That's how it plays in *Stranger on the Run*, an early made-for-television movie. It is a survival drama between boots in the dust and steel wheels that cut through anything, a clash between individualism and the new conglomerate. Mr. Gorman (Lloyd Bochner) is the derby hat from the East with the talking briefcase that spells the law out for head law man, Vince McKay (Michael Parks) in the film's opening scene. The city slicker's credo will dictate everything that will happen in the movie.

McKay has been told by the Gorman to govern the railroad town to the railroad's satisfaction because the railroad is the law that puts the authority in his badge and the badges worn by his men, a vicious crew of craven outlaws played by Sal Mineo, Tom Reese, Zalman King, and Pepe Horn.

His right hand man is O.E. Hotchkiss (Dan Duryea), an over-the-hill gunslinger who uses his reputation to disguise the fact that he needs reading glasses. Without them, he is the gunslinger who can't shoot straight and this becomes apparent during a shootout between the law men and their prey, a stranger falsely accused of murder and the itinerant farmer who helps him through tough times in the desert.

*O.E. Hotchkiss (Dan Duryea) teaches his shooting technique to a young admirer (Michael Burns).* 1967, UNIVERSAL TELEVISION.

It starts when the fiefdom of the railroad town is upset by the arrival of a drunkard (Henry Fonda), after he is tossed off the train when it makes its stop. He earns his whiskey by working for Berk (Walter Burke), the merchant. It is when he mentions the name of Alma Britton (Madlyn Rhue) that he becomes a marked man. This sends ripples through the chain of power in the town and it takes the good ol' deputy boys to straighten things out.

*O.E. Hotchkiss (Dan Duryea) is a faded gunslinger hired by a railroad to keep law and order in a way station growing into a frontier town.* 1967, UNIVERSAL TELEVISION.

It is the residual heat of the beating of a saloon entertainer and her subsequent murder...justice is silence that absolves the railroad of any responsibility of the deputies who stepped over the line. Sequestering the victim (Madlyn Rhue) in a shack does not help because it becomes her tomb, something that turns into a murder charge for the stranger when the sheriff's posse tracks him down as he flees from the shack.

Protestations of innocence only buy him time in a game Hotchkiss calles 'Bear Dog'. It's a baiting game used to take the minds off of hard times to enjoy a good blood sport. It is a matter of time before the sheriff and his boys start tracking the stranger.

The sheriff will do anything to hold on to his job, trying to maintain control while dealing the board of directors' guidelines. He has to be tougher than his men and sometimes he needs to toss them a bone with some meat on it. The stranger is the bone that blesses them with absolution because they have found someone who has atoned for their sin of murder.

The killer deputies are a rambunctious gang: Tom Reese, Sal Mineo, Zalman King, and Pepe Horn. Hotchkiss (Dan Duryea) is the faded gunman who plays it big for Matt Johnson (Michael Burns), his green, adolescent protégé, someone the old man can teach and show off to. This does not bode well with the boy's mother, a sexy prairie woman played by Anne Baxter. She is an independent-minded and hard-driven woman who is not impressed with the creed of the hired killers. She looks at them as being mercenaries of the railroad bosses. It is the new metal mule train that is throwing everything out of kilter in the West and the prairie dogs are feeling the heat of the bankers back East.

Michael Parks is atypical of the young gunmen of his era, young and toughened by the viciousness of the killers' circle. He is the captain of the killers who are paid to keep the railroad town a quiet and productive place. The sadistic attack on the woman is not deplored because of its brutality; it is condemned because it can bring an indictment down on the railroad.

Hotchkiss is considered a has-been by the railroad people. He keeps his job because the sheriff vouches for him. The other deputies fear his reputation, but still goad into showing off his stuff. Sal Mineo, Tom Reese, Zalman King, and Pepe Hern are also terrorists, bending the will of the power to obey their new masters. It is Mineo and Reese who are responsible for the beating and the murder, something they need to make the stranger pay for.

Henry Fonda plays the dissolute hobo as a drunkard with an inflexible will to do what is right. He is not swayed by a beating from a deputy or harassment by the deputies-formed posse. Henry Fonda is the odd man out, someone who crosses a line few people care to acknowledge.

*In* Do You Know This Voice?, *John Hopta (Dan Duryea) is a repugnant kidnapper who can still be charming when it serves an underhanded purpose.*
1964, COLUMBIA PICTURES.

# Crime Post Script (3)

The Sixties spelled the end of the old studio system as trends and economics changed the dynamics of movie making. Big screen Westerns were passé by the mid-60s and only a handful of stars could get away with making them. Westerns still thrived on television and Duryea appeared on all of the popular shows of the era. Television is what kept Duryea's career alive because he was constantly working and continuing to create unique characters.

Dan Duryea was not like many of the stars of his era, either living off the rare continued success or dispersing into supporting big screen roles, television shots or an old actors' home. During the sixties, he continued to give stellar performances on television.

Duryea's sixties films are a motley bunch that included many obscure and low-budget Westerns. The non-Western films included *Do You Know This Voice?*, *Walk a Tightrope*, *Flight of the Phoenix*, *Five Golden Dragons*, and *The Bamboo Saucer*.

Duryea continued to freelance, as he had done in the 40s and 50s. This led him to England for two downbeat and intriguing mid-60s sordid thrillers. *Do You Know This Voice?* and *Walk a Tightrope* are bleak, black-and-white tabloid crime dramas. A child murderer and a paid assassin are Duryea's 60s Yanks in England. The lead characters are so loathsome that they are hypnotic in the way they draw you into their warped sensibilities.

In *Do You Know This Voice?* and *Walk a Tightrope*, one can sense the resentment toward the aging American in working class England. He was once part of the post-war effort but now is an unwelcome reminder of the Cold War. What makes matters worse is that both Americans are poison to British society, cold-blooded killers who learned their craft during the last big war and now ply it in the decaying rebirth of the last blitzkrieg.

*Do You Know This Voice?* is a grim and disturbing movie about John and Jackie Hopta (Dan Duryea and Gwen Watford), a couple of kidnappers who demand a ransom even though their victim, a boy, has died during the commission of the crime. A blown sting leads to a dragnet that tightens due to police procedure. A tape recording of a garbled and eerie voice gives them a clue. The dragnet and a guilty conscience turn into a lasso and a catch. This time it is due to gum soles and a glass of poison.

Dan Duryea is droll and vicious as John Hopta, the inept kidnapper. It is bad enough that he pulled off a kidnapping, but killing the victim

*Supt. Hume (Peter Madden) tries to jar Rosa Marotta's (Isa Miranda) memory for details about the kidnapper she unwittingly saw at the phone booth in a scene from* Do You Know This Voice? 1964, COLUMBIA PICTURES.

puts him further in peril. As he pushes his luck and demands a ransom, banking on the authorities' ignorance of the accidental death, he leaves a trail of clues for the police to follow.

A simple trace on the ransom call turns into a police investigation thanks to Mrs. Maloota (Isa Miranda), an elderly woman who is apprehended by the cops at the scene of the call. It helps the course of action that the woman is the neighbor of the culprits. It is something that is not lost on the guilty couple, because their neighbor has attracted attention from having been drawn into things because of happenstance. Call it serendipity for the cops, but for the couple it is bad luck.

Superintendent Hume (Peter Madden) is the chief cop and he looks like a beanstalk with a large head. His prominent forehead, furrowed brow,

CRIME POST SCRIPT (3)

thick eyeglasses, and droll speech give him an edge of authority. It is a change of pace from having a handsome leading man playing the head detective. His 'eureka!' moment comes when the cops sweep up an elderly woman who was using the telephone pinpointed by the trace. That meant that the previous user was one of the kidnappers and that the woman had to have seen him.

*John Hopta (Dan Duryea) confers with Jackie (Gwen Watford), his subservient wife, about how to handle Mrs. Marotta, the witness who lives next door to them.* 1964, COLUMBIA PICTURES.

They use her as bait and plant Detective Sergeant Connor (Barry Warren), a boarder in the home. The couple next-door is the guilty party, but knowing this does not ruin the suspense of the movie. This is due mainly to Dan Duryea's loathsome performance and the dry, matter-of-fact procedure of the British police. If you ever wondered what Johnny Prince would have become if he escaped the death penalty, take a look at Hopta. He is a charmer in public, but abusive to his wife Jackie (Gwen Watford) in private. She was his mainstay, but has now become a liability because of her skittishness and his paranoia.

Hopta goes to extreme lengths to eliminate his other liability, his next-door neighbor. He tries poison and garroting, but fails twice. He leaves his mark as a horrible looking man because of the stocking mask he wore during the attempted strangling. The attempted murder scenes are atmospheric and chilling.

Dan Duryea is truly tortured in this lurid thriller. He is repugnant and wicked, a bitter man who dominates his wife and forces her to be an accomplice in an unthinkable crime. Hopta is full of anger and rage, blaming others for his job as a hospital orderly. The kidnapping would net

*A stocking mask and a garrote are two props in one of many failed murder attempts on Mrs. Marotta.* 1964, COLUMBIA PICTURES.

him some money, or so he thought. It did not occur to him that he may not handle success because it would make him the object of a manhunt.

Duryea's Hopta character is a low-class hustler with a small-time way of scheming. The accidental death and insistent ransom demands further prove the extent of his small-mindedness. What makes him seem big is the magnitude of his wife's fear and devotion. She suffers his abuse, and has sacrificed her life to make him happy. She complied with his scheme, but now criticizes him because he has botched everything. Hopta thinks that he has turned drawbacks into bigger grades of success. Paranoia derails his plans, and it all backfires during an ill-fated toast.

Gwen Watford as Jackie is a study in hysteria. She is critical of her husband yet dons a trench coat and men's clothes when she makes her disguised calls. Though fearful of his violent outbursts, she is not resistant to his occasional embraces.

Isa Miranda's Mrs. Maloota stands out as a foreigner in xenophobic England even though Duryea, as an American, does not. She is introduced on-screen as she is being harassed by her next-door neighbor, who torments her cats and suggests that she return to Capistrano. A kindly woman, her courage controls her fear as she is stalked and marked for death by the maniacal kidnappers after telling the press that she saw the culprit in the phone booth. It never dawned on her that they were her next-door neighbors.

Duryea's British follow-up to *Do You Know This Voice?* is less turgid although his character, Carl Lutcher, is just as sleazy and offensive as Hopta. *Walk a Tightrope* is a short movie, one that could pass as an hour-long cop show like *Law and Order*. There is the commission of the crime, the arrest, and the trial. Ellen Shepherd (Patricia Owens) is a woman madly in love with her second husband. Her ex-spouse proves to be a bothersome problem so she decides to have him killed by Carl Lutcher, an unscrupulous American. He murders the wrong husband and this leads to the complications of his arrest and trial.

The trial basically consists of Lutcher trying to prove Ellen Shepherd's duplicity in the crime. Her angle is that she performs as an innocent babe in arms. She claims that she is being implicated by the crazy American and gains sympathy from the judge and jury. The only wrinkle to her alibi is the foggy memory of Doug Randle (Richard Leech), a family friend who was knocked out by Lutcher and awoke from his stupor after the murder. He thought that he heard Ellen and Lutcher speaking with each other, but cannot swear to it because of his head trauma.

The mystery to *Walk a Tightrope* is the trust that a friend lends to the wife of a man killed by a hired assassin in front of his spouse's eyes. The friend was knocked out by the killer when he came downstairs to see what the commotion was about. He is semi-conscious when he hears the assassin and the wife talk business about the contract. However, the wife is a good actress and leads everyone to believe that Lutcher is delusional. That is the basis of her trial, insanity, but on behalf of the murderer.

This strange hook gives Duryea an opportunity to beg for his life in a court of law, much like he did in *Scarlet Street*. This is amusing because he still is odious and frightening, but now pays the price of his own expertise. He carried out the hit but killed the wrong husband. That is why this is a mistaken-identity movie combined with a courtroom procedural and a drama queen's desperate soliloquy.

*Walk a Tightrope* is a stiffly-acted film with the exception of Dan Duryea, whose portrayal of a hired killer blows away his fellow cast members in multiple ways. His deranged personality makes all of the other performers seem like wooden dummies. They are stilted and constipated in comparison to Duryea's nihilistic killer.

He has been betrayed by the woman who hired him for a hit where the murder happened to be a case of mistaken identity. Collusion and an unusual eyewitness to the murder lands the unlikely couple in court. A

*Carl Lutcher (Dan Duryea) has a strained home life with a shrew in* Walk a Tightrope. 1963, PARAMOUNT PICTURES CORP.

strident Patricia Owens elicits sympathy from everyone with her insistence that she is a random victim of a lunatic-at-large.

Other cast characters include a prim police inspector, a gregarious first husband who returns to haunt the widow, and a family friend who was semi-conscious when the murder occurred. He witnesses the exchange between the killer and the widow but is dissuaded from his suspicions when she insists on her innocence.

There is not much to the movie other than the actual hit, Duryea's home life, and his turn on the stand as a defendant and lawyer defending himself. Everybody else is cardboard. Duryea is cool and calculated when he bursts in on the couple and shoots the husband after he is identified. The short puffs of the silencer are brutal.

*Ellen Shepherd (Patricia Owen) hires Carl Lutcher (Dan Duryea) to murder her intrusive first husband.* 1963, PARAMOUNT PICTURES CORP.

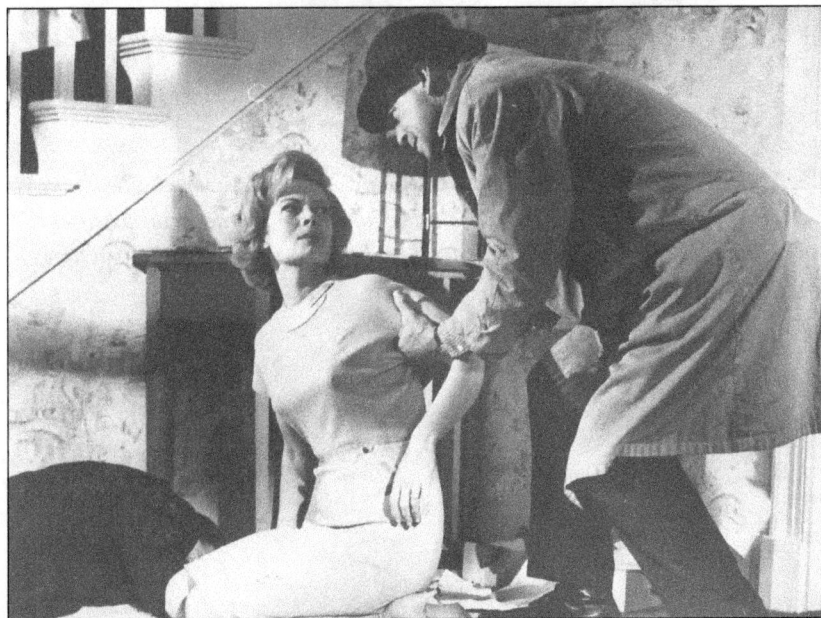

*Carl Lutcher (Dan Duryea) reminds Ellen Shepherd (Patricia Owen) that a deal is still a deal even though he has murdered the wrong husband.* 1963, PARAMOUNT PICTURES CORP.

The killer is a pigeon in a coop when he is at home with his shrewish girlfriend. She is dim-witted, but her buxom charm is enough to satisfy our sly villain. He is crude and direct with his interrogation and rebuttals.

The murder, betrayal, and trial are crucial steps in the resolution of the murder. They are ways to persuade or dissuade the jury from believing in Duryea's guilt or innocence. A tangent comes in the form of indicting Patricia Owens due to incriminating suppositions.

*Carl Lutcher (Dan Duryea) is the sole defendant in a murder trial when no one believes that he was hired by Ellen Shepherd.* 1963, PARAMOUNT PICTURES CORP.

# The Cold War

During the mid-60s, most of Duryea's time was spent playing parts on many of the popular shows of the era. It was the same thing as he had done during the 50s, when he first became familiar with the television audiences. His big-screen genres may have run the course of their popularity with the new young audiences, but the same crowd accepted him on the small screen.

*Checkmate, Route 66, Kraft Suspense Theater, Alfred Hitchcock,* and *Burke's Law* are some of the crime dramas Duryea worked on, and *Bonanza, Wagon Train, Daniel Boone,* and *The Virginian* are some of the Western shows from his long list of credits.

Dan Duryea was busy performing on television and gave many fine performances during the 60s, when his film career was drawing to a close. His last role was as Eddie Jacks on *Peyton Place,* a prodigal philanderer who returns to the woman he walked out on sixteen years ago.

His 60s movies were a strange blend of previous styles, mainly low-budget features including two British thrillers, a series of low budget Westerns, two early made-for-television Westerns, a small part in a Hollywood desert survival opus, a low-budget spy flick and a Cold War science-fiction adventure. His last big-screen non-Western films were *Flight of the Phoenix* and two low-budget espionage movies, *Five Gold Dragons* and *The Bamboo Saucer.*

*Flight of the Phoenix* featured an all-star international cast in a desert survival drama directed by Robert Aldrich. James Stewart stars as a gruff pilot who crash lands in the Sahara Desert with a motley group of passengers.

Disaster movies are dystopian critiques of technologically-advanced societies. It is not only a question of survival through primitivism, but the question of identity and the authority or lack thereof it accords. Superior strength or ultra-intelligence is the edge, but the unknown odd factors are the things that wind up creating or taking away good fortune.

In *Flight of the Phoenix,* Capt. Frank Towns (James Stewart) and Heinrich Dorfmann (Hardy Kruger) vie for the leadership of a band of C-82 Packet plane crash survivors in an attempt to beat the odds of surviving the Sahara Desert. They consist of a strange assortment of personalities.

Capt. Harris (Peter Finch) and Sgt. Watson (Ronald Fraser) are a staid and brave British officer and his munitions sergeant, a resentful weakling about to commit three acts of cowardice as a way of proving his independence. Trucker Cobb (Ernest Borgnine) is a roughneck with a few loose screws, accompanied by Dr. Reneaud (Christian Marquand), a company doctor who is accompanying the stressed-out worker back to the States.

"Ratbags" Crow (Ian Bannen) is the cynical tough guy with the sarcastic mouth and jittery attitude. Standish (Dan Duryea) is a quiet, Sunday-school-teacher type whose meekness and love for figs keeps him going. Mike Bellamy (George Kennedy) is the tough guy with the muscles that never quit. Gabriel (Gabriele Tinti) is a wounded young man whose love for his wife keeps him alive.

Poster for The Flight of the Phoenix, *a plane crash in the desert survival drama.* 1965, TWENTIETH CENTURY FOX CORP.

They were off-course when they crash landed, and it seems hopeless to think that they will be rescued. Vain attempts to find a remedy claim the lives of a few survivors. The odds change when the model-airplane designer suggests that they can build a smaller plane from the wreckage of the larger one.

It seems implausible, and this is the basis for a clash between old-school attitudes and new-school styles. It is a case of the crusty veteran who insists it can't be done, and the man with the calculations and the power of certainty who says that it can be accomplished. The movie ends with a smaller plane flying back to the oil field. The story of the movie is what happens in between the announcement of the possibility of building a Phoenix and the actual moment it takes off on the last cylinder.

One thing that enlivens the possible boredom of survival flicks is the clash of personalities. Getting on each other's nerves hampers and hastens project survival. The one-time passengers are now players in a real-life game of survival, and a miscue can mean a meal for the vultures.

It is inevitable that there are casualties, either through missteps with nature or Neanderthal bloodletting. This aspect is somewhat amusing because the victims are either known actors in small parts or nobodies who remained that way after the film. One thing was for sure, and that

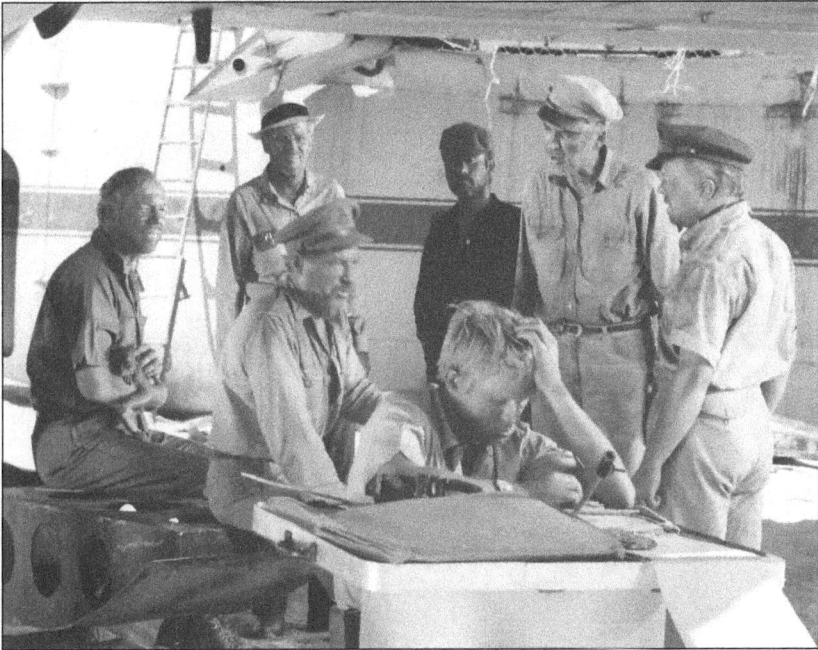

*Frank Towns (James Stewart) berates Sergeant Watson (Ronald Fraser) while Heinrich Dorfman (Hardy Kruger) works on his blueprints. Left to Right: George Kennedy, Dan Duryea, Gabrielle Tinti and Richard Attenbourough lend moral support.* 1965, TWENTIETH CENTURY FOX CORP.

was a forceful and victorious personality clash that would build a new plane and fly it out of the desert.

Disaster movies are adventure fantasies that jab at civilized mores and the false gravity of ranks and identities. Social standing and ultimately accepted authority are obliterated and everyone returns to the starting line in a primitive game of survival. A new social system arises, based on an individual's worth to the overall survival of the others.

In the case of *The Flight of the Phoenix*, it all comes down to the usual question of opposites. It's savvy hands-on experience versus cerebral cunning, with the outcome being the melding of the two. Frank Towns and

Heinrich Dorfmann are the old-school pilot and the young aeronautics designer who are faced with finding a solution for the crash landing in the desert. It is the designer's belief that they can build a smaller plane from the wreckage that sets off a bitter survival drama in which a disparate group of desperate people fight the slim to conquer death against slim odds of survival.

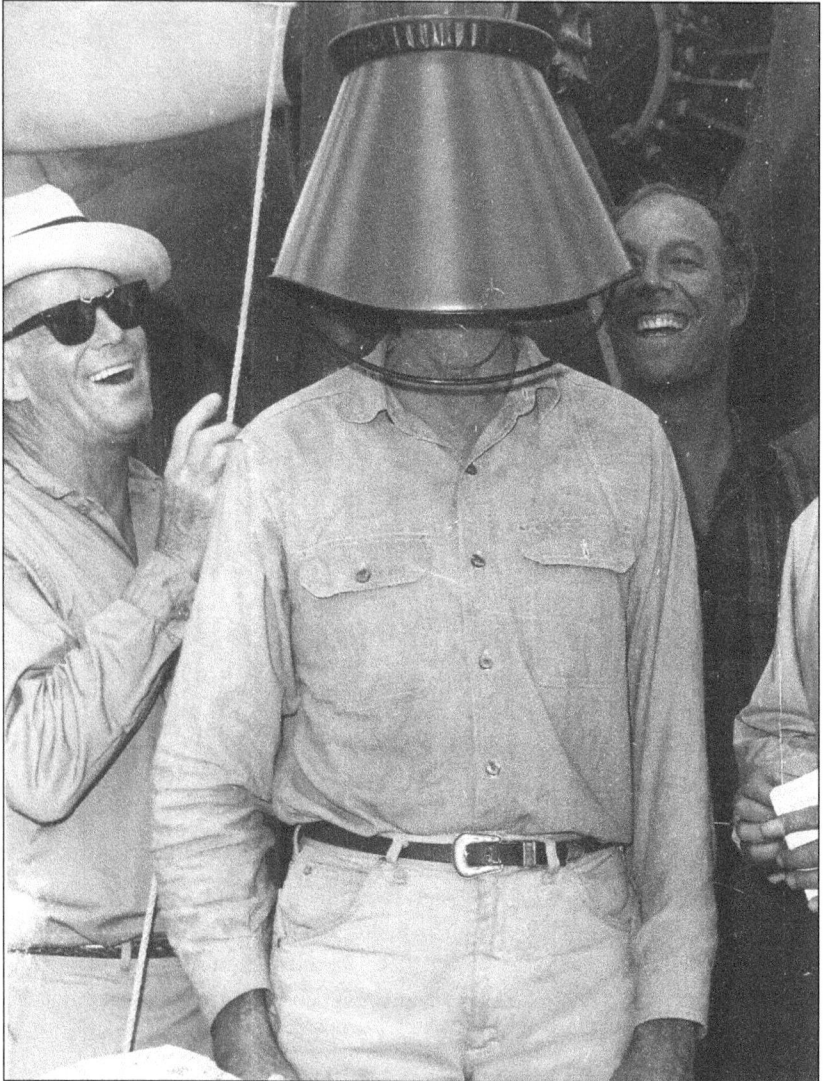

*During a break on the set of* Flight of the Phoenix, *Dan Duryea (left) plays a joke on James Stewart (center) while George Kennedy (right) has a good laugh.*
1965, TWENTIETH CENTURY FOX CORP.

Harry Alan Summers was a successful British producer whose main achievements were the Fu Manchu films. In *Five Golden Dragons*, he capitalizes on the dying secret-agent film craze. He assembled many notable names for the film, which was made in conjunction with the Shaw Brothers, who would later be noted for their kung-fu exploitation flicks.

Bob Cummings is Bob Mitchell, the smiling, smug, secret-agent star of *Five Golden Dragons*, a Filipino movie that found its way into the endless loop of Bond imitators that flooded late-night television in the late 60s and early 70s. Cummings was a popular actor in 40s films and gained fame in three success-ful sit-coms, *Love That Bob*, *The Bob Cummings Show*, and *My Living Doll*.

*The Five Golden Dragons* are a secret society comprised of former American screen hard-boiled tough guys. Dan Duryea, George Raft, and Brian Donlevy don cer-emonial costumes and plot crimes with a fourth member played by Christopher Lee. The fifth dragon is a mystery until his fatal recogni-tion in the film's countdown.

*Spanish poster for* Five Golden Dragons, *a Shaw Brothers spy comedy that plays like a weird spoof.* 1965, WARNER-PATHE DISTRIBUTORS LTD.

The British cult icon and the former crime king icons wear Japanese ceremonial gowns and don ornate dragon masks before grum-bling about how things aren't what they used to be. They look like ornaments at a Chinese New Year fireworks celebration. Fireworks are what one of the five dragons gets before the organization collapses in this bottom-of-the-barrel European espionage spy film.

*Five Golden Dragons* is the nadir of the spy genre, a hodge-podge mess of feeble espionage with a cast that had seen better days. Bob Cummings vir-tually resurrects his television personalities for this comedic spy film. One can't help but think of *Love That Bob*; instead of Ann B. Davis as Schultzy, we have Klaus Kinski as a chain-smoking killer with twisted nerves.

Bob Mitchell is a smug player whose perpetual smile and forced good humor help him to mug his way through this spy adventure. He somehow gets mixed up with the Five Golden Dragons and actually has a hand in their demise. They are trying for one last grand scheme and it involves doing business with a Mafia-type organization and a band of local thugs.

The action starts with a defenestrated tourist who passed a cryptic note to a taxi driver before being murdered. It reads, "Five Golden Dragons." The note winds up on the desk of Commander Sanders (Rupert Davies),

*Gert (Klaus Kinski) toys with Magda (Margaret Lee) when she becomes his captive.* 1965, WARNER-PATHE DISTRIBUTORS LTD.

who enlists the aid of his top cop, Inspector Chiao (Roy Chiao).

Bob Mitchell gets mixed up in the action when he flirts with Ingrid (Maria Rohm) and Margret (Maria Perschy) at a resort. They are amused but unimpressed by his one-liners and annoying smile. It is when Margret is found dead in bed that Mitchell is implicated in the investigation.

The action is centered around the European cabaret run by the perpetually-smiling Peterson (Siegardt Rupp), who has a mysterious hold over his sexy chanteuse, Magda (Margaret Lee). She, too, brings Mitchell deeper into the mystery that also involves Gert (Klaus Kinski), a vicious enforcer, and The Five Golden Dragons.

Everyone bumbles around in this chaotic, badly-edited-and-dubbed fiasco until it builds up to a twist ending that wakes the viewer up with a bang. The surprise dragon's loss is inconsequential to the viewer because of the apprehension of the former Hollywood heavyweights and the British cult idol.

Unintentional humor pervades this Summers-Shaw Brothers spy flick. The aftermath of an unlucky cab driver's interrogation by Gert is funny because it happens to someone else. Gert's propensity for dispatching the

*Four of the Five Golden Dragons are rounded up by Comm. Sanders (Rupert Davies).* 1965, WARNER-PATHE DISTRIBUTORS LTD.

players is matched only by his chain-smoking. He winds up being short of breath when he tangles with the wrong sidekick who prefers garrotes to neck ties.

Margaret Lee is seductive as Magda, a duplicitous nightclub singer. Maria Perschy is along for the ride until her character, Margret, has served her purpose. Her sister, Ingrid, is played by Maria Rohm.

Rupert Davies appears to be grateful for the role of Commandant Sanders, a flustered British police inspector working in Hong Kong. Sieghardt Rupp is Peterson, a strange, narcissistic villain who gets his shot at being a dragon although it will serve him no purpose. Roy Chiao plays Inspector Chiao, a resolute Filipino officer who investigates the odd goings on that place Mitchell at their center.

Dan Duryea fares much better in his last film role as Hank Peters, a snub-nosed CIA man ready to outdo the Commies in a battle to commandeer a downed UFO in Red China. In *The Bamboo Saucer*, he is tough with the phone decisions and the snap commands that make staying alive in the field his first priority. He leads an American contingent consisting of an astronaut and scientists that will match wits

*Hank Peters (Dan Duryea) is a two-fisted State Department man who goes toe-to-toe with the Russians and Red Chinese in* The Bamboo Saucer. *Bob Hastings (left) watches his back.* 1968, WORLD ENTERTAINMENT CORP.

and brawn with a Russian group made up of belligerent comrades and a sensitive beautiful scientist.

The psychedelic era dominated the late sixties, and everything that existed out of that warped sensibility was considered plastic and quaint. The past was negated by the new hip and former icons and attitudes were now ridiculed, challenged, and discarded. Movies like *The Bamboo Saucer* were considered insufficient blips on the new radar. Today, they embody the 60s more than most of the tripe that symbolized the era at the time.

Red, white, and blue are some of the colors of this trip inside Red China to destroy a flying saucer that may put an end to American technological dominance as we know it. It's not just the American team that wants to find the saucer but a Russian expedition that collides with the capitalists in intent and motive.

The Russian Communists are not as tight-knit with their Chinese counterparts as one would think, and they have to forge an uneasy alliance with the westerners. The scientists on both sides overrule the military authority and the movie becomes an ode to mutual understanding and international peace by the time it ends. Until then, the nod goes to the Americans thanks to Hank Peters (Dan Duryea), a state depart-

*Hank Peters (Dan Duryea) keeps an eye on advancing Red Chinese troops as the survival team (left to right: Vincent Beck, Rico Cattani and James Hong) share their last laugh at Dave Ephram's (Bernard Fox) joke.* 1968, WORLD ENTERTAINMENT CORP.

ment man who leads the Americans with the aid of a Chinese scout named Sam Archibald (James Hong).

*Collision Course* is the alternate title of this movie and could well be used to describe the antagonism that exists between Hank Peters and Zagersky, the militaristic officers played by Dan Duryea and Vincent Beck. Duryea has the edge because he is wilier and tougher. The Russian is blustery and comes off the way a peasant in uniform would if he had power.

The main mover in his expedition is Anna Karachev (Lois Nettleton), a Russian scientist. She bonds with Norwood (John Ericson), the American test pilot, and they provide the balance of power to the international minded scientists in the group. This includes Bob Hastings and Bernard

Fox for the Americans and British and Nick Katurich and Rico Cattani for the Russians. Only Peters and Zagersky have any enmity toward each other.

They finally trust each other until Zagersky tries to hijack the saucer back to Moscow. One of his men is killed trying to figure out a way to fly the saucer. As a result, a blood-and-guts battle goes down to provide cover for the saucer's takeoff.

The military men revert to their valiant combative stance against a column of Red Chinese soldiers, as does one of the peaceniks. In the end, universal peace is experienced when three of the survivors take a tour of the universe before deciding to land at Geneva as a display of international cooperation.

Duryea's last screen role is a tough-guy-of-valor part that lets him boss people around and defend his mission with his deadly machine-gun aim. He barks orders and shoots under duress with equal aplomb. Peters is fiercely American and does not trust the touchy-feely demeanor of everyone else. It is not his mission to share credit and knowledge with anyone for any reason.

He turns out to be right as the Russian leader tries to pull a *coup de etat*, but fails. It does not matter because the final victory flight is an international affair. All conventions are shattered when the Geneva-bound Bob Hastings' final "Amen" puts a damper on nationalism.

John Ericson is Fred Norwood, the test pilot who first encounters the UFO. He travels to China with Peters' team and gets to take a test run of the craft across the universe before flying to Geneva in a statement about international cooperation. Ericson had been the co-star with Anne Francis on *Honey West*, a hard-driving sensual private eye show that was short-lived and ahead of its time.

Lois Nettleton affects a thick Russian accent as Anna Karachev. Vincent Beck is Zagersky, the Boris Badenov-cartoon-stereotype Russian operative. Bob Hastings is Jack Garson and Bernard Fox is Dave Ephram, both specialists in their respective fields. James Hong is Sam Archibald, Peters' inside man in Red China.

# Film Credits

## The Little Foxes
*(1941, RKO Radio Pictures — 115 min.)*
*Regina Giddens:* Bette Davis. *Horace Giddens:* Herbert Marshall. *Alexandra Giddens:* Teresa Wright. *David Hewitt:* Richard Carlson. *Birdie Hubbard:* Patricia Colinge. *Leo Hubbard:* Dan Duryea. *Ben Hubbard:* Charles Dingle. *Director:* William Wyler. *Screenplay:* Lillian Hellman, based on her play. *Additional dialogue:* Arthur Kober, Dorothy Parker, and Alan Campbell. *Producer:* Samuel Goldwyn. *Cinematographer:* Gregg Toland. *Musical Score:* Meredith Willson. *Editor:* Daniel Mandell.

## Ball of Fire
*(1941, MGM — 111 min.)*
*Professor Bertram Potts:* Gary Cooper. *Katherine "Sugarpuss" O'Shea:* Barbara Stanwyck. *The Professors:* Oskar Homolka, Henry Travers, S.Z. Sakall, Tully Marshall, Aubrey Mather, Leonid Kinsky and Richard Hayden. *Joe Lilac:* Dana Andrews. *Duke Pastraimi:* Dan Duryea. *Garbageman:* Allen Jenkins. *Director:* Howard Hawks. *Screenplay:* Charles Bracket and Billy Wilder. *Story:* Billy Wilder and Thomas Monroe. *Producer:* Samuel Goldwyn. *Musical Score:* Alfred Newman. *Cinematography:* Greg Toland. *Editor:* Daniel Mandell.

## Pride of the Yankees
*(1942, MGM — 128 min.)*
*Lou Gehrig:* Gary Cooper. *Eleanor Twitchell:* Teresa Wright. *Babe Ruth:* Himself. *Sam Blake:* Walter Brennan. *Hank Hanneman:* Dan Duryea. *Christina "Ma" Gehrig:* Elsa Janssen. *Henry "Pop" Gehrig:* Ludwig Stoesell. *Myra Tunsely:* Virginia Gilmore. *Bill Dickey:* Himself. *Director:* Sam Wood. *Screenplay:* Jo Swerling and Herman J. Mankiewicz. *Story:* Paul Gallico. *Prologue:* Damon Runyon. *Producer:* Samuel Goldwyn. *Musical Score:* Leigh Hairline. *Cinematography:* Rudolph Mate. *Editor:* Daniel Mandell.

## That Other Woman
*(1942, 20th Century Fox — 75 min.)*
*Emily Borden:* Virginia Gilmore. *Henry Summers:* James Ellison. *Ralph Cobb:* Dan Duryea. *Constance Powell:* Janis Carter. *Grandma:* Alma Kruger. *George:* Bud McAllister. *Mrs. MacReady:* Minerva Urecal. *Bailey:* Charles Arnt. *Director:* Ray McCarey. *Screenplay:* Jack Jungmeyer. *Producer:* Walter Morosco. *Cinematography:* Joseph MacDonald. *Editor:* J. Watson Webb, Jr.

## Sahara
*(1943, Columbia Pictures — 97 min.)*
*Sgt. Joe Gunn:* Humphrey Bogart. *Waco Hoyt:* Bruce Bennett. *Jimmy Doyle:* Dan Duryea. *Giuseppe:* J. Carrol Naish. Sgt. Maj. Tambul: Rex Ingram. *Capt. Jason Halliday:* Richard Nugent. *Jean Leroux (Frenchie):* Louis Mercier. With: Lloyd Bridges, Carl Harbord, Patrick O'Moore. *Capt. Von Schletow:* Kurt Krueger. *Director:* Zoltan Korda. *Screenplay:* John Howard Lawson and Zoltan Korda. *Short Story:* Philip MacDonald. *Producer:* Harry Joe Brown (uncredited). *Score:* Miklos Rozsa. *Cinematography:* Rudolph Mate. *Editor:* Charles Nelson.

## Man From Frisco
*(1943, Columbia Pictures — 97 min.)*
*Matt Braddock:* Michael O'Shea. *Diana Kennedy:* Anne Shirley. *Joel Kennedy:* Gene Lockhart. *Jim Benson:* Dan Duryea. *Russ Kennedy:* Tommy Bond. *Johnny Rogers:* Ray Walker. *Martha Kennedy:* Ann Shoemaker. *Director:* Robert Florey. *Screenplay:* Ethel Hill and Arnold Manoff. *Story and Adaptation:* George Carleton Brown and George Worthing Yates. *Producer:* Albert J. Cohen. *Musical Score:* Marlin Skiles. *Cinematography:* Jack Marta. *Editor:* Ernest Nims.

## Mrs. Parkington
*(1944, MGM — 124 min.)*
*Susie "Sparrow" Parkington:* Greer Garson. *Major Augustus "Gus" Parkington:* Walter Pidgeon. *Armory Stilham:* Edward Arnold. *Baroness Aspasia Conti:* Agnes Moorehead. *Edward, Prince of Wales:* Cecil Kelloway. *Alice, Duchess of Bramount:* Gladys Cooper. *Jack Stilham:* Dan Duryea. *With:* Frances Rafferty, Tom Drake, Peter Lawford, Hugh Marlowe, Selena Royale and Fortunio Bonanova. *Director:* Tay Garnett. *Screenplay:* Robert Thoeren and Polly James. *Novel:* Louis Bromfield. *Producer:* Leo Gordon. *Musical Score:* Stanislaw Kaper. *Cinematography:* Joseph Ruttenberg. *Editor:* George Boemler.

## Ministry of Fear

*(1944, Paramount Pictures — 87 min.)*
*Stephen Neale:* Ray Milland. *Carla Hilfe:* Marjorie Reynolds. *Willi Hilfe:* Carl Esmond. Mrs. *Bellane #2, the spiritualist:* Hillary Brooke. *Inspector Prentice:* Percy Waram. *Cost'Travers, the tailor:* Dan Duryea. *Dr. Forrester:* Alan Napier. *George Rennit, private investigator:* Erskine Sanford. *Director:* Fritz Lang. *Screenplay:* Seton I. Miller. *Novel:* Graham Greene. *Producer:* Seton I. Miller. *Musical Score:* Victor Young and Miklos Rozsa (uncredited). *Cinematography:* Henry Sharp. *Editor:* Archie Marshek.

## None But The Lonely Heart

*(1944, RKO Pictures — 113 min.)*
*Ernie Mott:* Cary Grant. *Ma Mott:* Miss Ethel Barrymore. *Henry Twite:* Barry Fitzgerald. *Ada Brantline:* June Duprez. *Aggie Hunter:* Jane Wyatt. *Jim Mordinoy:* George Coulouris. *Lew Tate:* Dan Duryea. *Direction and Screenplay:* Clifford Odets. *Novel:* Richard Llewellyn. *Producer:* David Hempstead. *Musical Score:* Harris Eisler. *Cinematography:* George Barnes. *Editor:* Roland Gross.

## Woman in the Window:

*(RKO Pictures, Inc. — 1945 — 99 min.)*
*Professor Richard Wanley:* Edward G. Robinson. *Alice Reed:* Joan Bennett. *DA Frank Lalor:* Raymond Massey. *Heidt:* Dan Duryea. *Director:* Fritz Lang. *Screenplay:* Nunnally Johnson. *Novel:* J.H. Willis. *Producer:* Nunnally Johnson. *Cinematography:* Milton R. Krasner. *Music:* Arthur Lange. *Editor:* Gene Fowler Jr. and Marjorie Johnson.

## Main Street After Dark

*(1945, MGM — 57 min.)*
*Lt. Lorgan:* Edward Arnold. *"Ma" Dibson:* Selena Royale. *Lefty Dibson:* Tom Trout. *Jessy Bell Dibson:* Audrey Totter. *Posey Dibson:* Dan Duryea. *Keller, the pawnbroker:* Hume Cronyn. *Rosalie Dibson:* Dorothy Ruth Morris. *Director:* Edward L. Cahn. *Story:* John C. Higgins. *Screenplay:* John C. Higgins and Karl Kamb. *Producer:* Jerry Bresler. *Musical Score:* Jackson Rose. *Editor:* Harry Koner.

## The Great Flamarion

*(1945, Republic Pictures — 78 min.)*

*The Great Flamarion:* Erich Von Stroheim. *Connie Wallace:* Mary Beth Hughes. *Al Wallace:* Dan Duryea. *Eddie Wheeler:* Stephen Barclay. *Director:* Anthony Mann. *Screenplay:* Anne Wigton. *Story:* The Big Shot by Vicki Baum. *Producer:* William Wilder. *Musical Score:* Alexander Laszlo. *Cinematography:* James Spencer Brown, Jr. *Editor:* John F. Link.

## The Valley of Decision

*(1945, MGM — 119 min.)*

*Mary Rafferty:* Greer Garson. *Paul Scott:* Gregory Peck. *William Scott:* Donald Crisp. *Pat Rafferty:* Lionel Barrymore. *Jim Brennan:* Preston Foster. *Constance Scott:* Marsha Hunt. *Clarissa Scott:* Gladys Cooper. *William Scott, Jr.:* Dan Duryea. *Director:* Tay Garnett. *Screenplay:* Sonya Levien and John Mehan. *Novel:* Marcia Davenport. *Producer:* Edwin H. Knopf. *Music:* Herbert Stothart. *Cinematography:* Joseph Ruttenberg. *Editor:* Blance Sewell.

## Along Came Jones

*(1945, RKO — 90 min.)*

*Melody Jones:* Gary Cooper. *Cherry de Longpre:* Loretta Young. *George Fury:* William Demerast. *Monte Jarrod:* Dan Duryea. *Avery de Longpre:* Frank Sully. *Director:* Stuart Heisler. *Screenplay:* Nunnally Johnson. *Novel:* Alan Le May. *Producer:* Gary Cooper. *Music:* Walter Lange. *Cinematography:* Milton R. Krasner. *Editor:* Thomas Neff.

## Lady on a Train

*(1945, Universal — 94 min.)*

*Nikki Collins:* Deanna Durbin. Jonathan *Waring:* Ralph Bellamy. *Wayne Morgan:* David Bruce. *Mr. Sanders:* George Coulouris. *Danny:* Allen Jenkins. *Arnold Waring:* Dan Duryea. *Mr. Haskell:* Edward Everett Horton. *Margo Martin:* Maria Palmer. *Director:* Charles David. *Screenplay:* Edmund Beloin and Robert O'Brien. *Story:* Leslie Charteris. *Producer:* Felix Jackson. *Music:* Miklos Rozsa. *Cinematography:* Elwood Bredell. *Editor:* Ted J. Kent.

# The Black Angel

*(1946, Universal Pictures — 81 min.)*

*Martin Blair:* Dan Duryea. *Catherine Bennett:* June Vincent. *Marko:* Peter Lorre. Captain *Flood:* Broderick Crawford. *Mavis Marlowe:* Constance Dowling. *Joe:* Wallace Ford. *George Mitchell:* Archie Twitchell. *Director:* Roy William Neill. *Screenplay:* Roy Chanslor. *Novel:* Cornell Woolrich. *Producers:* Tom McKnight and Roy William Neal. *Cinematography:* Paul Ivano. *Musical Score:* Frank Skinner. *Editor:* Sal A. Goodkind.

# Scarlet Street

*(1945, Fritz Lang Productions — 103 min.)*

*Christopher Cross:* Edward G. Robinson. *Katharine "Kitty" March:* Joan Bennett. *Johnny Prince:* Dan Duryea. *Milly Ray:* Margaret Lindsay. *Janeway:* Jess Barker. *Patch — Eye Higgins:* Charles Kemper. *Director and Producer:* Fritz Lang. *Screenplay:* Dudley Nichols. *Novel and Play ("La Chienne"):* Georges De La Fouchadiere and Mouezy — Eon. *Music:* H.J. Salter. *Cinematography:* Milton Krasner. *Editor:* Arthur Hilton.

# White Tie and Tails

*(1946, Universal-International — 81 min.)*

*Charles Dumont:* Dan Duryea. *Louise Bradford:* Ella Raines. *Larry Lundie:* William Bendix. *George:* Frank Jenks. *Archer:* Richard Gaines. *Nat Romero:* Donald Curtis. *Director:* Charles Barton. *Screenplay:* Bertram Millhauser. *Novel:* ("The Victoria Docks at Eight"): Charles Beakon and Rufus King. *Producer:* Howard Benedict. *Music:* Milton Rosen. *Cinematography:* Charles Van Enger. *Editor:* Ray Snyder.

# Black Bart

*(1948, Universal-International — 80 min., Color)*

*Lola Montez:* Yvonne De Carlo. *Charles E. Boles (Black Bart):* Dan Duryea. *Lance Hardeen:* Jeffrey Lynn. *Jersey Brady:* Percy Kilbride. *Sheriff Godon:* Lloyd Gough. *Director:* George Sherman. *Screenplay:* Lucy Ward, Jack Natteford, and William Bowers. *Short Story:* Lucy Ward and Jack Natteford. *Producer:* Leonard Goldstein. *Music:* Uncredited. *Cinematography:* Irving Glassberg. *Editor:* Russell Scoengarth.

## Another Part of the Forest

*(1948, Universal-International — 107 min.)*
*Marcus Hubbard:* Fredric March. *Oscar Hubbard:* Dan Duryea. *Ben Hubbard:* Edmond O'Brien. *Regina Hubbard:* Ann Blyth. *Lavinia Hubbard:* Florence Eldridge. *John Bagtry:* John Dall. *Laurette Sincee:* Dona Drake. *Birdy Bagtree:* Betsy Blair. *Director:* Michael Gordon. *Screenplay:* Vladimir Pozner. *Play:* Lillian Hellman. *Producer:* Jerry Bresler. *Music:* Daniele Amfitheatrof. *Cinematography:* Hal Mohr. *Editor:* Milton Carruth.

## River Lady

*(1948, Universal-International — 78 min., Color)*
*Sequin:* Yvonne De Carlo. *Beauvais:* Dan Duryea. *Dan Corrigan:* Rod Cameron. *Stephanie Morrison:* Helena Carter. *Mike Riley:* Lloyd Gough. *Ma Dunnegan:* Florence Bates. *H.L. Morrison:* John McIntire. *Director:* George Sherman. *Screenplay:* D.D. Beauchamp and William Bowers. *Novel:* Houston Branch and Frank Wuter. *Producer:* Leonard Goldstein. *Music:* Paul Sawtell. *Cinematography:* Irving Glassberg. *Editor:* Otto Ludwig.

## Larceny

*(1949, Universal-International — 89 min.)*
*Rick Mason:* John Payne. *Deborah Owens Clark:* Joan Caulfield. *Silky Randall:* Dan Duryea. *Tory:* Shelly Winters. *Madeline:* Dorothy Hart. *Charlie Jordan:* Percy Helton. *With:* Dan O'Herlihy, Russ Conway, Paul Brinegar, and Don Wilson. *Director:* George Sherman. *Screenplay:* D.D. Beauchamp and William Bowers. *Novel:* Houston Branch and Frank Waters. *Producer:* Leonard Goldstein. *Musical Score:* Paul Sawtell. *Cinematography:* Irving Glassberg. *Editor:* Otto Ludwig.

## Criss-Cross

*(1949, Universal-International — 87 min.)*
*Steve Thompson:* Burt Lancaster. *Anna Dundee:* Yvonne De Carlo. *Slim Dundee:* Dan Duryea. *Det. Lt. Pete Ramirez:* Stephen McNally. *Vincent:* Tom Pedi. *Frank:* Percy Helton. *Finchley:* Alan Napier. *Pop:* Griff Barnett. *With:* Esy Morales and his Rhumba Band, Meg Randall, Richard Long, Joan Miller, Edna Holland, John Doucette, Marc Krah, James O'Rear, John Skins Miller and Tony Curtis (unbilled). *Director:* Robert Siodmak. *Screenplay:* Daniel Fuchs. *Novel:* Don Tracy. *Producer:* Michel Kraike. *Musical Score:* Miklos Rozsa. *Cinematography:* Frank Planer. *Editor:* Ted J. Kent.

# Manhandled

*(1949, Paramount — 97 min.)*

*Merl Kramer:* Dorothy Lamour. *Joe Cooper:* Sterling Hayden. *Karl Benson:* Dan Duryea. *Ruth/Mrs. Alton Bennett:* Irene Hervey. *Lt. Dawson:* Art Smith. *Dr. Redman:* Harold Vermilyea. *Alton Bennett:* Alan Napier. *Guy Bayard:* Phillip Reed. *Director:* Lewis R. Foster. *Screenplay:* Whitman Chambers and Lewis R. Foster. *Novel ("The Man Who Stole A Dream"):* L.S. Goldsmith. *Producer:* William H. Pine and William C. Thomas. *Music:* Darrell Calker. *Cinematography:* Ernest Laszlo. *Editor:* Howard Smith.

# Too Late For Tears *aka* Killer Bait

*(1949, United Artists — 99 min.)*

*Jane Palmer:* Lizabeth Scott. *Don Blake:* Don DeFore. *Danny Fuller:* Dan Duryea. *Alan Palmer:* Arthur Kennedy. *Kathy Palmer:* Kristine Miller. *Lt. Breach:* Barry Kelly. *Director:* Byron Haskin. *Screenplay and Story:* Roy Huggins. *Producer:* Hunt Stromberg. *Music:* Dale Butts. *Cinematography:* William Mellor. *Editor:* Harry Keller.

# Johnny Stool Pigeon

*(1949, Universal-International — 76 min.)*

*George Morton:* Howard Duff. *Terry Stewart:* Shelley Winters. *Johnny Evans:* Dan Duryea. *Joey Hyatt:* Anthony (Tony) Curtis. *Nick Avery:* John McIntire. *Sam Harrison:* Gar Moore. *Pringle:* Leif Erickson. *Director:* William Castle. *Screenplay:* Robert L. Richards. *Story:* Henry Jordan. *Producer:* Aaron Rosenberg. *Cinematography:* Maury Gertsman. *Editor:* Ted J. Kent.

# One Way Street:

*(1950, Universal-International — 76 min.)*

*Dr. Frank Matson:* James Mason. *Laura Thorson:* Marta Toren. *John Wheeler:* Dan Duryea. *Father Moreno:* Basil Ruysdael. *Ollie:* William Conrad. *Director:* Hugo Fregonese. *Screenplay:* Laurence Kimble. *Producer:* Leonard Goldstein. *Music:* Frank Skinner. *Cinematography:* Maury Gertsman. *Editor:* Milton Carruth.

## Winchester '73

*(1950, Universal-International — 92 min.)*

*Lin McAdam:* James Stewart. *Lola Manners:* Shelly Winters. *Waco Johnnie Dean:* Dan Duryea. *Dutch Henry Brown:* Stephen McNally. *High Spade Frankie Wilson:* Millard Mitchell. *With:* Charles Drake, John McIntire, Will Geer, Jay C. Flippen, Rock Hudson, Tony Curtis, Abner Biberman and James Best. *Director:* Anthony Mann. *Screenplay:* Robert L. Richards and Borden Chase. *Story:* Stuart N. Lake. *Producer:* Aaron Rosenberg. *Cinematography:* William Daniels. *Editor:* Edward Curtiss.

## The Underworld Story

*(1950, Allied Artists — 91 min.)*

*Mike Reese:* Dan Duryea. *E.J. Stanton:* Herbert Marshall. *Catherine Harris:* Gale Storm. *Carl Durham:* Howard Da Silva. *DA Ralph Munsey:* Michael O'Shea. *Molly Rankin:* Mary Anderson. *Clark Stanton:* Gar Moore. *Mrs. Eldridge:* Frieda Inescourt. *George "Parky" Parker:* Harry Shannon. *With:* Alan Hale, Jr., Roland Winters and Jay Adler. *Director:* Cy Endfield. *Screenplay:* Henry Blankfort. *Story:* Craig Rice. *Adaptation:* Cy Endfield. *Producer:* Hal E. Chester. *Music:* David Rose. *Cinematography:* Stanley Cortez. *Editor:* Richard Heermance.

## Al Jennings of Oklahoma

*(1951, Columibia Pictures — 79 min., Color)*

*Al Jennings:* Dan Duryea. *Margo St. Clare:* Gale Storm. *Frank Jennings:* Dick Foran. *Alice Calhoun:* Gloria Henry. *Lon Tuttle:* Guinn "Big Boy" Williams. *Judge Jennings:* Raymond Greenleaf. *Fred Salter:* Harry Shannon. *Tom Marsden:* John Dehner. *Director:* ray Nazarro. *Screenplay:* George Bricker. *Book:* Al J. Jennings and Will Irwin. *Producer:* Rudolph C. Flothow. *Music:* George Duning and Paul Mertz. *Cinematography:* Howard Greene. *Editor:* Richard Fantl.

## Chicago Calling

*(1952, Arrowhead Pictures — 75 min.)*

*Bill Cannon:* Dan Duryea. *Mary Cannon:* Mary Anderson. *Bobby:* Gordon Gebert. *Jim:* Ross Elliot. *Nancy Cannon:* Melinda Plowman. *Babs Kimball:* Judy Brubaker. *Peggy:* Marsha Jones. *Pete:* Roy Engel. *Director:* John Reinhardt. *Screenplay:* Peter Berneis and John Reinhardt.

## Thunder Bay

*(1953, Universal-International — 103 min., Color)*
*Steve Martin:* James Stewart. *Stella Rigaud:* Joanne Dru. *Teche Bossier:*
Gilbert Roland. *Johnny Gambi:* Dan Duryea. *Kermit MacDonald:* Jay C.
Flippen. *Francesca Rigaud:* Marica Handerson. *Phillipe Bagard:* Robert
Monet. *Dominique Rigaud:* Antonio Moreno. *Director:* Anthony Mann.
*Screenplay:* Gil Doud and John Michael Hayes. *Producer:* Aaron Rosenberg.
*Cinemtography:* Wiiliam Daniels. *Music:* Frank Skinner. *Editor:* Rossell
Schoengarth.

## Sky Commando

*(1953, Columbia — 69 min.)*
*Col. Ed (E.D.) Wyatt:* Dan Duryea. *Jo McWerthy:* Frances Gifford. *Lt.
Holstein "Hobbie" Lee:* Touch (Mike) Connors. *Major Scott:* Michael Fox.
*With:* William Bryant, Selmer Jackson and Morris Ankrum. *Director:* Fred
J. Sears. *Screenplay:* Samuel Newman. *Story:* Samuel Newman, Arthur E.
Orloff and William Sackheim. *Producer:* Sam Katzman. *Cinematography:*
Lester White. *Editor:* Edwin H. Bryant.

## 36 Hours *aka* Terror Street

*(1953, Hammer Films — 85 min.)*
*Major Bill Rogers:* Dan Duryea. *Katherine "Katie" Rogers:* Elsy Albin.
*Sister Jenny Miller:* Ann Gudrun. *Slossen, the smuggler:* Eric Pohlman.
*Henry Slossen:* Kenneth Griffith. *Director:* Montgomery Tully. *Screenplay
and Story:* Steve Fisher. *Producer:* Anthony Hinds. *Music:* Ivor Slaney.
*Cinematography:* Walter Harvey. *Editor:* James Needs.

## World For Ransom

*(1954, Allied Artists — 82 min.)*
*Mike Callahan:* Dan Duryea. *Alexis Pederas:* Gene Lockhart. *Julian
March:* Patric Knowles. *Major Bone:* Reginald Denny. *Frennessey March:*
Marian Carr. *Sear O'Connor:* Arthur Shields. *Inspector McCollum:* Douglas
Dumbrelle. *Wong:* Keye Luke. *Chan:* Clarence Lung. *Guzik:* Lou Nova.
*Dancer:* Carmen D'Antonio. *Director:* Robert Aldrich. *Screenplay:* Hugo
Butler and Lindsay Hardy. *Producer:* Robert Aldrich and Bernard Tabakin.
*Cinematography:* Joseph F. Biroc. *Editor:* Michael Luciano.

## Ride Clear of Diablo

*(1954, Universal-International — 80 min., Color)*
*Clay O'Mara:* Audie Murphy. *Laurie Kenyon:* Susan Cabot. *Whitey Kincaide:* Dan Duryea. *Kate:* Abbe Lane. *With:* Russell Johnson, Paul Birch, Jack Elam and Denver Pyle. *Director:* Jesse Hibbs. *Screenplay:* George Zuckeman. *Additional Dialogue:* D.D. Beauchamp. *Story:* Ellia Marcus. *Producer:* John W. Rogers. *Music:* Milton Rosen and Herman Stein. *Cinematography:* Irving Glassberg. *Editor:* Edward Curtiss.

## Rails Into Laramie

*(1954, Universal-International — 80 min., Color)*
*Jefferson Harder:* John Payne. *Lou Carter:* Mari Blanchard. *Jim Shanessy:* Dan Duryea. *Helen Shanessy:* Joyce Mackenzie. *Lee Graham:* Barton MacLane. *With:* Harry Shannon, Lee Van Cleef and Myron Healey. *Director:* Jess Hibbs. *Screenplay:* D.D. Beauchamp, Borden Chase and Joseph Hoffman. *Producer:* Ted Richmond. *Music:* Henry Mancini, Milton Rosen and Herman Stein. *Cinematography:* Maury Gertsman. *Editor:* Ted J. Kent.

## Silver Lode

*(1954, RKO Pictures — 81 min., Color)*
*Dan Ballard:* John Payne. *Rose Evans:* Lizabeth Scott. *Ned McCarty:* Dan Duryea. *Dolly:* Dolores Moran. *Sheriff Wooley:* Emile Meyer. *Judge Cranston:* Robert Warwick. *Director:* Allan Dwan. *Screenplay:* Karen DeWolf. *Producer:* Benedict Bogeaus. *Music:* Louis Forbes. *Cinematography:* John Alton. *Editor:* James Leicester.

## This Is My Love

*(1954, RKO Radio Pictures — 91 min., Color)*
*Vida Dove:* Linda Darnell. *Murray Myer:* Dan Duryea. *Glenn Harris:* Rick Jason. *Evelyn Myer:* Faith Domergue. *Eddie Collins:* Hal Baylor. *Connie Russell:* Herself. *With:* Jerry Mathers, Susie Mathers, William Hopper and Carl "Alfalfa" Switzer. *Director:* Stuart Heisler. *Screenplay:* Hugh Brooke and Hogan Wilde. *Short Story ("Fear Has Black Wings"):* Hugh Brooke. *Producer:* Hugh Brooke. *Music:* Franz Waxman. *Cinematography:* Ray June. *Editor:* Otto Ludwig.

# Foxfire

*(1955, Universal-International — 87 min., Color)*
*Amanda Lawrence:* Jane Russell. *Jonathan Dartland:* Jeff Chandler. *Hugh Slater:* Dan Duryea. *Maria:* Mara Corday. *Mr. Mablett:* Barton MacLane. *Mrs. Lawrence:* Frieda Inescourt. *Director:* Joseph Pevney. *Screenplay:* Ketti Frings. *Producer:* Aaron Rosenberg. *Music:* Frank Skinner. *Cinematography:* William Daniels. *Editor:* Ted J. Kent.

# Storm Fear

*(1955, United Artists — 88 min.)*
*Charlie:* Cornel Wilde. *Elizabeth:* Jean Wallace. *Fred:* Dan Duryea. *Edna:* Lee Grant. *David:* David Stollery. *Hank:* Dennis Weaver. *Benjie:* Steven Hill. *Director and Producer:* Cornel Wilde. *Screenplay:* Horten Foote. *Novel:* Clinton Seeley. *Music:* Elmer Bernstein. *Cinematography:* Joseph LaShelle. *Editor:* Otto Ludwig.

# The Marauders

*(1955, MGM — 80 min., Color)*
*Mr. Avery:* Dan Duryea. *Corey Everett:* Jeff Richards. *Hook:* Keenan Wynn. *Hannah Ferber:* Jarma Lewis. *Roy Rutherford:* Harry Shannon. *Albie Ferber:* David Kasday. *Louis Ferber:* James Anderson. *Ramos:* Peter Mamkos. *Director:* Gerald Mayer. *Screenplay:* Jack Leonard and Earl Felton. *Novel:* Alan Marcus. *Cinematography:* Harold Marzorati, A.S.C. *Music:* Paul Sawtell. *Editor:* Russell Selwyn.

# Battle Hymn

*(1957, Universal-International — 108 min., Color)*
*Col. Dean Hess:* Rock Hudson. *En Soon Yang:* Anna Kashfi. *Sgt. Herman:* Dan Duryea. *Capt. Skidmore:* Don DeFore. *Mary Hess:* Martha Hyer. *Maj. Moore:* Jock Mahoney. *Mess Sergeant:* Alan Hale, Jr. *Director:* Douglas Sirk. *Screenplay:* Vincent B. Evans and Charles Grayson. *Novel:* D.E. Hess. *Producer:* Ross Hunter. *Cinematography:* Russell Metty. *Music:* Frank Skinner. *Editor:* Russell Schoengarth.

## Night Passage

*(1957, Universal-International — 90 min., Color)*
*Grant McLaine:* James Stewart. *The Utica Kid:* Audey Murphy. *Whitey Harbin:* Dan Duryea. *Charlotte Drew:* Dianne Foster. *Verna Kimball:* Elaine Stewart. *Ben Kimball:* Jay C. Flippen. *Will Renner:* Herbert Anderson. *Jeff Kurth:* Hugh Beaumont. *Shotgun:* Jack Elam. *Director:* James Neilson. *Screenplay:* Borden Chase. *Producer:* Aaron Rosenberg. *Music:* Dimitri Tiomkin. *Cinematography:* William Daniels. *Editor:* Sherman Todd.

## The Burglar

*(1957, Columbia Pictures — 90 min.)*
*Nat Harbin:* Dan Duryea. *Gladden:* Jayne Mansfield. *Della:* Martha Vickers. *Baylock:* Peter Capell. *Dohmer:* Mickey Shaughnessy. *Police Captain:* Wendell K. Phillips. *Sister Sara:* Phoebe Mackay. *Charlie:* Stewart Bradley. *News Commentator:* John Fracenda. *Newsreel Narrator:* Bob Wilson. Director and Editor: Paul Wendkos. Screenplay: David Goodis, based on his novel. *Producer:* Louis W. Kellman.. *Cinematography:* Don Malkames. *Musical Score:* Sol Kaplan.

## Slaughter on 10th Avenue:

*(1957, Universal-International — 103 min.)*
*William "Bill" Keating:* Richard Egan. *Madge Pitts:* Jan Sterling. *John Jacob Masters:* Dan Duryea. *Daisy "Dee" Paisly:* Julie Adams. *Al Dahlke:* Walter Matthau. *Lt. Anthony Vasnick:* Charles McGraw. *Howard Rysdale:* Sam Levene. *Solly Pitts:* Mickey Shaughnessy. *Benjy Karp:* Harry Bellaver. *Midget:* Nick Dennis. *Director:* Arnold Laven. *Screenplay:* Lawrence Roman. *Novel:* William J. Keating and Richard Carter, "The Man Who Rocked the Boat." *Producer:* Albert Zugsmith. *Music:* Herschel Burke Gilbert — Richard Rodgers — Henry Mancini (uncredited). *Cinematography:* Fred Jackman, Jr. *Editor:* Russell F. Shoengarth.

## Kathy O

*(1958, Universal-International — 99 min., Color)*
*Harry Johnson:* Dan Duryea. *Celeste Saunders:* Jan Sterling. *Kathy O'Roarke:* Patty McCormack. *Helen Johnson:* Mary Fickett. *Ben Melnick:* Sam Levene. *Aunt Harriet:* Mary Jane Croft. *Direction and Screenplay:* Jack Sher. *Producer:* Sy Gomberg. *Music:* Frank Skinner. *Cinematography.:* Arth E. Arling. *Editor:* George A. Gittens.

## Showdown at Sandoval

*(1959, Walt Disney Productions — 63 min.)*
*Texas John Slaughter:* Tom Tryon. *Ben Jenkins:* Harry Carey, Jr. *Dan Trask:* Dan Duryea. *Mrs. Barko*: Beverly Garland. *Adeline Harris:* Norma Moore. *Captain Cooper:* Judson Pratt. *Director:* Harry Keller. *Producer:* James C. Pratt.

## Platinum High School

*(1960, MGM — 95 min.)*
*Steven Conway:* Mickey Rooney. *Jennifer Evans:* Terry Moore. *Maj. Redfern Kelly:* Dan Duryea. *"Crip" Hastings:* Warren Berlinger. *Lorinda Nibley:* Yvette Mimieux. *Hack Marlow:* Richard Jaeckel. *With:* Christopher Dark, Conway Twitty, Jimmy Boyd, Jack Carr, Elisha Cook, Jr. and Harold Lloyd, Jr. *Director:* Charles F. Haas. *Screenplay:* Howard Breslin. *Story:* Robert Smith. *Producer:* Red Doff. *Executive Producer:* Albert Zugsmith. *Music:* Van Alexander. *Editor:* Gene Ruggiero.

## Six Black Horses

*(1962, Universal-International — 80 min., Color)*
*Ben Lane:* Audie Murphy. *Frank Jesse:* Dan Duryea. *Kelly:* Joan O'Brien. *Boone:* George Wallace. *Mustanger:* Roy Barcroft. *Charlie:* Dick Pascoe. *Puncher:* Bob Steele. *Cantina Dancer:* Charlita. *Director:* Harry Keller. *Screenplay:* Burt Kennedy. *Producer:* Gordon Kay. *Cinematographer:* Maury Gertsman. *Editor:* Aaron Stell.

## He Rides Tall

*(1964, Universal — 84 min.)*
*Marshal Rocklin:* Tony Young. *Bart Thorne:* Dan Duryea. *Ellie Daniels:* Madlyn Rhue. *Kate McCloud:* Jo Morrow. *Josh McCloud:* R.G. Armstrong. *Dr. Sam:* Joel Fluellen. *Director:* R.G. Springsteen. *Screenplay:* Charles W. Irwin and Robert Creighton Williams. *Producer:* Gordon McKay. *Cinematographer:* Ellis W. Carter. *Musical Score:* Irving Gertz.

## Do You Know This Voice?

*(1964, Columbia Pictures — 80 min.)*
*John Hopta:* Dan Duryea. *Rosa Marotta:* Isa Miranda. *Jackie Hopta:* Gwen Watford. *Supt. Hume:* Peter Madden. *Det. Sgt. Connor:* Barry Warren. *Judy:* Jean Aubrey. *Director:* John Nesbitt. *Screenplay:* Neil McCallum. *Novel:* Evelyn Berckman. *Producer:* Jack Parsons. *Music:* Carlo Martelli. *Cinematography:* Arthur Lavis. *Editor:* Robert Winter.

## Taggert

*(1964, Universal — 85 min., Color)*
*Taggart:* Tony Young. *Jason:* Dan Duryea. *Stark:* Dick Foran. *Consuela:*
Elsa Cardenas. *Miriam:* Jean Hale. *Ben Blazer:* Emil Meyer. *Director:*
R.G. Springsteen. *Screenplay:* Robert Creighton Williams. *Novel:* Louis
L'Amour. *Producer:* Gordon McKay and Associates. *Cinematography:* Will
Margulies. *Musical Score:* Herman Stein. *Editor:* Tony Martinelli.

## Walk A Tightrope

*(1965, Paramount Pictures — 69 min.)*
*Carl Lutcher:* Dan Duryea. *Ellen Sheppard:* Patricia Owen. *Jason Sheppard:*
Terence Cooper. *Doug
Randle:* Richard Leech. *Counsel:* Neil McCallum. *Director:* Frank Nesbitt.
*Screenplay:* Jann Rubin. *Story:* Neil McCallum. *Producer:* Jack Parsons.
*Music:* Buxton Orr. *Cinematography:* Basil Emmott. *Editor:* Robert Winter.

## The Bounty Killer

*(1965, Embassy Pictures — 93 min., Color)*
*Willie Duggan:* Dan Duryea. *Johnny Liam:* Rod Cameron. *Carole:* Audrey
Dalton. *Rideway:* Richard Arlen. *Luther:* Fuzzy Knight. *Youth:* Peter
Duryea. *Pianist:* Eddie Quillan. *Inister:* Grady Sutton. *Waiter:* Tom
Kennedy. *Red:* Bob Steele. *Seddon:* Boyd "Red" Morgan. *Mike Clayman:*
Larry "Buster" Crabbe. *Sheriff Green:* Johnny Mack Brown. *Director:*
Spencer Gordon Bennett. *Screenplay:* Leo Gordon. *Producer:* Alex Gordon.
*Cinematographer:* Frederick E. West. *Musical Score:* Ronald Stein. *Editor:*
Ronald Sinclair.

## Flight of the Phoenix

*(1965, 20th Century Fox — 147 min., Color)*
*Frank Towns:* James Stewart. *Lew Moran:* Richard Attenbourough.
*Captain Harris:* Ptere Finch. *Heinrich Dorfmann:* Hardy Kruger. *Trucker
Cobb:* Ernest Borgnine. *Crow:* Ian Bannen. *Sergeant Watson:* Ronald Fraser.
*Dr. Renaud:* Christian Marquand. *Standish:* Dan Duryea. *Bellamy:* George
Kennedy. *Gabriele:* Gabriele Tinti. *Carlos:* Alex Montoya. *Tasso:* Peter
Bravos. *Farida :* Barrie Chase. *Director and Producer:* Robert Aldrich.
*Screenplay:* Lukas Heller. *Novel:* Elleston Trevor. *Cinematography:* Joseph
Biroc. *Music:* DeVol. *Editor:* Michael Luciano.

# The Hills Run Red
*(1967, United Artists — 103 min., Color)*
*Jerry Brewster:* Thomas Hunter. *Mendez:* Henry Silva. *Col. Getz:* Dan Duryea. *Seagall:* Nando Gazzolo. *Mary Ann:* Nicoletta Machiavelli. *Director:* Albert Lattuada. *Screenplay:* Dean Craig, Jack Pulman, Luigi Malerba and Alberto Lattuada. *Producers:* Ermanno Donati and Luigi Carpentieri. *Cinematography:* Toni Secchi. *Musical Score:* Enrico Morricone. *Editor:* Ornella Micheli.

# Incident at Phantom Hill
*(1966, Universal — 88 min., Color)*
*Captain Matt Martin:* Robert Fuller. *Memphis:* Jocelyn Lane. *Joe Barlow:* Dan Duryea. *Adam Long:* Tom Simcox. *Dr. Hannaford:* Linden Chiles. *Krausman:* Claude Akins. *O'Rourke:* Noah Beery, Jr. *Gen. Hood:* Paul Fix. *Frontiersman:* Denver Pyle. *Trader:* William Phipps. *Sheriff Drum:* Don Collier. *Director:* Earl Bellamy. *Screenplay:* Frank S. Nugent and Ken Pettus. *Producer:* Harry Tatelman. *Cinematographer:* William Marguiles, A.S.C. *Musical Score:* Hans J. Salter. *Musical Supervision:* Joseph Gershenson. *Editor:* Gene Milford.

# Winchester '73
*(1967, Universal — 97 min. — TVM — C)*
*Lin McAdam:* Tom Tryon. *Dakin McAdam:* John Saxon. *Bart McAdam:* Dan Duryea. *Preacher:* John Drew Barrymore. *Larouge:* Joan Blondell. *High — Spade Johnny Dean:* John Dehner. *Meriden:* Barbara Luna. *Ben McAdam:* Paul Fix. *Dan McAdam:* David Pritchard. *Jake Starret:* John Doucette. *Scots:* Jack Lambert. *Sunrider:* John Hoyt. *Director:* Herschel Daugherty. *Teleplay:* Richard L. Adams, based on screenplay by Bordern Chase. *Producer:* Richard E. Lyons. *Cinematography:* Bud Thackery. *Musical Score:* Sol Kaplan. *Editor:* Richard G. Wray.

# Five Golden Dragons
*(1967, Commonwealth United Entertainment — 104 min.)*
*Bob Mitchell:* Bob Cummings. *Magda:* Margaret Lee. *Comm. Sanders:* Rupert Davies. *Gert:* Klaus Kinski. *Ingrid:* Maria Rohm. *Margret:* Maria Perschy. *Five Golden Dragons:* Dan Duryea, Brian Donlevy, George Raft, Christoper Lee and ??????? *Director:* Jeremy Summers. *Screenplay:* Harry Alan Towers. *Story:* Edgar Wallace. *Producer:* Peter Welbeck (Harry Alan Towers). *Music:* Malcolm Lockyer. *Cinematography:* John Von Kotze. *Editor:* Donald J. Cohen.

## Stranger On The Run

*(1967, Universal — 97 min. — TVM — C)*
*Ben Chamberlain:* Henry Fonda. *Valverde Johnson:* Anne Baxter. *Vince McKay:* Michael Parks. *O.E Hotchkiss:* Dan Duryea. *George Blaylock:* Sal Mineo. *Mr. Gorman:* Lloyd Bochner. *Matt Johnson:* Michael Burns. *Leo Weed:* Tom Reese. *Dickory:* Bernie Hamilton. *Larkin:* Zalman King. *Alma Britten:* Madlyn Rhue. *Berk:* Walter Burke. *Director:* Don Siegal. *Screenplay:* Dean Riesner. *Story:* Reginald Rose. *Producer:* Richard E. Lyons. *Cinematography:* Bud Thackeray. *Music:* Leonard Rosenman. *Editor:* Richard G. Wray.

## The Bamboo Saucer *aka* Collision Course

*(1968, World Entertainment Corp. — 100 min.)*
*Hank Peters:* Dan Duryea. *Fred Norwood:* John Ericson. *Anna Karachev:* Lois Nettleton. *Jack Garson:* Bob Hastings. *Zagersky:* Vincent Beck. *Dave Ephram:* Bernard Fox. *Sam Archibald:* James Hong. *Director:* Frank Telford. *Screenplay:* Frank Telford. *Story:* Frank Telford and Rip (Alfred) Van Ronkel. *Producers:* Charles E. Burns and Jerry Fairbanks. *Music:* Edward Paul and Raoul Kraushaar. *Cinematography:* Hal Mohr. *Editor:* Richard Harris.

# Index

# Bear Manor Media

FOXY LADY
This Authorized Biography of **Lynn Bari**

ALSO STARRING...
FORTY BIOGRAPHICAL ESSAYS ON THE GREATEST CHARACTER ACTORS OF HOLLYWOOD'S GOLDEN ERA, 1930-1965
CYNTHIA AND SARA BRIDESON

Affectionately, Jayne Mansfield
RICHARD KOPER

THE MAN OF A THOUSAND VOICES
Mel Blanc
BY BEN OHMART

## Classic Cinema.
## Timeless TV.
## Retro Radio.

WWW.BEARMANORMEDIA.COM

THE SILVER AGE OF COMICS
Fantastic Four
WILLIAM SCHOELL

THE OMNI-DIRECTIONAL THREE-DIMENSIONAL VECTORING PAPER PRINTED OMNIBUS FOR BEWITCHED ANALYSIS A.K.A. THE Bewitched HISTORY BOOK
BY DAVID L. PIERCE

NORTH BY NORTHWEST
THE MAN WHO HAD TOO MUCH
JAMES STRATTON

VERNON DENT
STOOGE HEAVY
SECOND BANANA TO THE THREE STOOGES AND OTHER FILM COMEDY GREATS BY BILL CASSARA

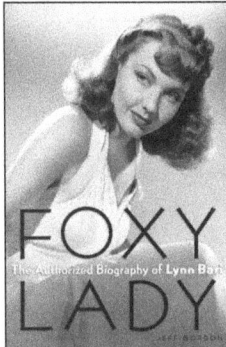

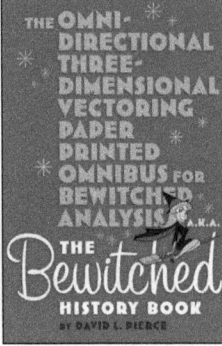

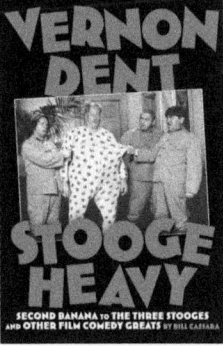

www.ingramcontent.com/pod-product-compliance
Lightning Source LLC
Chambersburg PA
CBHW060328100426
42812CB00003B/913